Inhalt

Vocabulary

Gastronomisches Fachvokabular

Short forms and abbreviations used in the dictionary

AE	Amercian English
BE	British English
e.g.	for example (abbreviation of Latin "exempli gratia")
pl	plural
sg	singular
sth	something
so	someone
sb	somebody

German – English

Deutsch - Englisch

A

Aal	eel
– in Aspik	eel in jelly (aspic)
–, geräucherter	smoked eel
– vom Spieß	eel on the spit
Aalragout	eel stew, matelote of eel
abbrühen	to scald
ABC-Pflaster	heat plaster
Abendessen	dinner
Abendessen im Freien	al fresco dining
Abendessen mit Tanz	dinner dance
Abendessen, spät	supper
Abendkarte	tonight's specials
Abendmenü	set dinner
Abfall	litter
Abflug, Abreise	departure
Abflugbereich	boarding area
Abfluss	drain
Abgang	aftertaste, finish
abgerundet mit	complemented by
abgestanden, altbacken (Brot)	stale
abhaken	to tick
abhängig	dependent
abhäuten, schälen	to skin
abheben (Hörer)	to lift the receiver
abheben, starten (Flugzeug)	to take off
abkühlen	to chill
Abkürzung	abbreviation

Ablagerungen	sediment
Ablauf	procedure
Ablaufdatum	expiry date
ablöschen (Braten, mit Wein oder Wasser)	to add liquid to a roast
ablösen	to become detached
abnehmbar	removable
Abreisedatum	date of departure
abschäumen	to skim
Abschied	farewell
Abschlussarbeiten	finishing touches
abschmecken	to season to taste
abschrecken	to rinse with cold water
abschwarten	to remove rind
abseihen	to drain, strain
absplittern	to chip off
abspülen	to rinse
abstauben	to dust
abstreifen	to strip off
Absturzsicherung	safety rail
abtauen	to defrost
abtropfen	to drain, to strain
abwaschen	to rinse
Abwasch	sink
abwechseln	to alternate
abwechselnd	alternately
abwechslungsreich	varied
abwischen	to wipe (clean)
Adapter	adapter
ähnlich	similar
Ahornsirup	maple syrup
Aiolisauce	aioli sauce (garlic mayonnaise)
Akazienhonig	acacia honey
Aktenvernichter	paper shredder
alarmieren	to alert
Alge	seaweed
Alkohol	alcohol
alkoholfrei	non-alcoholic
alkoholfreies Getränk	soft drink, (aerated) lemonade
Alkoholgehalt	alcohol concentration
alkoholisch	alcoholic
alkoholische Getränke	alcoholic drinks, liquors
allergisch auf	allergic to
Allerheiligen	All Saints' Day
alles inklusive	all-inclusive
allgemeine Geschäftsbedingungen	terms and conditions
Alpenvorland	foothills of the Alps
Alptraum	nightmare
Alufolie	aluminium foil, tinfoil

Amarant	amaranth
Amaretti	macaroons
Amaretto	amaretto (almond-flavoured liqueur)
Ampel	traffic lights
Amsel	blackbird
Ananas	pineapple
–, gebacken	pineapple fritters
anbieten	to offer
(scharf) anbraten	to sear
Anchovis	*siehe Sardellen*
andalusische Sauce	Andalusian sauce (tomato-based mayonnaise)
Änderung	amendment
Anforderung	requirements
Anfrage	inquiry, query
Angebot	offer
angenehm	pleasant
angereichert, verstärkt	enhanced
angerichtet in	dressed in
Angestellte/r	clerk
angrenzend	adjoining
anhäufen	to heap
animierend	zappy
Anis	aniseed
Anisschnaps	aniseed brandy
anklicken	to click on
Ankunft	arrival
Anlass	occasion
Anleitung	instruction, manual
anmelden	to register
Anna-Kartoffeln	potatoes Anna (potato cake)
anregend	zappy
Anreise	check-in
–, frühe	early check-in
–, späte	late check-in
Anreisedatum	date of arrival
anrichten	to dress
Anrichteplatte	oval eared dish
Anruf	call
Ortsgespräch	local call
Ferngespräch	long-distance call
Anrufbeantworter	answering machine
anstellen	to queue up
Anstellung	employment
Antialkoholiker	teetotaller
Antragsformular	application form
Bewerbung	application
Anzahlung	deposit

Anzeige	advertisement
Aperitif	aperitif, before-dinner drink
Apfel	apple
Apfelkren	horseradish with apple
Apfelkuchen, gestürzt (Tarte Tatin)	upside-down cake
Apfelmus	apple purée, apple sauce
Apfelstrudel	apple strudel
Apfeltasche	apple turnover
Appetithäppchen	finger food, snacks
appetitlich	appetising
April	April
Aranzini	candied orange peel
Arbeiterschaft	workforce
Arbeitgeber/in	employer
arbeitslos	unemployed
Arbeitsplatz	kitchen counter
Arbeitszeiten	working hours
Armer Ritter	French toast
Aroma	aroma, flavourings
aromatisch	aromatic, well-flavoured
Artischocke	artichoke
Artischockenboden	artichoke base, artichoke bottom
Artischockenherz	artichoke heart
Äsche (Fisch)	grayling
Aschenbecher	ashtray
Aspik	jelly, aspic
atmen	to breath
ätzend	corrosive, acidly
Aubergine	eggplant, aubergine
Auerhahn	capercaillie, mountain cock, woodgrouse
auf Anfrage	on request
auf den Grund gehen	to look into sth
auf die Rechnung setzen	to place charges on
auf Eis	on the rocks
auf Wunsch des Kunden	custom-made
Aufenthalt	stay
–, angenehmer	pleasant stay
auffüllen	to fill up, to restock, to replenish
aufgehen	to rise
aufgeregt	excited
aufgeschäumt	foamed
aufgießen (z. B. den Braten)	to baste
aufkochen	to bring to the boil
Auflauf	soufflé, bake
– Auflaufkartoffeln	soufflé potatoes
Auflaufform	soufflé dish
auflegen	to hang up

German	English
auflösen	to dissolve
aufmerksam	vigilant
–aufmerksam machen	to alert
Aufmerksamkeit	attention
Aufpreis	additional charge
– für Haustier	pet's supplement
aufrichtig	sincere
aufsaugen	to absorb
Aufschlag	supplement
Aufschlag für Einzelzimmer	single supplement
aufschlagen	to break
Aufschnitt	assorted sliced, cold meats, cold cut
Aufschnittmaschine	slicer
aufschreiben	write down
aufspießen	to skewer, to spear
aufstehen	to get up
Aufstrich	spread
auftauen	to thaw
auftreten (Problem)	to occur
aufwischen	to sweep
August	August
Aurorasauce	Aurore sauce
Ausbeinmesser	boning knife
Ausbildung	education
Ausbildungsprogramm	training programme
ausbreiten (Tischtuch)	to spread out (a tablecloth)
Ausbruch	outbreak
auschecken	check out
ausdehnen	distend
ausfüllen	to fill in
Ausgabe	serving
ausgeben (Getränke)	to dispense (drinks)
ausgebucht	fully booked
ausgeglichen	balanced, well-balanced
ausgelöst	boneless
ausgerollter Teig	rolled pastry
ausgestattet	equipped
ausgestellt	issued
ausgewogen	balanced, well-balanced
ausgiebig	extensive
ausgießen	to pour
auslassen (Speck)	to render down
ausleeren	to pour
auslösen	to bone
ausnehmen	gut
auspressen	to squeeze
Ausrüstung	equipement
ausrutschen	to slip

Außenseite	exterior
Ausstattung	fittings
Ausstellung	exhibition
Auster	oyster
Austernmesser	oyster knife
Austernpilz	oyster mushroom
Austernsauce	oyster sauce
Austernschiffchen	oyster boats
Auswahl an ...	choice of ...
Ausweis	mean of identification, identity card
Ausziehcouch	convertible sofa
Autovermietung	car rental, car-hire company
Avocado	avocado

B

Baba mit Rum	baba, rum baba (small yeast-raised cake soaked in rum syrup)
Babybett	baby cot
Babysittervermittlung	babysitting service
Bachforelle	brown trout, brook trout
backen	to bake
Back(ofen)temperatur	oven temperature
Backblech	cake pan
Backerbsen	fried batter drops, profiteroles (pea-sized balls of choux pastry)
Backform (flach)	flat baking tin
Backgeschirr	baking dishes
Backhuhn	fried chicken
Backpapier	baking paper, cookie sheet
Backpinsel	pastry brush
Backpulver	baking powder
Backrohr	oven
Backteig	batter (egg) drops, frying batter
Backwerk, Gebäck	pastry
Bäckerin-Kartoffeln	boulangère potatoes (baked with onions)
Bademantel	dressing gown, bathrobe
Bådematte	bath mat
Badetuch	bath towel
Badewanne	bath
Bagel	bagel (round roll with a hole in the middle)
Baguette	French bread, baguette
Baisermasse	meringue mixture
Baisertorte	meringue pie
Bakterie	bacterium

German	English
Ballaststoffe	fibres
Bambussprossen	bamboo shoots
Banane	banana
–, gebackene	banana fritters
Band	ribbon
Bandnudeln	ribbon noodles, flat noodles, tagliatelle
Bankett	banquet
Bankkonto	bank account
Bankomat	ATM (automated teller machine), cash machine/dispenser
Bankverbindung	bank connection
bar	(in) cash
Bar	bar, counter
Barhocker	bar stool
Barkarte	bar menu
Barkeeper/in	barman, barkeeper
Barsieb	bar strainer
Bartuch	bar towel
Barbarie-Ente	musk duck
Barbe	barbell, mullet
bardieren	to wrap in bacon
Bärlauch	wild/wood garlic, ramson
Bärlauchbutter	wild garlic butter
Bärlauchsauce	wild garlic sauce
Barsch, Flussbarsch	perch
Basilikum	basil
Basmatireis	basmati rice
Bauch	belly
Bauchspeck	streaky bacon
Bauernbrot	country/farmhouse loaf
Bauernomelette	country omelette (bacon and potatoes)
Bauernschmaus	garnished sauerkraut, smoked and roast pork, sausage and bread dumpling with sauerkraut
Bauernsuppe	peasant-style soup (vegetable soup)
bayerische Creme	Bavarian cream
beachten	to bear in mind
Beamer	projector
bearbeiten	to work on sth
beaufsichtigen	to supervise
Béchamelsauce	milk sauce, béchamel sauce (basic white sauce)
Becher	mug
Bedarf	need
bedecken	to coat, to cover
bedeckt mit ...	topped with ...

German	English
Bedienung	service
Bedienungsanleitung	server's manual
Bedienungsfeld	control panel
Bedienungsgeld (nicht) inbegriffen	service (not) included
Bedienungsgeld, -zuschlag	service (charge)
Bedürfnisse	needs
Beefsteak tatare	tartar steak, steak tartare
Beeren	berries
befestigen	to attach
befeuchten	to wet
begehren	to adore
begeistert	enthusiastic, excited
begierig	anxious
begleichen	to settle
begleiten	to accompany
begleitet von	accompanied by
Begleitperson	accompanying person
Begrüßung	salutation
Behälter	container
behandeln	to treat
Behandlung	treatment
behaupten	to claim
Beherbergung	accommodation
behindert	disabled
behinderte Person	disabled person
behindertengerechte Zimmer	handicap accessible rooms
behindertengerechter Zugang	disabled access
Beifuß	mugwort
Beignet	beignet, fritter
Beilage	side dish
Beinfleisch	boiled ribs of beef
beinhalten	to contain
Beiried	sirloin, entrecôte
beizen	to cure
Bekleidung	garment
Belag	coating (BE), topping (AE)
belegtes Brot	open sandwich
Belegung	occupation
belesen	knowledgeable
beraten	to advise
Bercy-Sauce	Bercy sauce (butter, shallots, white wine)
Berliner	*siehe Krapfen*
Berliner Leber	calf's liver with apple
berücksichtigen	to bear in mind
Beruf	profession, job
Berufsschule	vocational school
beschäftigen mit	to bother with

German	English
beschlagen (Dampf)	to steam up
beschreiben	to describe
Beschreibung	description
beschriftet	labelled
Beschwerde	complaint
(sich) beschweren	to complain
besetzt	engaged
Besitzer	owner
besprühen	to drizzle
Bestätigung	confirmation
bestäuben	to dust, to dredge
Besteck	cutlery
bestellen	to order
Bestellung	order
bestreuen	to sprinkle, to dredge
bestreut mit	sprinkled with
betont durch	accented by
Betrachtung	consideration
beträufeln	to drizzle
betreuen	to look after
betriebsfremd	external
Betriebsurlaub	plant holidays
Bett	bed
Bettüberwurf	bedspread
beurteilen	to evaluate
Beuschel (Lamm)	lamb pluck
Beuschel (Kalb)	stewed calf's heart and lights
Beutel	bag
bevorzugen	to prefer
bewerben für (einen Job)	to apply for (a job)
bewundern	to admire
bezahlen	to settle
Konto ausgleichen	to settle an account
beziehen auf	to refer to
Bibernelle	burnet
Bibliothek	library
Bier	beer
Bier vom Fass	draught beer
Bier-, Maßkrug	stein
Bierdeckel	beer mat
Bierglas (groß)	beer tumbler
Bierhefe	brewer's yeast
Bierkrug	beer jug, mug
Biersauce	beer sauce
Biertulpe	Pilsner glass
helles obergäriges Hefebier	ale, lager, pale ale
–, dunkles	stout, porter, dark beer, brown ale

Bigarade-Sauce	bigarade sauce (flavoured with bitter oranges)
Bildschirm	monitor, screen
billiger Wein	plonk
Bindemittel	thickening agent
binden (z. B. mit Mehl oder Stärke)	to bind, thicken
Bindfaden	string
bio(logisch)	organic, organically
Bio-Brot	biological bread
biologisch abbaubar	biodegradable
Birne	pear
Birne Alma	pear Alma (stewed in port wine, decorated with whipped cream)
Birne Helene	pear Helena (pear on vanilla ice cream with hot chocolate sauce)
Biskotte	sponge biscuits, sponge finger, lady fingers
Biskuitroulade	rolled sponge cake, Swiss roll
Biskuittorte	sponge cake
Bismarckhering	Bismarck herring (marinated herring fillet)
Bissen	mouthful
Bitok	Bitoke (kind of Hamburg steak)
Bitter	bitter
blanchieren	to blanch
Blase	bladder, blister
blass	pale
Blatt	leaf
Blattkohl	*siehe Grünkohl*
Blattsalat	mesclun salad
Blätterteig	flanky, puff pastry
Blätterteigpastete	vol-au-vent (patties filled with fine [veal, chicken, game, ham ...] stew)
– mit Geflügel	chicken vol-au-vent
– mit Meeresfrüchten	seafood vol-au-vent
– mit Pilzen	mushroom vol-au-vent
blau gekocht	cooked au bleu
Blaukraut	red cabbage
Blaubeere(n)	bilberry, -ies (pl) (BE), blueberry, -ies (pl) (AE)
Blauschimmelkäse	blue cheese
Bleistift	pencil
Bleistiftmine	pencil lead
Blesshuhn	coot
Blini	blini (small buckwheat pancakes)
Blitz	lightening

German	English
blumig	flowery, floral
Blumengeschäft	flower shop
Blumenschmuck	floral decoration
Blumenstrauß	flower bouquet
Blumenvase	flower vase
Blüte	blossom
Blütenblatt	petal
blutig	rare, underdone
Blutwurst	black pudding, blood sausage
Bockshornklee	fenugreek
Boden	soil
Bodensatz	sediment
böhmischer Knödel	diced bread dumpling
Bohnen	beans
Bohnenkraut	savory
Bordeauxwein	Bordeaux
–, rot	– red Bordeaux, claret
–, weiß	– white Bordeaux
Bordelaise-Sauce	bordelaise sauce (wine sauce with beef marrow)
Bordkarte	boarding pass
Borretsch	borage
Bouillabaisse	Bouillabaisse, fish soup (French style), French fish soup with saffron
Bouillonkartoffeln	bouillon potatoes
Bouquet	bouquet
Bowle	cup (chilled drink of wine and fruits)
Brandteig	choux pastry
Brandteigkrapferln	profiteroles
Branntwein	spirit
Brasse	bream
Bratapfel	baked apple
braten	to fry
–, im Ofen	to roast
–, in der Pfanne	to pan-fry
Braten	roast ...
Bratenfett	dripping
Bratengitter	roasting rack
Bratenpfanne	roasting pan
Bratensaft	gravy
Bratenspieß	spit
Bratenwender	roasting spit, turnspit
Bräter	roasting dish
bratfertig	oven-ready
Bratkartoffeln	pan-fried potatoes
Bratpfanne	frying pan

German	English
Bratwurst	brat, bratwurst, roast pork sausage
– mit Sauerkraut	fried pork sausage with sauerkraut
brauchen	to require
Brauerei	brewery
bräunen	to brown
braune Butter	brown/black butter
brauner Fond	brown stock
braune Sauce	brown sauce
breites Angebot	wide range of
Brennnessel	nettle
Brett	board
Brettljause	snack on a wooden platter
Brezel	pretzel (crispy knot-shaped biscuit), bretzel
Bridiernadel	trussing needle
Briefpapier (vorgedruckt)	letterhead paper
Briefwaage	postal scales
Bries	sweetbread
Brimsen	cream cheese made of ewe's milk
Brioche	brioche
Brokkoli	broccoli
– mit Butterbröseln	– with breadcrumbs and butter
Brokkoliröschen	broccoli florets
Brombeere(n)	blackberry, -ies (pl), brambleberry, -ies (pl)
Brösel	breadcrumbs
Brot	bread
–, selbst gebacken	home-baked bread
–, ungesäuert	unleavened bread
–, weiß	white bread
Brotkorb	bread basket
Brotsauce	bread sauce
Brotwürfel	bread cubes
Brunch	brunch (BReakfast + lUNCH)
Brunnenkresse	watercress
Bruschetta	bruschetta (toasted garlic bread)
Brüsseler Spitzen	Belgian endive
Brust	breast of ...
Bruststück	brisket
gefüllte Kalbsbrust	roast stuffed breast of veal
brutto	gross
Bücherregal	bookshelf
Buchhaltung	accountancy
Buchladen	bookstore
Büchsenfleisch	preserved meat
Buchteln	yeast buns
Buchung	booking
Buchungsformular	booking form

Buchweizen	buckwheat
Buchweizenpfannkuchen	buckwheat pancake
Bückling	bloater, buckling, kipper
Büffel-Mozzarella	buffalo mozzarella
Bügeleisen	iron
Bügelservice	iron service
Bühne	stage
Bulette	*siehe Fleischlaibchen*
Bundesland	province
Bündner Fleisch	Grisons air-dried beef
bunter Salat	fancy salad
Burgunder	Burgundy
Burgunderbraten	boeuf bourguignon (beef stew in red wine), Burgundy beef stew
Burgundersauce	burgundy sauce (red wine sauce)
Büroklammer	paper clip
Bürolager	supply cabinet
Bürste	brush
Bürzel	parson's nose
Bus erreichen	to catch the bus
Busecca	busecca (tripe and bean soup)
Butter	butter
–, gesalzen	salted butter
–, geklärt	clarified butter
–, grün	green butter
Butterfisch	butter fish
Butterkeks	butter biscuit
Buttermesser	side knife, butter knife, spreader
Buttermilch	buttermilk
Buttermischungen	savoury butters
Buttersauce	butter sauce
Butterteller	side plate, bread and butter plate
in Butter schwenken	to butter

C

Calvados	calvados (apple brandy)
Campingplatz	camping site
Canapés	canapés
Cannelloni	cannelloni (stuffed rolls of noodle dough)
Caprese Salat	tomato and mozzarella salad
Carmen-Suppe	Carmen soup (cream of rice coloured with tomato purée)
Carpaccio	carpaccio, beef carpaccio (thin slices of raw beef seasoned with oil and Parmesan)
Cashewnuss	cashew (nut)

German	English
Cassata	cassata (slice of ice cream with candied fruit)
Cassis	cassis (liqueur made from blackcurrants)
Cayenne(-pfeffer)	cayenne (pepper)
Champagner	champagne
Champagnersauce	champagne sauce
Champagnertulpe	champagne tulip
Champignon	mushroom, white mushroom
–, gebacken	deep-fried breaded mushrooms
Champignonsauce	champignon sauce
Chantilly-Sauce	Chantilly sauce
charmant	charming
Chateaubriand	double fillet steak
Chauffeur	driver
Cheddarkäse	cheddar cheese
Chef	manager, boss
Chefkoch, -köchin	executive chef
Chefportier	hall porter (BE), bell captain (AE)
Chefsalat	chef's salad
Chesterstangen	chester straws
Chicorée	chicory
Chili	chili, chilli
Chili con Carne	chili con carne (chili stew of minced beans and beef)
Chili(-pulver)	chili powder
Chilisauce	chili sauce
Chinakohl	Chinese cabbage
Chips	crisps
Choron-Sauce	Choron sauce (Béarnaise sauce with tomato purée)
Christi Himmelfahrt	Ascension Day
Cioppino	cioppino (stew of fish and shellfish in tomato sauce)
circa	roughly
Clementine	clementine
Clubsandwich	club sandwich
Cockpit	cockpit
Cocktail	cocktail
– mischen	to mix a cocktail
– mit Früchten	cobbler
– mit Gingerale	cooler
– mit Sahne	flip
– mit Zuckerrand	crustas
Cocktailkarte	cocktail list
Cocktailkirschen	maraschino cherries
Cocktailschale	cocktail glass
Cocktailtulpe	hurricane glass

German	English
Cognac	cognac
Cognacschwenker	brandy snifter
Colbert-Sauce	Colbert sauce (maître d'hôtel butter blended with meat jelly)
Collinsglas	Collins glass
Computerarbeitsplatz	workstation
Cordon bleu	escalope of veal cordon bleu (filled with ham and cheese)
Cornflakes	cornflakes
Couscous	couscous
Couvertteller	side plate, bread and butter plate
Crème brûlée	crème brûlée, burnt cream
Cremeschnitte	cream slice, millefeuille, napoleon (AE)
Cremesuppe	cream soup, cream of ..., bisque
Spargelcremesuppe	cream of asparagus
Karfiolcremesuppe, Blumenkohlcremesuppe	cream of cauliflower
Geflügel-/Hühnercremesuppe	cream of chicken
Lauchcremesuppe	cream of leek
Champignon-/Pilzcremesuppe	cream of mushroom
Erbsencremesuppe	cream of pea
Kartoffelcremesuppe	cream of potato
Gemüsecremesuppe	cream of vegetable
Wildcremesuppe	cream of venison
cremig	creamy
Crêpe Suzette	crêpe suzette (with flaming orange liqueur)
Crostini	croutes, toast
Croûtons	croutons
Cumberlandsauce	Cumberland sauce (redcurrant jelly, mustard, orange juice and port)
Curry(pulver)	curry (powder)
Currysauce	curry sauce

D

German	English
Damentoilette	ladies (toilet)
Damhirsch	fallow deer
dämpfen	to steam
Dampfkartoffeln	steamed potatoes
Dämpfer	steamer
Darblay-Suppe	Darblay soup (potato soup with shredded vegetables)
Darm	intestine
darunterziehen (z. B. Eischnee unter die Masse ziehen)	to fold in

German	English
das Geschäft/Hotel leiten	to run the business/hotel
Dattel	date
Dattelmuscheln	piddocks
Datum	date
Dauphine-Kartoffeln	dauphine potatoes, potato croquettes
Debreziner	debreziner (sausage)
Decke	blanket
Deckel	lid
deftig	substantial
dekantieren	to decant
dekorieren	to decorate
desinfizieren	to disinfect
Dessert	dessert, sweets
Dessertgabel	dessert fork, salad fork, pudding fork
Dessertgebäck	dessert pastry
Dessertlöffel	dessert spoon
Dessertmesser	dessert knife
deutsche Sauce	German sauce (with veal stock)
deutscher Kaviar	roe lumpfish
Dezember	December
Diaprojektor	slide projector
Diät	diet
Diäteinschränkungen	dietary restrictions
dick	thick, stout
dickmachend	fattening
dick werden lassen (z. B. Milch)	to clot
Dickmilch	curdled milk
Diebstahlversicherung	theft protection
Diener	valet
Dienstag	Tuesday
Dienstplan	duty roster
Digitalkamera	digital camera
Dill	dill
Dillbutter	dill butter
Dillsauce	dill sauce
Dinkel	spelt
Dinkelnudeln	spelt noodles
Diskretion	discretion
Donnerstag	Thursday
Donut	doughnut
Doppeldecker	double-decker
doppelte Lendenschnitte	double tenderloin steak
doppelter Scotch	double Scotch
doppeltes Zwischenrippenstück	double sirloin steak
Doppelzimmer	double room
Dorade	*siehe Goldbrasse*
Dörrpflaume	prune

Dorsch	cod, codling, codfish
Dose	tin (BE), can (AE)
Dosenbier	tinned beer
Dosenöffner	tin opener (BE), can opener (AE)
Drachenkopf	scorpion fish
Drahtgestell	wire rack
drahtlose Internetverbindung	wireless internet connection
drehen	to turn
Drehstuhl	swivel chair
Drehtür	revolving door
Dreieck	triangle
Dreikönig	Epiphany
dressieren (Geflügel)	to truss
Drosseln	thrushes
Druck	pressure
Druckbleistift	drop action pencil, retractable pencil, mechanical pencil
Drucker	printer
Druckerpatrone	print cartridge
Duchesse-Kartoffeln	duchess potatoes (potato croquettes browned in the oven)
dunkles Bier	dark beer
dünsten	to smother
dünsten (Kasserolle)	to pot roast
Durchfall	diarrhoea
durchgegart	well-done
Durchreiche	serving hatch
Durchsage	public announcement
durchsichtig	transparent
durchstreichen	to cross out
durchwachsen	streaky, marbled, pancetta
Durchwahl	extension
durstig	thirsty
Duschkabine	shower cubicle
Duschkopf	shower head
Duschschlauch	shower hose
Duschvorhang	shower curtain
Düse	nozzle
Dutzend	a dozen of
DVD-Spieler	DVD player

E

Éclairs	éclairs (small cakes of choux pastry filled with cream and chocolate glazing)
Ecke	corner
–, an der	at/on the corner

German	English
Edamer	edam (AE)
edel	noble
Edelstahl	stainless steel
ehemalig	former
ehrgeizig	ambitious
Ei	egg
– aus Freilandhaltung	free-range eggs
–, florentinisch	eggs Florentine, poached (eggs on bed of leaf-spinach)
–, gefüllt	stuffed egg, eggs mimosa
–, hart gekocht	hard-boiled egg
– in Cocotte (pochiert)	en cocotte
– in Mayonnaise	egg in mayonnaise
– nach Wunsch	eggs any style, cooked to order
–, pochiert	poached egg
–, russisch	stuffed eggs, Russian style
–, wachsweich	medium-boiled egg
–, weich gekocht	soft-boiled egg
Eier Benedikt	eggs Benedict (poached egg with ham and hollandaise sauce)
Eier Bercy	eggs Bercy, fried (with grilled sausage and tomato sauce)
Eier Chimay	eggs Chimay, stuffed (eggs au gratin with mushroom stuffing)
Eier Mornay	eggs Mornay, poached (au gratin)
Eier Turbigo	eggs Turbigo, fried (with sausage)
Eierspeise	scrambled egg
Eierfrucht	eggplant, aubergine
Eidotter, Eigelb	egg yolk
Eiernudeln	egg noodles
Eiersauce	egg sauce
Eierschale	eggshell
Eierschneider	egg slicer
Eierschwammerl	chanterelles
Eierschwammerlsauce	chanterelles sauce
Eieruhr	egg timer, kitchen timer
Eiweiß	egg white
Eichenfass	oak barrel
eifrig	keen
Eigenschaft	characteristic
Eimer	bucket
einarbeiten	to incorporate, to fold in
Einbahn(-straße)	one-way street
Einbrenn	roux
–, dunkel	dark roux
–, hell	clear roux
Einbrennsuppe	brown soup

Eincheckschalter	check-in counter
einfach	simple
einfetten	to grease
einfrieren	to freeze
Eingang	entrance
Eingangshalle	entrance hall
eingeben (Tastatur)	to key in
eingelegt	pickled
eingemacht	potted
Eingeweide	guts
einheimisch	native, local
Einheimische/r	local
einhüllen	to wrap
Einkauf	purchase
einkaufen	to purchase
Einlage	additions
einlegen	to souse
Einmach	*siehe Einbrenn*
Einmachglas	preserving jar
Einmachsuppe	thick soup
einölen	to rub oil into sth
einreiben	to rub in
Einrichtung	facility
einschalten (Licht)	to switch on
einschätzen	to evaluate
Einschätzung	assessment
einsteigen	to board
einstreichen	to brush
einstreichen (mit Öl)	to oil
eintauchen	to dip
–, in Backteig	to batter
einteilen	to arrange
Eintopf(gericht)	hot pot, hotchpotch, single-dish meal
eintragen (mit Tastatur)	to enter
Eintrittsdatum	entry date
Einwanderung	immigration
Einwegflasche	non-returnable bottle
einweichen	to soak
Einwohner/in	resident
Einzelhandel	retail
Einzelnutzung	single use
Einzelzimmer	single room
Eisbecher	sundae, coupe, ice cream tub
Eisbein	pickled leg of pork
Eisbergsalat	iceberg lettuce
Eiscreme	ice cream
Eisenkrauttee	vervain tea
eisgekühlt	iced, chilled

Eiskübel	ice bucket
Eismaschine	ice cream maker, ice machine
Eisomelette (mit Baiserhaube)	ice omelette, baked Alaska (ice cream covered with meringue)
Eisschaufel	ice scoop
Eiswasser	iced water
Eiswürfel	ice cube
Eiszange	ice tongs (pl)
ekelhaft	revolting
elastisch	elastic
Elch	elk, moose
elegant	sleek
Elektriker/in	electrician
Emmentaler	Emmenthal
Empfang	reception
Empfänger (Brief)	recipient
Empfänger	receiver
Empfangsdame/-herr	receptionist
empfehlen	to recommend
Empfehlung	recommendation
Empfehlung des Hauses/ Küchenchefs	chef's recommendation
emulgieren	to emulsify
Endivie	endive (BE), chicory (AE)
Endstück	end piece
eng	narrow
Enoki Pilz	enoki mushroom
Ente	duck
Entenküken	duckling
enteisen	to defrost
entfernen	to take away, to remove
entfetten	to remove fat from
entgräten	to bone
enthülsen	to pod
entkalken	decalcify
entkernen	to core, to stone
entkernt	stoned (BE)
entkorken	to uncork
Entrecote Mirabeau	sirloin steak Mirabeau (with anchovy fillets and olives)
Entrecote nach Lyoner Art (mit Zwiebeln)	sirloin steak lyonnais (with fried onions)
Entrecote nach Tiroler Art (mit Tomaten und Zwiebelringen)	Tyrolean sirloin steak (with tomatoes and fried onion rings)
entschäumen	to remove the froth
entschlossen	unflinching
entschuppen (Fisch)	to scale
Entschuppungsgerät	fish scaler
entsteinen	to stone

German	English
entstielen	to destalk
enthusiastisch	enthusiastic
Entwurf	layout
entzündlich	inflammable
Enziansauce	gentian sauce
Enzianschnaps	gentian
Erbsen	peas
Erbsenpüree	pea purée, pease pudding
Erbsenpüreesuppe (frisch, getrocknet, grün)	green pea purée soup (fresh, dried, green)
Erbsenschoten	sugar peas, mangetout peas
Erdapfel	*siehe Kartoffel*
Erdbeere(n)	strawberry, -ies (pl)
Erdbeereis	strawberry ice cream
erdig	earthy
Erdnuss	peanut
Erdnussbutter	peanut butter
Erdnusssauce	peanut sauce
Erfahrung	experience
Erfrischung	refreshment
Erfrischungsraum	refreshment room
erfrischend (Wein)	refreshing
erhalten	to receive
erhitzen	to heat, to scald
Erholung	recreation
Erklärung	explanation
Ermäßigung	reduction
Ernährungslehre	nutritional science
Ersatz	substitute
Erscheinung(sbild)	appearance
erschöpft	exhausted
erschöpflich	exhaustible
erschwinglich	affordable
ersetzen	to replace, to substitute
Erstattung	reimbursement
Erste Hilfe	first aid
Erste-Hilfe-Kasten	first aid kit
erste Klasse	business class
erwärmen	to warm
Espresso	espresso
Essig	vinegar
Essig-(Öl-)Karaffe	oil and vinegar cruet set
Essigessenz	vinegar essence
Essiggurken	cornichons, gherkins (BE), pickles (AE)
Esslöffel voll	tablespoonful (tbs)
Estragon	tarragon
Estragonbutter	tarragon butter
Estragonsauce	tarragon sauce

Etikette	label
etikettiert	labelled
Euter	udder

F

fad (geschmacklos)	unsavoury
fad (langweilig)	boring
Faden	thread
Fadennudeln, Vermicelli	vermicelli
Fähigkeit	ability, skill
zu etwas fähig sein	to be skilled
Fahrstuhlführer	liftboy
falten	to fold
Familienprogramm	family plan
Familienstand	marital status
fantastisch	fancy
färben	to dye
Färbung	colouring
Fasan	pheasant
faschieren (Fleisch)	to mince
faschieren (Nüsse)	to grind
faschierter Braten	meat loaf
Faschiertes	minced meat
Faschingskrapfen	*siehe Krapfen*
Fass	barrel
Fastenspeise	Lenten dish
Fastensuppe	Lenten soup, soup maigre
Faxgerät	facsimile transmitter, fax machine
Februar	February
Feder	feather
Feiertag, Urlaub	holiday
staatlicher Feiertag	public holiday
religiöser Feiertag	religious holiday
Feige	fig
fein	elegant
Feinschmecker	gourmet
auf Feinschmeckerart	for gourmets
Feldthymian	wild thyme
Fenchel	fennel
Fenchelsauce	fennel sauce
Fenster	window
Ferienhaus	cottage
Fermentation, Gärung	fermentation
Fernbedienung	remote control
Fertiggerichte	instant meal, food
fest füllen	to stuff, to fill
feste Reservierung	firm reservation

festgehalten	laid down
Festigkeit	firmness
Festsaal	ballroom
Fettabscheider	fat separator
fettarm	low-fat
Fettgehalt	fat content
feucht	damp
Feuchttuch	wet tissue, wipe
Feueralarm	fire alarm
feuerfest	fireproof, ovenproof
Feuerleiter	fire escape
Feuerlöscher	fire extinguisher
Feuerwehr	fire brigade
Feuerzeug	lighter
Fieber	fever
Filet	fillet of ...
filetieren	to fillet
Filetiermesser	filleting knife
Filetsteak	fillet steak, prime steak
kleines Filetsteak	tournedo
Filterkaffee	filtered coffee, regular coffee, percolated coffee drip coffee (AE)
Filterpapier	filter paper
Finanzmannsauce	sauce financière (Madeira sauce flavoured with truffle)
Fingerschale	finger bowl, finger glass
Finnenbrot	Finnish rye
Fisch	fish
–, fangfrisch	catch of the day
– in Muschelschalen	scalloped fish
Fischersauce (à la pecheur)	fisher sauce
Fischfond	fishstock, court-bouillon
Fischgabel	fish fork
Fischgericht	fish dish
Fischgeschirr	fish dish
Fischhändler	fishmonger
Fischkochtopf	fish kettle
Fischmesser	fish knife
Fischstäbchen	fish finger
Fisolen (grüne Bohnen)	green/French/string beans
Fitnessraum, Turnsaal	gym
flach	flat
Fladenbrot	focaccia, flat bread
flambieren	to flambé
Flammeri	flummery
Grießflammeri	flummery of semolina
Flasche	bottle
Flaschenbier	bottled beer
Flaschenöffner	bottle opener

German	English
Flaschenportionierer	measure pourer
Flaschenwein	bottled wine
flaumig	fluffy
flechten	to weave
Fleisch	flesh
Fleischabfälle	meat scraps
Fleischfond	gravy
Fleischgabel	cook's/dinner fork
Fleischgericht	meat dish
Fleischklopfer	mallet
Fleischklöße, Fleischlaibchen	meatballs, hamburger
fleischlos	meatless
Fleischmesser	dinner meat knife
Fleischpastete	Cornish pasty
Fleischwolf	meat mincer/grinder
fleißig	diligent
Fliege (Kleidungsstück)	bow tie
Fliese	tile
Fließband	conveyor belt
Flipchart	flip chart
Flitterwochen	honeymoon
Flocken	flakes
Flosse	fin
Flug	flight
Inlandsflug	domestic flight
Auslandsflug	international flight
Flugangst	aerophobia, fear of flying
Flugbegleiter/in	flight attendant
Flughafenzubringer	airport shuttle (service)
Fluglinie	airline
Fluglinienangestellte/r	airline representative
Flugsteig	gate
Flugstrecke	routing
Flugzeug	airplane, plane
Flügel	wing, winglet
Flunder	flounder
Flüssigkeit	liquid
Fogosch	fogas
Fohlen (Fleisch)	colt
folgen	to follow
Folienkartoffeln	baked potatoes, potatoes en papillote
Fön	hairdryer
Fond	stock
fordern	to stipulate
Forelle	trout
Forellenbarsch	black bass
Form	shape
Becherform	mould

German	English
Foyer	lounge
Fragebogen	questionnaire
Frankfurter Würstel	Frankfurters, frankfurter sausage, Wieners
französische Zwiebelsuppe	French onion soup
frei (auf das Haus)	complimentary
frei (verfügbar)	vacant
Freibad	outdoor pool
freie Stelle	vacancy
Freigepäck	baggage allowance
Freitag	Friday
Freizeit	leisure, spare time
Freizeiteinrichtungen	recreation facilities
Freizeitkleidung	casual clothes
Fremdartigkeit	foreignness
Fremdwährung, in einer	foreign currency, in a
Freude	pleasure
freundlich	kind
Frikassee	fricassee
frisch	fresh
Frische	freshness
Frischhaltefolie	plastic wrap, cling film, wrapping film
Frischkäse	fresh cheese
Frischling	young wild boar
Friseur	hairdresser
Frittaten	sliced pancakes
Frittatensuppe	consommé Célestine (with shredded pancake)
Fritteuse	deep fryer, fryer
frittieren	to fry, to deep-fry
Fronleichnam	Corpus Christi
Froschschenkel	frog legs
Früchte	fruits
– in Backteig	fruits in batter
Fruchtcocktail	fruit cocktail
Früchtegelee(s)	fruit jelly, -ies (pl)
Fruchtsaft	fruit juice
Fruchtmark	fruit purée
Früchtekompott	stewed fruit, compote
Früchtespiegel	fruit coulis
Fruchtfleisch	fruit flesh, pulp
Fruchtlikör	fruit-flavoured brandy
fruchtig	fruity
fruchtiger Abgang (Wein)	fruity finish
Frühgemüse	early vegetables
Frühkartoffeln	new potatoes
Frühlingsgemüse	spring vegetables
Frühlingsrolle	spring roll, egg roll

German	English
Frühlingszwiebel	spring onions (BE), scallion (AE)
Frühstück	breakfast
Frühstücksbuffet	breakfast buffet
Frühstückskarte	breakfast menu
Führerschein	driving licence
Fülle	filling, stuffing
füllen	to fill
Füllung	stuffing
Fundbüro	lost and found
Fundsache	lost property
Fußballplatz	football pitch
Fußgängerübergang	pedestrian crossing
Fußgängerzone	pedestrian zone

G

German	English
Gabel	fork
Gabelmakrele	pompano
Galantine	galantine
Galgant	galangal
Galle	gall bladder
Gämse	chamois
Gämsenpfeffer	jugged chamois
Gang	aisle
Gang (erster, zweiter ...)	course (first, second ...)
3-gängiges Abendessen	3-course dinner
gängig	major
gängige Kreditkarten	major credit cards
Gans	goose, geese (pl)
Gänseleber	goose liver, foie gras
Gänseleberpastete	goose liver pâté
Gänsefleischpastete	goose paste
Gänseconfit	confit of goose (goose preserved in fat)
ganz	whole
Garantie	warranty
Gardemanger	larder
Garderobe	cloakroom, wardrobe
Garderobenfrau	cloakroom attendant
Garmethode	cooking method
Garnele, Krevette	prawn, shrimp
Garnelencocktail	prawn cocktail, shrimp cocktail
Garnelensauce	prawn sauce
Garnelenbutter	shrimp butter
garnieren	to garnish
Garnitur	garnishing
Gartenkresse	garden cress
Gasherd	gas cooker

German	English
Gast	guest
Gästeblatt	registration form
Gästebuch	hotel register
Gästezimmer	guest room
Gastfamilie	host family
Gastfreundschaft	hospitality
Gasthaus	inn, country-inn
(Gäste) empfangen	to receive (guests)
Gazpacho	Gazpacho (soup of uncooked vegetables with vinegar and oil)
Gebäck	plaited rolls
gebackene Apfelspalten	apple fritters
gebeizt	graved
gebildet	educated
Gebrauch	use
Gebühr	fee
gebührenfrei	free of charge
Gedeck	place setting
Gedeck (Kosten)	cover service
Geduld	patience
geeignet	suitable
geeist	iced, chilled
Geflügel	poultry, fowl
Geflügelleber	poultry liver
Geflügelauflauf	chicken soufflé
Geflügelfond	chicken stock
Geflügelklein	giblets
Geflügelkroketten	chicken croquettes
Geflügelmagen	gizzard
Geflügelragout	chicken stew
Geflügelsalat	chicken salad
Geflügelschere	poultry shears
Geflügelsuppe mit Tomaten	consommé madrilène (chicken broth with tomatoes)
Gefrierschrank	freezer
Gegenstand	item
gegenüber	opposite of
Gehalt	salary
gehaltvoll	full-bodied
gehen	to go
gehen lassen (Teig)	to prove
Gehirn	brain
Geld abheben	to withdraw
Geldwechsel	currency exchange
Gelee	jelly, -ies (pl)
Früchtegelees	fruit jellies
Weingelee	wine jelly
Gelegenheit	occasion
Geliermittel	gelling agent

German	English
Gelierzucker	preserving sugar
gemäß den Jahreszeiten	seasonal, in season
gemischt	mixed, assorted
gemischter Salat, Beilagensalat	assorted salad
Gemüse	vegetables, veggies
Gemüsesäfte	vegetable juices
Gemüsemesser	vegetable knife
Gemüseschäler	vegetable peeler
Gemüsefond	vegetable stock
Gemüsestreifen	vegetable stripes
Gemüsepaprika	sweet pepper
Gemüsepfanne	stir-fry (vegetables)
gemütlich	cosy
genannt	quoted
genau	accurate
Genauigkeit	accuracy, precision
Genfer Sauce	genevoise sauce (red wine sauce with anchovy butter)
genügend	sufficient
Gepäck	luggage, baggage
Gepäckabholbereich	baggage claim area
Gepäckausgabe	baggage claim
Gepäcksschild	luggage tag
Gepäckswagen	luggage carrier
gepflegt	soigné
gepökelt	cured
geradeaus	straight ahead
Gerät	utensil, appliance
gereift	aged
Gericht	meal
gerinnen	to coagulate
Germ	yeast
Germknödel	yeast dumpling
Germteig	yeast dough
Germiny-Suppe	germiny soup (sorrel soup bound with egg yolks and cream)
Gerste	barley
Gerstensuppe	barley soup
Geruch	scent, smell
Gesamtbetrag	total amount
Gesamtschule	comprehensive school
gesättigt	saturated
gesättigte Fettsäuren	saturated fatty acids
Geschäftsessen	business lunch/meal, company dinner
geschieden	divorced
Geschirr	crockery, china
Geschirrspüler	dishwasher

German	English
Geschirrspülraum	washing-up room
Geschirrtuch	tea cloth, towel
Geschmack	flavour, taste
Geschmacksverstärker	flavour enhancer
geschmacklos	unsavoury, insipid, tasteless
geschmackvoll	tasty
Geschwister	siblings
Geselchtes	smoked pork
Gesetz	law
Gesicht	face
gespritzt (Obst, Gemüse)	sprayed
gesund (Essen)	wholesome
Gesundheitszustand	state of health
gesurt	gammon
Getränk	beverage, drink
–, begleitendes	corresponding drink
Kreation des Barkeepers	fancy drink
Getränkekarte	drink list
Getreide	cereals
getrocknete Früchte	dried fruits
Gewährleistung	guarantee
Gewicht	weight
nach Gewicht	by weight
Gewinn	profit
Gewinnspanne	profit margin
Gewitter	thunderstorm
Gewohnheit	habit
Gewürze	spice
Gewürzfruchtpastete	chutney
Gewürzsenf	German mustard
gezuckert	sweetened
gießen	to pour
– einschenken	to pour in
– begießen	to pour on, to pour over
– aufgießen	to pour onto
– mit etwas übergießen	to pour over with sth
Gitterbett	crib
glacieren	to glaze
Glanz	brightness
glänzend	shiny
Glas	jar
Glasaal	elver, silver eel
Glasnudeln	Chinese noodles
Glasur	glazing, glaze, icing, frosting
glatt	even
Glattbutt	brill
Glätteisen	(smoothing) iron
Glatthai	smooth hound, dogfish
gleichzeitig	simultaneous

German	English
Gleitzeit	flexitime
Gliederung	grouping
Glocke	bell
Glühbirne	light bulb
Glühmost	mulled cider
Glühwein	mulled wine
Golatsche	sweet roll
Goldbarsch	red perch, redfish, rosefish, bergylt
Goldbrasse	dorado, gilthead
Golfplatz	golf course
Grad	degree
Grahambrot	Graham bread, whole wheat bread (AE)
Grammeln	cracklings, greaves
Grammelknödel	dumplings with pork cracklings
Granatapfel	grenadine, pomegranate
Granatapfelsauce	pomegranate sauce
Grand-veneur-Sauce	sauce grand-veneur (poivrade sauce with game extract and redcurrant jelly), venison sauce
Grapefruit	grapefruit
grasig	grassy
gratinieren	to gratinate
Graupen	pearl barley
Gribiche-Sauce	gribiche sauce (tartare sauce with capers)
Grieß	semolina
Grießbrei	semolina pudding
Grießknödel	semolina dumpling
Grießpudding	semolina pudding
grillen	to barbecue, to grill, to broil (AE)
mit Holzkohle grillen	to charcoal broil
Grill	griddle
Griller	barbecue, BBQ
Grillgerichte, Grilladen	grills, grilled meats, grilled dishes
Grissini	grissini (crisp bread in long thin sticks)
grob	coarse
grobkörniges Salz	coarse salt
Großhandel	wholesale
Großmarkt	wholesale market
großzügig	generous
gründlich	thorough
Gründling	gudgeon
Grundriss	floor plan
grundsätzlich	genuinely
Grünkern	unripe grain (of spelt)
Grünkohl	kale, green cabbage
Gruppenleiter	group leader

German	English
Gruppentarif	group rate
Gruß	regard
Gugelhupf	gugelhupf, gugelhopf, ring cake
Gulasch	goulash, stewed beef or veal in paprika sauce
Gulaschsuppe	goulash soup (highly seasoned soup of beef and potatoes)
Gummimatte	rubber mat
Gurke	cucumber
Gurkensauce	cucumber sauce
Gurt	seat belt
Gusseisen	cast iron
gut aufgelegt	cheerful
gut aussehend	well-presented
gut gelaunt	good-humoured
gut organisiert	well-organised
Gütesiegel	seal of quality
Gutschein	voucher
Gymnasium	grammar school (BE), high school (AE)

H

German	English
hacken, klein hacken	to chop up
Hackbeil	chopper, cleaver
Hackbrett	chopping board
Hackmesser, Wiegemesser	chopping knife
Hackstock	chopping block
Hafer	oats
Haferflocken	oat flakes, rolled oats
Hafergebäck	oat cakes
Haferbrei	porridge, oatmeal
Haferflockensuppe	oatmeal soup
Haferschrot	grits
Haftnotizzettel	post-it notes
Hagebutte	rosehip
Hagel	hail
Hagelzucker	sugar crystals
Haggis	haggis (sheep's offal boiled in the animal's stomach)
Hahn	cock
–, jung	cockerel
Hahnenkamm	cockscomb
Hai	shark
Häkchen	tick
halbe-halbe	fifty-fifty
halbfest	semi-hard

German	English
Halbpension	half board, part board, demi pension
halbsüß	medium sweet, semi-sweet
halbtrocken	medium dry
Halle	terminal
Hallenbad	indoor pool
Halstuch (Koch)	chef's kerchief
Halstuch, Schal	scarf
Haltbarkeit	shelf life
Haltbarkeitsdatum	sell-by date
Hammelfleisch	mutton
Hammelbrust	breast of mutton
Hammelkeule	leg of mutton
Hammelkarree	rack of mutton, loin of mutton
Hammelkotelett	mutton chop
Hammelragout	mutton stew
Hammelrippenstück	rib of mutton
Hammelbraten	roast mutton
Hammelschulter	saddle of mutton, shoulder of mutton
Hammelfüße	mutton trotters
Handelsakademie	commercial college, business school
Handelsschule	commercial school
Handgepäck	carry-on bag, hand luggage
Handgepäcksablage	overhead compartment
handhaben	to handle
Handlauf	handrail
Handmühle	hand mill
Handschuh	glove
Handtuch	(hand) towel
Handtuchhalter	towel rack, towel rail
Handy	cell phone, mobile phone
Hanföl	hemp seed oil
Hanfsamen	hemp seed
Harfe (Küchengerät)	guitar cutter
Harissa	harissa (chilli sauce)
hart werden	to become hard, to become tough
Hartkäse	hard cheese
Hartweizen	durum wheat
Hase	hare
Haselnuss	hazelnut, filbert, noisette
Haselnussauflauf	filbert soufflé
Haselnusscreme	hazelnut cream
Hasenpfeffer	jugged hare
Haube	wooly hat
Häuptelsalat	lettuce
Hauptgang	main course
Hauptgericht	main dish

German	English
Hauptsaison	peak period
Hauptschule	secondary (modern) school (BE), junior high school (AE)
Hausbote	pageboy
Hausdame, Haushälter/in	executive housekeeper
hausgebeizt	home-marinated
hausgemacht	homemade
Hausmädchen/-bursche	floor maid/attendant
Hausmannskost	plain cooking, plain food
Haut	skin
HBLA	college for home economies
Hebel	lever
Hecht	pike
Hefe	yeast
Hefegebäck	yeast pastry
Hefekuchen	yeast cake
Heidelbeere(n)	bilberry, -ies (pl) (BE), blueberry, -ies (pl) (AE)
Heilbutt	halibut
heimisch	domestic
heiße Schokolade	hot chocolate
Heizung	heating
helles Bier	light (pale) beer
herb	dry
Herbe	bitterness
Herd	(kitchen) range, stove
–, freistehend	central stove
Hering	herring
–, geräuchert	smoked herring
–, mariniert	marinated herring
Heringssalat	herring salad
Heringshai	porbeagle, mackerel shark
Herkunft	origin
Herkunftsbezeichnung	mark of origin
Herkunftsnachweis	proof of origin
Herkunftsort	point of origin
Herrenfriseur	barber's shop
Herrentoilette	gents (toilet)
herstellen	to produce
Hersteller	manufacturer
Herstellungsdatum	manufacturing date
Herz	heart
herzhaft	hearty, savoury
Herzmuschel	cockle
Heurige (Kartoffeln)	new potatoes
Heuriger (Wein)	young, new wine
Heuriger (Lokal)	wine tavern
Heuschnupfen	hay fever
Hilfskellner/in	assistant waiter/waitress

German	English
Hilfskoch, Küchenhilfe	assistant chef, assistant cook
Himbeere(n)	raspberry, -ies (pl)
hinaufgehen	to go upstairs
hinten	at the rear
hinter	behind
hinteres Viertel	hindquarters
Hintergrundmusik	background music
hinuntergehen	to go downstairs
Hinweis	indication
hinzufügen	to add
Hirn mit Ei	calf's brain with egg
Hirsch	deer, stag
Hirschfilet	fillet of deer
Hirschkalb	fawn
Hirschkeule, -schlegel	leg of deer
Hirschkotelett	deer chop
Hirschschnitzel	escalope of deer
Hirschsteak	deer steak
Hirschragout	deer stew, ragout of deer
Hirse	millet
Hirtenpastete	shepherd's pie (minced meat topped with mashed potato) cottage pie
hitzebeständig	heatproof
H-Milch	long-life milk
Hochrippe	prime rib of beef
Hochsaison	high season
Hochzeit	wedding
Hochzeitssuite	bridal suite
Hochzeitstag	wedding anniversary
Höflichkeit	courtesy, politeness
aus Höflichkeit	by courtesy
höflich	courteous, polite
höhere Schule	senior high school
Hollandaise Sauce	hollandaise sauce (yolks of egg, melted butter, lemon juice)
holländischer Käse	Dutch cheese, edam (AE)
Holunder, Holler	elderberry, -ies (pl)
Holunderblütensirup	elderberry blossom syrup
Holundersauce	elderberry sauce
Holzofen	wood-burning oven
Holzofen-Brot	wood-stove baked bread
Holzofen-Pizza	wood-stove baked pizza
Honig	honey
Honigmelone	honeydew melon
Hopfen	hop
Hörnchen	elbow macaroni
Hornhecht	needlefish, garfish
Hotel am Flughafen	terminal hotel

German – English

Hotelhalle	lobby
Hotelkette	hotel chain
HTL	technical college
Huchen, Donaulachs	huchen, Danube salmon
Hüferschwanzel	aitchbone of beef
Huhn	chicken
–, gebacken	fried chicken
Junghuhn	spring chicken
Hühnerbrust	chicken breast
Hühnercurry	chicken curry
Hühnerflügel	chicken wings, winglets
Hühnergalantine	chicken galantine
Hühnerkeule	(chicken) thigh, drumsticks
Hühnerklein	chicken giblets (and trimmings)
Hühnerkraftsuppe	chicken broth
Hühnerleber	chicken liver
Hühnerpastete	chicken pâté
Hühnersuppe mit Lauch	cock-a-leekie (soup of chicken and leeks)
Hülsenfrüchte	pulses
Hummer	lobster
– amerikanische Art	American style lobster (in rich tomato sauce)
–, flambiert	lobster flambé
–, gefüllt	stuffed lobster
Hummerbisque	lobster bisque
Hummerbutter	lobster butter
Hummercocktail	lobster cocktail
Hummergabel	lobster pick
Hummerkrabben	red prawns
Hummermayonnaise	lobster mayonnaise
Hummersalat	lobster salad
Hummersauce	lobster sauce
Hummerzange	lobster cracker
Thermidor	thermidor (lobster meat baked in the lobster shell)
hungrig	hungry
Hustenstiller	cough reliever
Hüttenkäse	cottage cheese

I

Imbiss, Jause	snack
Impfung	vaccination
in Folie, in Papier	en papillote (in paper casing)
in Form bringen	to shape
in Kürze	in brief
Induktionsplatte	induction cooktop

German	English
Information	information desk
Informationsständer	information rack
Ingwer	ginger
Ingwersauce	ginger sauce
Inhalt, Gehalt	content
Inneneinrichtung	interior
Innereien	offals, giblets, pluck
– vom Lamm	– lamb pluck
innerhalb	within
Insassenversicherung	PAI (personal accident insurance)
Installateur/in	plumber
Instantbrühe	instant broth
Internat	boarding house/school
Internet	internet
Irish-Coffee-Glas	Irish coffee glass
Irish Stew (Hammelfleischeintopf)	Irish stew (mutton stew with onions and potatoes)
(sich) irren	to be mistaken
italienische Sauce	Italian sauce
italienische Teigwaren	Italian pasta
italienisches/offenes Omelette	frittata

J

German	English
Jacke	jacket
Jägerart	chasseur
Jägersauce (Champignons, Weißwein, Tomatensauce), Sauce Chasseur	hunter sauce, sauce chasseur (mushrooms, white wine, tomato sauce)
Jahresurlaub	annual holiday
Jahrgang (Wein)	vintage (year)
Jahrgangsangabe	year of production
mit Jahrgangsangabe	indicating the year of production
Jakobsmuschel	scallop
Jakobsmuschelspießchen	scallop brochettes
Jänner, Januar	January
japanische Mispel	loquat, Japanese medlar
jeden zweiten Tag	every second day
Johannisbeere (rot, schwarz)	currant (red, black)
Johannisbeersaft	currant juice
Johannisbeersauce	redcurrant sauce
Johannisbrot	carob
Joinville-Sauce (Fischsauce mit Garnelenbutter)	Joinville sauce (fish sauce with shrimp butter)
Jugendherberge	youth hostel
Juli	July
jung	young
jung, neu	nouveau

German	English
Junggesellenabend	stag night
Junggesellinnenabschied	hen night
Jungkoch	commis-chef
Juni	June
Jus	gravy
Juweliergeschäft	jeweller's shop

K

German	English
Kabel	cord
Kabeljau	cod, codling, codfish
Kaffee	coffee
–, schwarz	black coffee
–, koffeinfrei	decaffeinated coffee, caffeine-free coffee
– mit Sahne (Obers)	coffee with cream
– mit Milch	coffee with milk
Kaffeebecher	coffee mug
Kaffeekanne	coffee pot
Kaffeetasse	coffee/tea cup
Kaiserpilze, Kaiserlinge	imperial mushrooms
Kaiserschmarren	cut up pancake, kaiserschmarren
Kakao	cocoa
Kaki, Kakipflaume	persimmon
Kaktusfeige	prickly pear
Kalb	calf
Kalbshirn	calf's brains
Kalbsbackerln	calf's cheeks
Kalbskopf	calf's head
Kalbsherz	calf's heart
Kalbsnieren	calf's kidneys
Kalbsnuss	veal noisette
Kalbsleber	calf's liver
Kalbsbries	calf's sweetbread
Kalbszunge	calf's tongue
Kalbfleisch	veal
Kalbspüreesuppe	veal (purée) soup
Kalbskotelett	veal chop
Kalbsmedaillons	veal medallions
Kalbsnuss	veal noisette
Kalbssteak	veal steak
Kalbsragout	veal stew
Kalbsgulasch	veal stew in paprika sauce
Kalbsfond	veal stock
Kalbfleischpastete	veal and ham pie
Kalbsbraten	roast veal
Kalbsbrust, gefüllte	stuffed breast of veal
Kalbskarree	best end neck of veal (loin of veal)

German	English
Kalbsleberwurst	calf's liver sausage
Kalbsnierenbraten (gerollt)	roast (rolled) loin of veal with kidneys
Kalbsnuss	topside of veal
Kalbsragout	ragout of veal
Kalbsragout in weißer Sauce	blanquette of veal
Kalbsrouladen	veal roulades (slice of veal cutlet rolled up with stuffing and stewed)
Kalbsschnitzel	escalope of veal, veal cutlet
Kalbsvögerl	knuckle of veal (braised)
Kalmar	calamary, squid
kalorienarm	low-calorie
kalt	cold
kalter Braten	cold roast meat
kalte Jause (mit großen Stücken Brot, Käse, Speck...)	ploughman's lunch (BE)
kalte Platte	assorted sliced, cold meats, cuts
kalte Vorspeisen	cold appetizers (starters)
kaltgepresst	cold-pressed
Kamille	Camomile
Kamillentee	camomile tea
Kamin	fireplace
Kamm	comb
Kammmuscheln	queen scallops
Kamut	kamut
kandieren	to crystallise
Kandiszucker	rock candy
Kaninchen	rabbit
Kapaun	capon
Kapazität, Volumen	capacity
Kaper	caper
Kapernsauce	caper sauce
Kapuze	hood
Kapuzinerkresse	Indian cress, nasturtium
Karambole, Sternfrucht	carambola, star fruit
Karamellzucker	caramel sugar
Kardamom	cardamom
Kardinalsauce (Béchamel und Hummerbutter)	cardinal sauce (bechamel and lobster butter)
Kardone, Gemüseartischocke	cardoon
Karfiol, Blumenkohl	cauliflower
–, gebacken	deep-fried breaded cauliflower
–, gratiniert	cauliflower cheese
Karfiolauflauf	cauliflower mould/pudding
Karfiol-/Blumenkohlcremesuppe	Du Barry soup, cream of cauliflower soup
Karfreitag	Good Friday
Kärntner Kasnudeln	Carinthian pasta

German	English
Karotte, Gelbe Rübe	carrot
Karottensauce	carrot sauce
Karpfen	carp
Karree, Lende	loin of ...
Schweinskarree	loin of pork
karrierebewusst	career-minded
Kartäuser-Art (mit verschiedenem Gemüse, in Becherform gekocht)	chartreuse (with mixed vegetables cooked in moulds)
Kartoffel, Erdapfel	potato
–, gewürfelt	diced potato
–, in der Schale	jacket potatoes, potatoes in their jacket
Kartoffelbällchen	potato balls
Kartoffelkroketten	potato croquettes
Kartoffelgerichte	potato dishes
Kartoffelknödel	potato dumpling
Kartoffelnudeln	potato noodles
Kartoffelfladen, Kartoffellaibchen	galette (potatoes)
Kartoffelgnocchi	potato gnocchi
Kartoffelgulasch	potato goulash
Kartoffelnester	potato nests
Kartoffelpuffer	potato fritters
Kartoffelpüree, -brei	mashed potatoes
Kartoffelkroketten	potato croquettes, dauphine potatoes
Kartoffelsalat	potato salad
Lorette-Kartoffeln (Käsekroketten)	lorette potatoes (cheesy potato croquettes)
Lyoner Kartoffeln (mit Zwiebeln gebraten)	lyonnaise potatoes (fried with onions)
Macaire-Kartoffeln (Kartoffelkuchen, in der Pfanne gebraten)	macaire potatoes (potao cake fried in butter)
Karussell	carousel
Käse	cheese
Käseglocke	cheese cover
Käsehobel	cheese slicer
Käsekrainer	cheese kransky
Käsemesser	cheese knife
Käsereibe	cheese grater
Käseschneider	cheese cutter
Käsespätzle	cheese spaetzle
Käsestange (mit Blätterteig)	cheese straw (with puff pastry)
Käsetörtchen, Ramequins	cheese tartlets, ramekins
Käsewindbeutel	cheese puffs, choux buns with cheese
Kassa	cash desk, cashier's office
Kasserolle	casserole

German	English
Kastanienreis	rice of chestnuts with whipped cream
Katzenhai	dogfish
Kaufhaus	department store
Kaviar	caviar
Kaviarbutter	caviar butter
Kaviarsauce	caviar sauce
kehren	to sweep
Keim	germ
Keimlinge	seedlings
kein Fleisch essen	to abstain from meat
Keks	biscuit (BE), cookie (US)
Kelchglas	goblet
Keller, Untergeschoß	basement
Kellermeister/in	head of wine cellar
Kellner	waiter
Kellnerin	waitress
kennzeichnen	to denote
gekennzeichnete Felder sind verpflichtend	denoted are required fields
Keramik	pottery
Kerbel	chervil
Kerbelbutter	chervil butter
Kern	seed
kernlos	seedless
Kerze	candle
Kerzenhalter	candlestick, candleholder
Kerzenleuchter	candelabrum
Kessel	kettle
Keule	haunch
Keule, Unterschenkel	shank
Kfz-Kennzeichen	licence plate number
Kichererbsen	chickpeas, garbanzo
Kidneybohnen, rote Bohnen	kidney beans, red beans
Kind, Kinder	child, children (pl)
Kinderbetreuung	childcare
Kinderstuhl	high chair
Kipferl	crescent, croissant
Kippbratpfanne	tilting frying pan
Kippkochkessel	tilting kettle
Kir (Weißwein und Cassis)	kir (white wine and cassis)
Kir Royal (Champagner und Cassis)	kir royal (champagne and cassis)
Kirsche(n)	cherry, -ies (pl)
Kirschwasser	kirsch, kirschwasser
Kirschtomaten	cherry tomatoes
Kissenüberzug	pillow case
Kiste	box
Kitz, Zicklein (Fleisch)	kid

German	English
Kiwi	kiwi
Klammer	bracket
Klammermaschine	stapler
klammern	to staple
Klapptisch	tray table
klären	to clarify
Klarsichtfolie	transparent film
Klatsch, Tratsch	gossip
kleben	to stick
Kleber, Uhu®	glue
Klebestreifen	adhesive tape
Klecks	dallop
Kleiderbügel	coathanger
Kleie	bran
Kleinkind	toddler
Klemmbrett	clipboard
Kletzenbrot	fruit loaf
Klimaanlage	air conditioning, AC
Klimaschrank	wine storage cabinet
Klinke, Griff	handle
Klobürste	toilet brush
klopfen (Steak)	to beat, to tenderise
Klumpen	lump
klumpig	lumpy
Knabbergebäck	breadsticks
Knäckebrot	crispbread (Swedish wholemeal crackers), rye crisps (AE)
knapp an Personal	short-staffed
kneten	to knead
Knoblauch	garlic
Knoblauch(-zehe)	garlic (clove)
Knoblauchbutter	garlic butter
Knoblauchpresse	garlic press
Knoblauchsauce	garlic sauce
Knoblauchwurst	garlic sausage
Knöchel	ankle
umknicken	to twist the ankle
Knochen	bone
Knochenmark	bone marrow
Rückenmark	spinal marrow
Knödel	dumpling
Knollenkartoffel, Knollenziest	Japanese artichokes
Knorpel	cartilage
Knurrhahn	gunard
Knusperreis	puffed rice, rice crispies
knusprig	crunchy, crispy
Kochbuch	cookery book
kochen	boil
kochen (Tee)	to brew (tea)

German	English
kochfertig	ready to cook
Kochlöffel	(wooden) spoon
Kochmesser	cook's knife, chef's knife
Kochmethode	cooking method
Kochnische	kitchenette
Kochplatz	kitchen range
Koffer	suitcase
Kohl, Wirsing	savoy cabbage
Kohlrouladen	meat-filled cabbage rolls
Kohlensäure	carbon dioxide
Kohlrabi	kohlrabi, turnip cabbage
Kohlsprossen, Rosenkohl	Brussels sprouts
Kokosnuss	coconut
Kokosfett	coconut fat
Kokosnusscreme/-sirup	coconut cream
Kokossauce	coconut sauce
Kommode, Schubladenschrank	dresser, chest of drawers
komplex	complex
Kondensmilch	condensed/evaporated milk
Konditor, Zuckerbäcker	confectioner
Konditoreiware	confectionary
Konferenz-, Besprechungs-raum	conference room
Konferenzmappe	organisation file
Königsberger Klopse	meatballs in savoury sauce
konsequent, beständig	consistent
konservieren	to conserve
konserviert	tinned (BE), canned (AE)
Konserven	preserves
Konservierungsmittel	preservative
Kontamination, Verschmutzung	contamination
Kontonummer	account number
kontrollieren	to inspect, to check, to control
unter Kontrolle haben	to have under control
Kontrolllampe	pilot light, warning lamp
Kontrollturm	control tower
Konvektomat	convection oven
Konzentrat	concentrate
Kopfhörer	earphones, headset
Kopfpolster	pillow
Kopfsalat	*siehe Häuptelsalat*
Kopfschmerzen	headache
kopieren	to copy
Kopie	copy
Kopierer	photocopier, photocopying machine
Koriander	coriander
Koriandersauce	coriander sauce
Korinthen	currants
Korkenzieher	corkscrew

korkig	corky
Korn, Getreide	grain
Korn(schnaps)	schnapps
Körper	body
koscher	kosher
Kostenersparnis	cost saving
kostenpflichtiges Fernsehen	pay TV
Kostenvoranschlag	estimate
Kotelett (mit Knochen)	chop
Kotelett (ohne Knochen)	cutlet
Kotelettmanschette	paper-frill, chicken-frill
Krabbe	crab
Krabbencocktail	crabmeat cocktail
Kraftsuppe, Kraftbrühe	broth, beef tea, consommé
Rinderkraftsuppe	beef broth
Kraftsuppe mit Eierstich	royale soup (with egg custard)
kräftig	powerful
Krankenstand	sick leave
Krankenversicherung	health insurance
Krankheit	disorder
Kranz, Ring	ring, wreath
Kranzkuchen	ring cake
Krapfen	Austrian doughnut, krapfen (doughnuts filled with apricot jam)
Krauseminze	frizzy mint
Kraut, Kohl	cabbage
Kraut, Weißkraut	white cabbage
Krautfleckerl	pasta squares with cabbage
Krautsalat	cabbage salad
Krautstrudel	cabbage strudel
Krautwickler	stuffed cabbage rolls
Kräuter, Gewürzkräuter	herbs, aromatic herbs
Kräuterbutter	herb butter, maître d'hôtel butter
nach Kräutern	herbaceous
Kräutersauce	herb sauce
Kräutersträußchen	bouquet of herbs
Krawatte	tie
Krebs	crayfish
Krebsbutter	crayfish (crab) butter
Krebssauce	crayfish sauce
Ragout von Flusskrebsen	crayfish stew
Krebssuppe	bisque of crayfish
Kreditkarte	credit card
Kren, Meerrettich	horseradish
Apfelkren	horseradish with apple
Krensauce, Semmelkren	horseradish sauce
Oberskren	creamed horseradish
Kreolensauce	creole sauce

kreolische Art (mit Reis, Tomaten, Paprikaschoten)	creole
Kresse	cress
Kressebutter	cress butter
Kressesauce	watercress sauce
Kreuzfahrt	cruise
Kreuzkümmel	cumin
Kreuzung	junction
Kristallzucker	refined sugar (crystals), castor/granulated sugar
Krokant	brittle, cracknel
Kroketten	croquettes
Krug	pitcher
Krustentier	crustacean, shellfish
Krustentiersauce	shellfish sauce
Kuchen, Torte	cake
Küchenbrigade	kitchen personnel
Küchenchef	head chef, chef de cuisine
Küchengarn	twine
Küchengehilfe	kitchen assistant
Küchengeräte	cooking utensils
Küchenjunge (veraltet)	scullion
Küchenkrepp	kitchen paper
Küchenmaschine	food processor
Küchenmesser	chef's knife
Kugelschreiber	ballpoint pen
kühlen	to cool
–, im Kühlschrank	to refrigerate
Kühlhaus	walk-in fridge
Kühlraum	cold store
Kühlschrank	refrigerator, fridge
Kühlung, Kühlverfahren	refrigeration
Kühlvitrine	cool counter
Kukuruz	Austrian term for: maize (BE), corn (AE)
kulinarisch	culinary
Kümmel	caraway seed
Kumquat, Zwergorange	kumquat
Kündigung, Bekanntmachung	notice
kündigen	to give notice
Kundschaft	customers
künstlich	artificial
Kürbis	pumpkin, (winter) squash
Gartenkürbis	marrow
Kürbiskerne	pumpkin seeds
Kürbiskernöl	pumpkin seed oil
Kurkuma, Gelbwurz	turmeric
Kurtaxe	visitor's tax
kurz anbraten	to stir-fry

kurzes Getränk	short drink
Kurzschluss	short circuit
Kutteln, Kaldaunen	tripe
Kuvert	envelope

L

Lachs	salmon
–, gekocht	boiled salmon
– in Blätterteig	salmon in pastry
– in Dillmarinade	dill marinated salmon
– in Salzkruste	salmon in salt crust
Lachsbutter	salmon butter
Lachsforelle	salmon trout
Lachsröllchen	salmon cornets
Lachstatar	salmon tartare
Lage	location, setting
–, historische	historic setting
Lager	storage
Lager, Vorratsraum	storage room, storeroom
Lagerbestände	food supplies
Lagerbier	lager (beer)
lagern	to store
Laib	loaf
Lammfleisch, Lamm	lamb
Lammbraten	roast lamb
Lammbrust	breast of lamb
Lammeingemachtes	white lamb stew
Lammkarree	rack of lamb, loin of lamb
Lammkeule	leg of lamb
Lammkotelett	lamb chop
Lammragout	lamb stew
Lammrücken	saddle of mutton
Lammschulter	shoulder of mutton
Lammviertel	quarter of lamb
Milchlamm	spring, baby lamb
Lampe	lamp
landen	to land
Landesvorwahl (Telefon)	country code
Landkarte	map
ländlich	rustic
Landwein	local wine
Landwirtschaftsschule	agricultural school
Langkornreis	long grain rice
längs, der Länge nach	lengthways
Languste	spiny lobster, langouste, crawfish
– Bellevue (Schwanzscheiben in Gelee)	– en Bellevue (lobster meat in jelly)

– Bellevue in Aspik	lobster in jelly
–, katalanisch	lobster Catalan style
–, mit Mayonnaise	spiny lobster mayonnaise
Langustine	rock lobster
LAP (Lehrabschlussprüfung)	final examination
Laptop	laptop
LAP-Zeugnis	certificate of apprenticeship
Lasagne	lasagne
Laserpointer	laser pointer
Lattenrost	duckboards, slatted frame
Lauch, Porree	leek
Lauchsauce	leek sauce
Läuterzucker	simple sugar syrup
Lautsprecher	speaker
Lautsprecheranlage	PA (public address) system
lauwarm	tepid, lukewarm
lauwarm werden	to become lukewarm
Lavendel	lavender
lebendig	alive, lively
Lebenslauf	CV (curriculum vitae) (BE), resume (AE)
lebenslustig	fun-loving, zestful
Lebensmittelfarbe	food colourant
Leber	liver
–, geröstet	sautéed liver
Leberkäse	meat loaf
Leberknödel	liver dumpling
Leberreis	shredded liver
Leberschädel	liver pie in pig's caul
Leberwurst	liver sausage, liverwurst
lebhaft, energisch	vigorous
Lebkuchen, Pfefferkuchen	gingerbread
lecker	scrumptious
ledig	single
leer	thin, thin-bodied
leeren	to pour
legen, geben, platzieren	to place, to put
legieren	to bind, to thicken
legiert, schaumig gerührt	creamed
Lehre	apprenticeship
Lehrling, Auszubildende(r)	apprentice
leicht	light
leicht beleuchtet	softly lit
leiden	to suffer
Leidenschaft	passion
leidenschaftlich	passionate
leider	unfortunately
Leinöl	linseed oil

German	English
Leintuch	fitted sheet
Leintücher	linen sheets
Leng, Lengfisch	ling
Leselampe	reading lamp
leserlich	legible
leuchtend bunt	brightly-coloured
Leute	people
lieblich	off-dry
Lieblings...	favourite
Liebstöckl	lovage
liefern, beliefern	to supply
Lieferant	supplier
Lieferung	supply
Lift	elevator, lift
Likör	liqueur
likörartig	liqueur-like
Likörglas	cordial glass
Limabohnen, Mondbohnen	Lima beans
Limande, Kliesche (Fisch)	dab
Limette	lime
Limettenbutter	lime butter
Limettensauce	lime sauce
Limonade	(aerated) lemonade, bottled soda, soft-drink
Lindenblüten	lime blossom
Linsen	lentils
Linsenpüreesuppe	lentil (purée) soup
Linzer Torte	linz cake (hazelnut cake with currant jam)
Lippfisch	wrasse
Liptauer (Frischkäse aus Schafmilch mit Paprika und Kümmel)	Liptauer (soft, white cheese of ewe's milk with paprika and caraway seeds)
Litschi	lychee
Liwanzen, Dalken	small yeast cake with filling
Locher	hole puncher
lockern, (sich) ablösen	to loosen
Löffel	spoon
Löffelbiskuits	sponge biscuits, sponge finger, lady fingers
Lohn	wages
Longdrink	long drink
Longdrinkglas	highball glass
Lorbeer	bay
Lorbeerblatt	bay leaf
Löwenzahnsalat	dandelion salad
Luft	air
lüften	to air
Luftfahrt	aviation

luftgetrocknet	air-dried
Lüftung	ventilation
lukrativ, einträglich	lucrative
Lumpfischrogen	roe lumpfish
Lunge	lights, lung
Lungenbraten, Rinderfilet	tenderloin
doppelte Lendenschnitte (Chateaubriand)	double tenderloin steak
Filetsteak	tenderloin/fillet steak
Tournedos	small fillet steak
Filet mignon	very small fillet steak
Filetgulasch	fillet goulash
lutschen, saugen	to suck
Luxushotel	luxury hotel
Lyoner Sauce (Zwiebelsauce)	lyonnaise sauce (onion sauce)

M

Macadamianuss	macadamia nut
Mädchenname	maiden name
Madeira	Madeira
Madeirasauce	Madeira sauce
Madrider Suppe	*siehe Geflügelsuppe mit Tomaten*
Magen	stomach
mager	lean
Magermilch	skim(med) milk
mahlen, gemahlen	ground
Mahlzeit zu einem festen Preis	fixed price meal
Mai	May
Maifisch, Alse	shad, allice shad
Maifischrogen	shad roe
Mais, Zuckermais	maize (BE), corn, sweetcorn
Maisgrießbrei (in Wasser oder Milch gekocht)	hominy (crushed maize cooked with water or milk)
Maiskolben	corn on the cob
Maismehl	cornflour (BE), cornstarch (AE)
Maisöl	corn oil
Maître-d'hôtel-Kartoffeln (mit Petersilbutter)	maître d'hôtel potatoes (with parsley butter)
Maître-d'hôtel-Sauce (Butter, Petersilie, Zitronensaft)	maître d'hôtel sauce (butter, parsley and lemon juice)
Majoran	marjoram
Makkaroni	macaroni
Makrele	mackerel
–, geräuchert	smoked mackerel
Malteser Sauce (Hollandaise mit Orangensaft)	Maltese sauce (hollandaise with orange juice)

German	English
Malz	malt
Malzkaffee	barley coffee
Manager im Dienst	manager on duty
Mandarine	mandarin, tangerine
Mandel	almond
Mandelsplitter	flaked almonds
Mandelsirup	orgeat syrup (almond flavoured)
Mandelkroketten (Kartoffelkroketten, mit Mandeln paniert), Berny-Kartoffeln	croquette potatoes amandine
Mandelmakronen	*siehe Amaretti*
Mango	mango, -es (pl)
Mangold	chard, Swiss chard
Mantel	coat
Maraschino	maraschino (liqueur from sour cherries)
Maraschinokirschen	maraschino cherries
Marengo (mit Tomaten und Weißwein)	marengo (with tomato and white wine)
Margarine	margarine
Margaritaschale	Margarita glass
Mariä Empfängnis	Immaculate Conception
Mariä Himmelfahrt	Assumption
Marille	apricot
Marillenauflauf	apricot soufflé
Marillenknödel	apricot dumplings
Marillenbrand	apricot brandy
Marinade	marinade
marinieren	to marinate, to souse
Marke	brand
Markenzeichen, Handelsmarke	trademark
Markknödel	marrow dumpling
Marksauce	marrow sauce
Marmelade	jam
Marmor	marble
Marmorgugelhupf	marbled gugelhupf
Marmorkuchen	marbled cake
Maroni, Kastanie	chestnut
Marsala	Marsala
Martiniglas	Martini glass
März	March
Marzipan	marzipan
Maßeinheit	measurement
mästen	to fatten
Masthuhn	pullet, fattened chicken
Matjeshering	pickled/matie herring
Matratze	mattress
Matrosensauce	matelote sauce
matschig	mushy

Maulbeere	mulberry, -ies (pl)
Maultier	mule
Maus	mouse
Mayonnaise(sauce)	mayonnaise (sauce)
–, grün	green mayonnaise (with purée of herbs)
Medaillon	medallion
Meer-, Steindatteln	date-shells
Meeraal	conger eel
Meeräsche	grey mullet
Meerblick	sea view
Meerbrasse, Wolfsbarsch, Loup	seabram, bass
Meeresfrüchte	seafood, shellfish
Meeresfrüchtesauce	seafood sauce
Meerforelle	sea trout
Meergrundel	goby
Meerohren	sea ears, ormers, abalones
Meersalz	sea salt
Mehl	flour
Mehlbutter	kneaded butter
mehlieren, mit Mehl bestreuen	to sprinkle with flour
mehlig	mealy
Mehlsieb	flour sifter, bolter
Mehlschwitze	*siehe Einbrenn*
Mehrkornbrot	multi-grain/multi-cereals bread
Mehrwertsteuer	VAT (value-added tax)
Melanzani	eggplant, aubergine
Melasse, Zuckersirup	treacle, golden syrup, molasses (AE)
Melone	melon
Menagen, Gewürzständer	cruet stands
Menge, Betrag	amount
Menü	set meal
Menü (gesetzt)	table d'hôte meal
Messbecher	measuring cup/jug
– an der Bar	jigger
Messer	knife, knives (pl)
Messerblock	knife block
Messer-, Scheidenmuscheln	razor shells, razor clams
Messlöffel	bar spoon
mieten	to hire
Mikrowelle	microwave oven
Milch	milk
–, geschäumt	foamed milk
–, pasteurisiert	pasteurised milk
Haltbarmilch	long-life milk
Milchbrötchen	milk roll
Milchkännchen	milk jug (BE), creamer (AE)
Milchprodukte	dairy foods/products

German	English
Milchpulver	milk powder
Milchrahmstrudel	milk and cream Strudel
Milchreis	rice pudding
mild	mild, soft
mild (Wein), ausgereift	mellow
Milz	spleen
Milzschnitten	milt on toast
Mindesthaltbarkeitsdatum	best before/by date
Mineralwasser	mineral water
Minestrone	Italian vegetable soup
Minizpizza	mini-pizza
Minze	mint
Minzsauce	mint sauce
Mirabelle	Mirabelle, yellow plum
mischen	to mix, to blend
gut verrühren, abtreiben	to mix thoroughly
mischen, kombinieren, zusammengeben	to combine
Mispel	medlar
mit Bad	en suite bath
mit Bankkarte	by debit card
mit Bindfaden umwickeln	bind with string
mit Butter und Bröseln (polnische Art)	à la polonaise
mit dem Auto/Bus/Flugzeug ...	by car/bus/plane ...
mit Kohlensäure	sparkling
mit Kreditkarte	by credit card
mit Mandeln	amandine
mitfühlend, sozial, liebevoll	caring
Mitgefühl, Verständnis, Beileid	sympathy
Mittagessen	lunch
Mittagsmenü	set lunch
Mitte, mittel	middle
mittel	medium
Mittel, Möglichkeiten	means
Mittwoch	Wednesday
Mixer	blender, mixer
Modenschau	fashion show
Moderatorenkoffer	presenter's case
Mohn	poppy seeds
Mohnbrötchen	seed roll
Mohnnudeln	poppy seed noodles
Mohr im Hemd	steamed chocolate pudding with whipped cream (and vanilla ice cream)
Molke	whey
Molkerei	dairy
Montag	Monday

German	English
Montblanc (Kastanienpüree mit Schlagobers)	montblanc (mashed chestnuts with cream)
Morchel	morel
Morcheltörtchen	morel tartlet
Morchelsauce	morel sauce
Mörser	mortar
Mortadella	mortadella
Moselwein	moselle
Most, Apfelwein	cider, hard cider (AE)
Mousse (gefrorenes aromatisiertes Schlagobers)	mousse (frozen whipped cream mixture)
Mousseline-Sauce (Hollandaise mit geschlagenem Schlagobers), Schaumsauce	mousseline sauce (hollandaise sauce with whipped cream)
Muffin	muffin
–, sauer (Art Bagel)	English muffin
Muffinform, Muffinblech	muffin tray
Mufflon (Fleisch)	mufflon, mouflon
Mühle	mill
Müllbeseitigung	waste disposal
Mullbinde	gauze bandage
Müllerinnen-Art	shallow-fried
Mulligatawny-Suppe (Currysuppe mit Huhn)	mulligatawny (soup) (curry soup with chicken)
Mülltonne	dustbin, garbage bin
Multivitaminsaft	V-8 juice
mundgerecht	bite-sized
Münze	coin
Münztelefon	pay phone
Muräne	moray eel
Mürbteig	short crust pastry
Mürbteigkuchen	short cake
Muscheln	mussels
–, überbacken	gratinated mussels
Muschelbeignets	clam fritters
Muschelgarten	mussel-bed
Muschelsuppe (mit Venusmuscheln)	clam chowder
Miesmuschelsalat	mussel salad
Zuchtmuscheln	farmed mussels
Muskatblüte	mace
Muskateller	muscatel, muscat grapes
Muskatnuss	nutmeg
Muskatnussreibe	nutmeg grater
Müsli (Getreideflocken mit Nüssen und Früchten)	muesli (flakes of cereals with nuts and dried fruit), granola
Müsliriegel	granola bar
Müslischüssel	cereal bowl
Muster	sample

Mutterkümmel	cumin
Muttersprache	mother tongue

N

nach und nach	progressively
nachdenklich	contemplative
Nachgeschmack	aftertaste
nachgiebig	yielding
Nachname	surname, last name
Nachschlag	second helping, serving
nachteilig, schädlich	detrimental
Nachspeise	dessert, sweets
Nachttisch	bedside/night table
Nachttischlampe	bedside lamp
Nagelfeile	nail file, emery board
Nagelschere	nail scissors
Nagelzwicker	nail clipper
Nähe	vicinity
nahrhaft	substantial
Namensschild	name tag
Nantua-Sauce (Béchamel mit Krebsbutter)	Nantua sauce (béchamel with crayfish butter)
Napfkuchen, Gugelhupf	napfkuchen (yeast cake with raisins)
Napfschnecken	limpets
nappieren	to coat
Napron	slipcloth
Nasenspray	nasal spray
Nashi-Birne	apple/Asian pear
Nationalfeiertag	National Day
Nationalität	nationality
Natron	bicarbonate of soda
naturtrüb	unfiltered
Nebel	fog
neben	beside, next to
negativ, ungünstig, nachteilig	adverse
Nektar	nectar
Nektarine	nectarine
Nelke, Gewürznelke	clove
Nest	nest
netto	net
Netz, Darmnetz	omentum
neu zuweisen	to reallocate
Neue Mittelschule	new secondary school
neuer Wein, Primeur	young wine, green wine
Neujahrstag	New Year's Day
Neunauge	lamprey

German	English
Nieren	kidneys
Nockerln	quenelles, dumplings
normalerweise, gewöhnlich	usually
normannische Sauce (Weißwein-sauce mit Fischfond)	sauce normand (white wine sauce with fishstock)
Norweger-Sauce	Norwegian sauce
Notausgang, Fluchtweg	emergency exit
Notfall	emergency
notieren	to put down
Notiz	notes
Notizblock	notepad
Notizzettel	memo pad
Notruf	emergency call
Notwendigkeit	necessity
Nougat	nougat
November	November
nüchtern	sober
Nudeln	noodles
Nudelgratin	baked noodles
Nudelholz	rolling pin
Nuss	nut
Nussbutter	brown (black) butter
Nüsschen (z. B . Lammnüsschen)	noisette (e.g. lamb noisetts)
Nusskartoffeln (haselnussgroße Bratkartoffeln)	noisette potatoes (nut-shaped fried potatoes)
Nussknacker	nutcracker
Nutzinhalt	storage volume

O

German	English
Oberfläche	surface
obergärig (Bier)	top-fermented
Obers	cream
Oberskren	creamed horseradish
oberste Etage	top floor
Obstknödel	fruit dumpling
Obstler	fruit schnapps
Obstmesser	fruit knife
Obstkuchen	fruit pie
Obstsalat	fruit salad
Obsttorte	flan
Obsttortenring	flanring
obwohl	although
Ochsenmaulsalat	ox-cheek/muzzle salad
Ochsenschwanz	oxtail
klare/gebundene Ochsen-schwanzsuppe	(clear) oxtail soup
Ochsenzunge	ox-tongue

O | German – English

German	English
Ofenkartoffeln (in der Schale gebacken)	baked jacket potatoes (baked in their skin)
offen (Wein)	per glass, in carafe, from the cask
Öffnungszeiten	opening hours
ohne Kohlensäure	still
Okraschoten, Gombos	okra pods, gumbos
Oktober	October
Öl	oil
Olive	olive
grüne Olive	green olive
schwarze Olive	black olive, ripe olive
Olivenpaste	olive paste
gefüllte Oliven	stuffed olives
Olivenkartoffeln, Schlosskartoffeln (olivenförmig geschnitten und in Butter gebraten)	olive potatoes, chateau potatoes (olive-shaped fried potatoes)
Omelette	omelette
– auf savoyische Art (mit Kartoffeln und Käse)	cheese and potato omelette
– auf spanische Art (Eierkuchen mit Tomaten, Zwiebeln und Paprika)	Spanish omelette (flat omelette with onions, pimiento and tomatoes)
– mit Kräutern	herb/savoury omelette
– mit Spinat	Florentine/spinach omelette
– nach Bauernart (mit Speckwürfeln, Kartoffeln und Sauerampfer)	peasant's omelette (omelette with sorrel, potatoes and bacon, not folded)
– nach Försterinart (mit Waldpilzen)	wild mushroom omelette
– natur	plain omelette
– mit Hühnerleber	chicken liver omelette
Omelette Stephanie (mit Erdbeeren)	soufflé Stephanie (with strawberries)
Orange	orange
Orangensaft, frisch gepresst	orange squash
Orangemarmelade	marmalade
Orangenbutter	orange butter
Orangenlimonade	orangeade
Orangensauce	orange sauce
Orangenspalte	orange segment
Orchidee	orchid
ordentlich, sauber, hübsch	neat
Ordnerablage	file cabinet
Oregano	oregano, wild marjoram
Organigramm	organisation chart
Orlow (braisiert und mit Zwiebelmus glaciert), Kalbsrücken Orlow	Orlov (browned in hot oven with onion purée), saddle of veal Orlov

Ossobuco (Kalbshaxe, in Scheiben gedünstet)	ossobuco (braised slice of veal shank)
Ostermontag	Easter Monday
österreichisch	Austrian
Ostseelachs	salmon of the Baltic Sea
Overheadprojektor	overhead projector

P

Paar	couple, pair
Page	bellboy
Palatschinken	pancakes (filled with jam or curd cheese)
Palette	metal spatula
Pampelmuse	*siehe Grapefruit*
panieren	to bread
Paniermehl	breadcrumbs
Pansen	rumen
Papaya	papaya
Papiergeld, Geldschein	paper money
Papierkorb	waste basket, wastepaper bin
Papierschneider	paper cutter, guillotine
Papiertaschentuch	tissue
Paprika (Gewürz)	paprika
Paprikahuhn	paprika chicken
Paprikasauce	paprika sauce, sweet pepper sauce
Paprika (grün, rot, gelb)	pepper (green, red, yellow), bell pepper
gefüllte Paprika	braised stuffed green peppers
Paprikaschote	pepper pod
Paranuss	Brazil nut
Parasolpilz, Schirmpilz	parasol mushroom
Parfait, Halbgefrorenes	parfait
parieren, zuputzen	to prepare for cooking
Pariser Kartoffeln (Nusskartoffeln, in Fleischglace glasiert)	parisienne potatoes (noisette potatoes rolled in meat-glaze)
Pariser Schnitzel (in verquirltes Ei getaucht und gebacken)	escalope of veal, Parisienne (dipped in beaten egg and fried)
Parkplatz	parking area, parking lot, car parking
–, einzeln	parking space/spot
Parmaschinken	Parma ham
Parmentier-Kartoffeln (gebratene Kartoffelwürfel)	parmentier potatoes (cube-shaped and fried)
Parmesanspießchen	parmesan en brochettes
Partner/in	associate

Passagier/in	passenger
Passagierschiff	liner
passen zu	to go with
passieren, filtern, abseihen	to strain
Passionsfrucht	passion fruit
Paste	paste
Pastete	pâté
Pasteten	pies
Pastetchen	patty, -ies (pl), bouchée
Pastinake	parsnip
Pauschale	flat rate
Pauschale, Paket	package
Pauschalreise	package tour
peinlich	embarrassing
Pekannuss	pecan nut
Pektin	pectin
Pellkartoffeln	jacket potatoes
Penthouse, Luxussuite im obersten Stockwerk	penthouse
perfektionistisch	perfectionist
Perlhuhn	guinea fowl, guniea hen
Perlhuhnragout	salmi of guinea hen
Perlzwiebel, Silberzwiebeln	pearl onion, pickled onions
Personal	staff
Personalausweis	identity card
Pestosauce (Basilikumpaste in Olivenöl)	pesto sauce (basil paste in olive oil)
Petermännchen, Drachenfisch	weever, greater weever
Petersfisch, Heringskönig	John Dory, Dory
Petersilie	parsley
Petersilienkartoffeln	parsley potatoes
Petersiliensauce	parsley sauce
Petersilwurzel	parsley root
Petits fours, Teegebäck	petits fours, fancy biscuits
Pfanne	pan
Pfannkuchen, Palatschinke	pancake
Pfeffer (ganz, geschrotet, gemahlen)	pepper (whole, crushed, ground)
Pfefferkorn	peppercorn
Pfeffermühle	pepper mill
pfeffern	to pepper
Pfeffersauce (mit Essig und Pfefferkörnern)	poivrade sauce (with vinegar and pepper), pepper sauce
pfeffrig	peppery
Pfefferminze	peppermint
Pfefferminztee	mint tea
Pfefferoni, Chilischote	chilli pepper
Pfeilwurz	arrowroot
Pferdefleisch	horse meat

German	English
Pfifferlinge	*siehe Eierschwammerl*
Pfingsten	Whitsun
Pfirsich	peach
Pfirsich Alexandra (auf Vanilleeis mit Erdbeermus)	peach Alexandra (on vanilla ice cream with strawberry purée)
pflanzlich	vegetable
Pflaster	band aid, adhesive bandage, plaster
Pflaume, Zwetschke	plum
pflegen	to groom
Pflicht	duty
Physalis	physalis, cape gooseberry, ground-cherry (AE)
Piccata (kleines Naturschnitzel mit Petersilie und Zitrone)	piccata (slice of veal fried in butter with parsley and lemon)
pikante Sauce (mit Essig, Essiggurkerln, Petersilie)	piquant sauce (with vinegar, gherkins, parsley)
Pilawreis	pilaw/pilaf/pilau rice
Pilot/in	pilot
Pilzsauce	mushroom sauce
Piment	allspice, pimento
Pimpinelle	burnet
Pinienkern	pine nut
Pinienkernsauce	pine nut sauce
Pinnwand	pin board
Pintglas	pint glass
Pinzette	tweezers
Pistazie	pistachio
Pizza	pizza
Pizzatasche	folded-over pizza
Planschbecken	toddler's pool
Planung	planning
Plastikbehälter	plastic container
Platte, Teller	plate
Platz (viereckig)	square
platzen	to burst, to split
Platzteller	cover plate
Plundergebäck	Danish pastry
pochieren	to poach
Pofese	French toast
pökeln	to pickle sth
Pökelfleisch	salt(ed)/pickled pork
Polenta, Sterz, Maisbrei	polenta (maize porridge)
Polizze	policy
Pollack	Pollack, green cod
Polsterzipf	cushion corners (deep fried pastry)
Poly(technische Schule)	polytechnical school

German	English
Pommes frites, Kartoffelstäbchen	chips (BE), French fried potatoes (AE)
–, selbst gemacht	homefries
Pommes-frites-Schneider	potato chipper
Porterhouse-Steak	porterhouse steak
Portier, Gepäckträger	porter
Portionsgröße	size of portion/serving
portugiesische Sauce	Portuguese sauce
portugiesische Suppe (Tomatensuppe)	Portuguese soup (tomato soup)
Portulak	purslane
Portwein	port (wine)
Portweinsauce	port wine sauce
Porzellan	porcelain
Postfach	PO Box
Postleitzahl	zip code, postal code
Pot-au-feu (Fleisch- und Gemüseeintopf)	pot-au-feu (broth with meat and vegetables)
Poularde	poussin
Poulette-Sauce (weiße Sauce mit Eigelb)	sauce poulette (white sauce with egg yolk)
Powidl	plum jam
Powidltascherl	plum jam pockets
Praktikant/in	trainee
praktisch, nützlich	handy
präsentieren	to present
präzise, exakt, genau	precise
Preiselbeere(n)	cowberry, cranberry, -ies (pl)
Preiselbeersauce	cranberry sauce
Preisliste, Tarif	tariff
Preisschild	price tag
Pressekonferenz	press conference
pressen, drücken	to press
kaltgepresst	cold-pressed
heißgepresst	hot-pressed
Presskopf	brawn, chopped pig's head (BE), headcheese (AE)
Pressschinken	pressed ham
prickelnd	prickly
Prinzessin-Suppe (Geflügelcremesuppe mit Spargelspitzen)	princess soup (cream of chicken soup with asparagus tips)
Prise	pinch, sprinkle
pro Erwachsenem	p.a. (per adult)
pro Portion	per serving
Prosecco	prosecco
Protokoll	minutes
provenzalische Sauce	provençale sauce
Prozent	percentage
Prüfer	auditor

Puffreis	puffed rice, rice crispies
Pumpernickel	pumpernickel (wholemeal ryebread)
Punsch	punch
pur, gerade	straight, neat, plain
Whiskey pur	a "straight" whiskey
pürieren	to mash
Püreesuppe	purée soup
Pute	turkey hen
putzen, reinigen	to clean
Putzmittel	cleaning agent

Q

Qualität	quality
Qualitätswein	quality wine
Qualle	jellyfish
Quantität	quantity
Quappe, Trüsche	burbot, eelpout
quellen (lassen)	to swell
Quiche Lorraine (Lothringer Specktorte)	quiche Lorraine (flan with bacon and cream)
Quinoa	quinoa
Quitte	quince
Quittung	receipt

R

Rabatt, Abzug	discount
Rad	wheel
Radicchio	radicchio (red-leaved chicory)
Radicchiosauce	radicchio sauce
Radiergummi	eraser
Radieschen	red radish
Radler (Bier mit Limonade), Alsterwasser	shandy
raffiniert	refined
Ragout, Eintopf	stew
Rahmenprogramm	Framework, supporting programme
Rahmkartoffeln	creamed potatoes
Rahmsauce, Sahnesauce	cream sauce
Rahmschnitzel, Kalbsschnitzel in Sahnesauce	creamed veal escalope, veal escalope in cream sauce
Rahmstrudel	cream strudel
Rahmsuppe	sour cream soup
Rambutan	rambutan

Rand	rim, edge
Salzrand	salt rim/edge
Zuckerrand	sugar rim/edge
ranzig	rancid
Rapsöl	rape (seed) oil
Rasierer	razor
Rasierapparat	shaver
Rasierschaum	shaving foam
raspeln, grob reiben	to rasp
rassig	racy
Rat(schlag)	advice
einen Rat geben	to give advice
Rathaus	town hall
Raucherbereich	smoking area/zone
räuchern, selchen	to smoke
Rauchmelder	smoke detector
Räumlichkeit	premise
Ravigote-Sauce (Vinaigrette mit Kapern und feinen Kräutern), Kräutersauce	ravigote sauce (vinaigrette with capers and fine herbs), herb sauce
Ravioli	ravioli
Rebhuhn	partridge
Rechnung	bill (BE), check (AE), invoice, account, receipt
Rechnung begleichen	to settle the account
Rechnungsbetrag	balance due
rechtmäßig, legitim	legitimate
Rednerpult	lectern
reduzieren	to reduce
Referenz	reference
Regal	shelf, shelves (pl)
Regen	rain
–, leicht	light shower
–, schwer	heavy shower
Regenschirm	umbrella
Regenbogenforelle	rainbow trout
Reh	roe, roebuck (male)
Rehkeule	leg of venison
Rehrücken	roast saddle of venison
Reibe, Reibeisen	grater
reiben	to rub
–, mit Reibeisen	to grate
geriebener Käse	grated cheese
reif	ripe, mature
reifen	to mature
Reife	ripeness
Reinanke	fera blue
Reindling	Carinthian raisin cake
reinigen	to clean

German	English
Reiniger (chemische Reinigung)	dry cleaner
Reinigung, Wäscherei	valet service
Reis	rice
–, parboiled	converted rice, minute rice
–, braun	brown rice
Basmatireis	basmati rice
Curryreis	curried rice
Vollreis	brown rice
Rundkornreis, Perlreis	short grain rice
Reisauflauf	rice soufflé
Reisfleisch	rice with meat
Reispudding	cold rice pudding
Reise	trip
Reise, Seereise, Törn	voyage
Reisebüro	travel agency
Reisedaten	travel data
Reisende/r	traveller
Reisepass	passport
Reisescheck	traveller's check
mit Reiseschecks zahlen	to pay in traveller's checks
Reißzwecke	pushpin
reizend, entzündend	quaint
Remoulade-Sauce (Mayonnaise mit Senf, Kapern und Essiggurkerln)	remoulade sauce (mayonnaise with mustard, capers and gherkins)
Rentier	reindeer
reservieren	to reserve
Reservierung, Bestellung	reservation
Reservierungsübersicht	reservation rack
Restaurant	dining room
Restaurantleiter	dining room manager, maître d'
Rettich (weiß, schwarz)	radish (white, black)
Rezept	recipe
Rezeption	front office, reception desk
Rhabarber	rhubarb
Rheinsalm	rhine salmon
Rheinwein	Rhine wine, hock
Ribisel (rot)	redcurrant
Richtlinie	guideline
riechen	to smell
riesen...	giant, jumbo
Riesengarnele, Hummerkrabbe	king prawn
Rillen	furrows
Rind	cattle
Rinderfiletspitzen	sirloin tips
Rinderschmor(saft)braten	braised beef
Rindfleisch	beef
Rindskarbonade	beef carbonade
Rindfleischsalat	beef salad/vinaigrette

Rindsragout	beef stew, stewed beef, ragout of beef
Rindssuppe	beef broth, bouillon, beef tea
Rindsroulade	beef roulades
gepökeltes Rindfleisch	corned beef
Rindsbraten, Roastbeef (kalt)	(cold) roast beef
Rindsherz	ox' heart
Rindsrose	*siehe Hüferschwanzel*
Rindsroulade	(braised) rolled stuffed fillet of beef
Ringelblume	marigold
Ringlotte	greengage
Ripperl(n)	spare ribs
Risipisi	rice with peas
Risotto	risotto (Italian rice dish)
Rissolen (frittierte Blätterteigtaschen)	rissoles (fried cakes with meat or fish stuffing)
Robert-Sauce (Zwiebel, Weißwein, Senf)	Robert sauce (onion, white wine, mustard)
Rochen	(sting) ray, skate
Rodel	toboggan
rodeln, Schlitten fahren	to toboggan
Rogen (vom Fisch)	roe
Roggen	rye
Roggenbrot	rye bread
roh, blau	raw
Rohkost	raw fruit and vegetables
Rohkost(platte)	assorted raw vegetables (crudities)
Rohschinken	raw ham
geräucherter Rohschinken	smoked raw ham
Rohwurst	raw sausage
Rohzucker	brown/unrefined sugar
Rohrzucker	cane sugar, demerara sugar
Rollbraten	rolled and boned roast beef
Rollmops	rollmops (rolled [pickled] herring)
Rollschinken	rolled boned ham
Rollstuhl	wheelchair
Römersalat	romaine, cos lettuce
Römertopf	earthenware pot
Röntgengerät	X-ray machine
Roquefortsauce	Roquefort sauce
Roséwein	rosé wine
Rosine	raisin
Roulade	roulade
Rosmarin	rosemary
Rosmarinsauce	rosemary sauce

German	English
rösten, braten (im Ofen)	to roast
Rösti (geraspelte Bratkartoffeln)	Rösti (fried pancake of grated potatoes)
Röstkartoffeln	hashed brown potatoes
Rotauge	roach
Rotbarbe	red mullet
Rotbarsch	sea perch
Rotbrasse	red sea-bram
Rotkraut	red cabbage
rote Bohnen	red beans
Rote Rübe, Rote Beete	beetroot (BE), red beet (AE)
Rote-Rüben-Sauce, Rote-Beete-Sauce	beetroot sauce
roter Schnapper	red snapper
Rotfeder	rudd
Rotwein	red wine
Rotweinbirnen	pears in red wine
Rotweinsauce	red wine sauce
Rotzunge	lemon sole
Rübenzucker	beet sugar
Rücken	rack/saddle of ...
Rückerstattung	refund
Rückruf	return call
Rucksack	backpack
Rückseite	backside
Rückverfolgbarkeit	traceability
Ruf	reputation
Rührei	scrambled egg
rühren	to stir
unter ständigem Rühren	stirring continually
Rührglas	mixing glass
Rührschüssel	mixing bowl
Rührstab	stirrer
Rührteigkuchen	creamed cakes
Rukola, Rauke	rocket, arugula
Rukola-/Raukepesto	rocket pesto
Rum	rum
Rumpf	torso
Rumpsteak	rump steak
rund	round
Rundumblick	all-around view
rupfen	to pluck
russische Eier	Russian eggs, eggs à la russe, stuffed egg, Russian style
rutschen	to slide, to slip
rutschig	slippery
Rutschen	slippage

S

German	English
...schulter	shoulder of ...
...stelze	leg of ...
Sachertorte	chocolate cake “Sacher”
Safe	safe
Safran	saffron
Safranfäden	saffron stigmas
Safransauce	saffron sauce
saftig	succulent
Saftigkeit	succulence
Saftpresse	juice extractor
Saftrinne	juice groove
Sägefisch	sawfish
Saibling	char
Saison	season
–, außerhalb der	off-season
saisonal	seasonal
Salamander, Grill mit Oberhitze	salamander
Salami	salami
Salat	salad
–, einfacher	plain salad
–, gemischter	mixed salad
–,,zusammengesetzter	assorted salad
Salat anmachen	to toss salad
Salatblätter	lettuce leaves
Salatschleuder	salad spinner
Salatteller	salad plate
Salbei	sage
Salbeibutter	sage butter
Salbeisauce	sage sauce
Saltimbocca (Schnitzel mit Salbei und Schinken)	saltimbocca (escalope with sage and ham)
Salz	salt
salzen	to salt
Salz- und Pfefferstreuer	salt and pepper shaker
Salzhering, Bückling, Räucherhering (getrocknet oder geräuchert)	kipper (kippered herring), bloater (dried or smoked)
Salzkartoffeln	boiled/plain potatoes
Salzkruste	salt crust
Salzlake, Pökel	brine, souse, pickle
Salzwasserfisch	saltwater/sea fish
Salzburger Nockerln	soufflé baked in the oven, baked sweet soufflé made of beaten egg whites
sämig	thick, stout
Sammelplatz	assembly point

German	English
Samstag	Saturday
samtig	velvety
Sanddorn	sea buckthorn
Sanduhr	hourglass
Sandwich	sandwich
sanfter Abgang (Wein)	tender finish
sanitäre Anlagen	sanitary facilities
Sardellen	anchovy, -ies (pl)
Sardellenbutter	anchovy butter
Sardellensauce	anchovy sauce
Sardinen	sardines, pilchards
–, in Öl	sardines in oil
Sättigung	saturation
Sauberkeit	cleanliness
Saubohnen, dicke Bohnen	broad beans, fava beans
Sauce	sauce
–, grün (Sauce verte)	green sauce
Sauce Béarnaise (Sauce hollandaise mit Estragon)	béarnaise sauce (hollandaise sauce with tarragon)
Sauce Chateaubriand (Fleischglace, Butter, Petersilie)	Chateaubriand sauce (meat glaze enriched with butter and parsley)
Sauce Demi-Glace, braune Grundsauce	demi-glace sauce, basic brown sauce
Sauce hollandaise	Dutch sauce
Sauce Mornay, Käsesauce (Béchamel mit Käse)	Mornay sauce, cheese sauce
Sauce suprême (Geflügeleinmachsauce)	suprême sauce (chicken stock with cream)
Sauce Tatar (Mayonnaise aus hart gekochtem Eigelb mit Schnittlauch)	tartare sauce (mayonnaise with chopped pickles)
Saucenschüssel	gravy boat
Sauciere	saucer, sauce boat, gravy boat
sauer, säuerlich	sour, acid
Säure	acid, acidity
säuerlich	acidic
Sauerampfer	sorrel
Sauerampfersauce	sorrel sauce
Sauerbraten (in Essigbeize vorbehandelter Schmorbraten)	sauerbraten (braised beef, previously marinated in vinegar)
Sauerkirsche(n)	sour cherry, -ies (pl)
Sauerkraut	sauerkraut
Sauermilch	acidophilus/sour milk
Sauerrahm	sour cream
Sauerrahmdip	sour cream dip
Sauerrahmsauce, Smitane	sour cream sauce
Sauerstoffmaske	oxygen mask
Sauerteig	buttermilk dough, sourdough

German	English
Sauna	sauna
sautieren, schwingend rösten	to sauté
Sautierpfanne	sauté pan
Savoyer Kartoffelgratin (mit Bouillon und Käse überbacken)	savoy potatoes (potatoes gratinated with broth and cheese)
Scampi, Kaisergranat	scampi, Dublin Bay prawns
schaben	to scrape
Schaber	scraper
Schächten	kosher butchering
schädlich	harmful
Schaffleisch	mutton
Schafmilch	ewe's milk, sheep's cheese
Schafskäse	sheep's cheese
Schale	rind (of fruit), shell, zest (of citrus fruit)
schälen	to pare, to peel
schälen (Eier, Nüsse)	to shell
schälen (Hülsenfrüchte)	to husk
Schäler	peeler
Schälmesser	peeling/paring knife
schalldicht	soundproof
Schalotte	shallot
Schalottenbutter	shallot butter
Schalottensauce	shallot sauce
Schalter	switch
Schaltjahr	leap year
Schankwein	house wine
scharfkantig	sharp-edged
Schaschlik	shashlik (meat on skewers), kebabs
schätzen	to estimate
schätzen, beurteilen	to assess
Schaufel	shovel
Schaum	froth
Schaumbad	foam bath
schäumen	to froth
schaumig	frithy, frothy
schaumig rühren, legieren, abrühren	to cream
schaumig schlagen	to beat into a foam
Schaumgebäck, spanischer Wind, Baiser	meringue
Schaumkartoffeln (Kartoffelpüree mit Schlagobers)	mousseline potatoes (mashed potatoes with whipped cream)
Schaumwein, Sekt	sparkling wine
Scheck, Rechnung (AE)	check
Scheibe/Schnitte von ...	slice of ...
scheinen	to seem

German	English
Scheinwerfer	spotlight
Scheiterhaufen	soufflé of white bread and stewed apples
Schellfisch	haddock
Schere	scissors
Schicht	layer
Schichtsalat	layer salad
Schicht (Job)	shift
schieben, stoßen	to push
Schiebetür	sliding door
Schildkröte	tortoise, turtle
Schildkrötensauce (Madeirasauce mit Auszug von Kräutern), Tortue	turtle sauce (Madeira sauce with essence of herbs)
Schildkrötensuppe	turtle soup, real
Schildkrötensuppe Lady Curzon (mit Curry gewürzt und mit Schlagobers bedeckt)	turtle soup Lady Curzon (flavoured with curry and covered with whipped cream)
falsche Schildkrötensuppe	mock turtle soup
schimmelig	mouldy
schimmeln	to go mouldy
Schinken	ham
–, dünn geschnitten	rasher
–, gekocht	boiled ham, cooked ham
–, geräuchert	smoked ham
Rohschinken	raw ham
Schinkenauflauf	ham soufflé
Schinkenfleckerl (überbackene)	pasta squares with ham (au gratin)
Schinken-Käse-Toast	sandwich toast (toasted ham and cheese sandwich)
Schinkenknödel	ham dumpling
Schinkenmousse	ham mousse
Schinkenröllchen	ham cornets, ham rolls
Schinkenwurst	ham sausage
schlachten	to slaughter
Schlafsaal	dormitory
Schlag	blow
schlagen (schaumig)	to whip
schlagen, klopfen	to beat
Eischnee schlagen	to beat egg whites
geschlagener Obers	whipped cream, Chantilly
Schlange (von Menschen)	queue
Schleie	tench
Schleife	ribbon
schleudern	to centrifuge
Schließfach	safe deposit box
Schloss	lock

German	English
Schlosskartoffeln (olivenförmig geschnitten und in Butter gebraten)	chateau/castle potatoes (olive-shaped fried potatoes)
Schlüsselwort	keyword
Schmalz	dripping, lard
Schmankerl, Leckerbissen	titbit, tasty (BE), tidbit (AE)
Schmarren	omelette which is torn into odd-shaped pieces with a fork
schmecken nach	to taste of
schmecken, kosten, abschmecken	to taste
schmelzen	to melt
geschmolzene Butter	melted butter
Schmelzkartoffeln	fondant potatoes
Schmerz	pain
Schmerzmittel	pain reliever
Schmerztabletten	pain killer
schmierig	greasy
schmoren, dünsten	to stew
schmoren, im Ganzen (braun) dünsten	to braise
Schmorgericht	casserole
Schmorkartoffeln	stewed potatoes
schmücken	to adorn
Schnapper	snapper
Schnaps	spirit
schnäuzen	to blow the nose
(Weinberg-)Schnecke	snail
Schneckenbutter	snail butter
Schnecke mit Kräuterbutter	snail with herb butter
Schneckenpfanne	snail pan
Schneckenzange	snail tongs
Schnee	snow
Schneehuhn	snow/white grouse, ptarmigan
Schneeregen, Graupel	sleet
Schneebesen	whisk
schneiden	to cut
in Scheiben/Streifen schneiden	to slice
in Würfel schneiden	to cube, to dice
zuschneiden	to cut to size
Schneide, Klinge	blade
Schneidebrett	cutting board
Schnellkochtopf	pressure cooker
Schnepfe	snipe, woodcock
schnittfest	semi-soft
Schnittlauch	chives
Schnittlauchbutter	chive butter
Schnittlauchkartoffeln	chive potatoes
Schnittlauchsauce	chive sauce
Schnitzel	escalope (of ...)
schnorcheln	to snorkel

Schnörkel	squiggle
schnurlos	cordless
Schöberln	sponge squares/biscuits
schockgefrieren	to quick-freeze
Schokoladenauflauf	chocolate soufflé
Schokoladenglasur	chocolate glaze
Schokoladenriegel	chocolate bar
Scholle	plaice
Schönheitspfleger	beautician
Schönheitssalon	beauty salon
Schopfbraten	roast neck of pork
schöpfen	to ladle
Schöpfer	ladle
Schöpsernes	*siehe Schaffleisch*
Schote	husk
(Erbsen-)Schote	(pea) pod
schottische Suppe (Hammel- oder Rindssuppe mit Graupen)	Scotch broth (soup of mutton or beef and pearl barley)
schräg	sloping
Schrank	closet
schrecklich, furchtbar	awful
Schreibpapier des Hotels	hotel stationery
Schreibtisch	desk
Schreibunterlage	desk pad
Schreibwaren	stationery
Schriftart	font type
Schriftgröße	font size
Schrot, grobes Mehl	shred, coarsely ground wholemeal
Schrot, Vollkorn	wholemeal
Schublade	drawer
Schüler/in	pupil
Schürze	apron
Schüssel	bowl
schütteln (gut)	to shake (well), to toss
schützen	to protect
Schutzhütte	shelter
Schutzkleidung	protective clothing
Schwalbennestersuppe	bird's nest soup
Schwamm	sponge
Schwanz	tail
Schwarte	rind
Schwarzbrot	brown/black bread
Laib Schwarzbrot	brown loaf
schwarze Butter	black butter
schwarze Liste	blacklist
Schwarzwälder-Kirsch-Torte	Black Forest cake (with morello cherries)
Schwarzwurzel	black salsify

German	English
Schwedenplatte (marinierte und geräucherte Fischspezialitäten)	Swedish platter (marinated and smoked fish specialities)
Schwein	pig
Schweinsherz	pig's heart
Schweinsnieren	pig's kidneys
Schweinsleber	pig's liver
Schweinszunge	pig's tongue
Schweinsfuß	pig's trotter
Schweinefleisch	pork
Schweinskotelett	pork chop
Schweinsragout	pork stew, stewed pork, ragout of pork
Schweinshaxe, -stelze	pork knuckle, leg of pork
Schweineschmalz, weißer Speck	lard
Schweinsbraten	roast pork
Schweinsfaschiertes	chopped pork
Schweinshaxelsulz	brawn of pig's trotters
Schweinskopfsülze	brawn (in aspic jelly)
Schweinsohren (Gebäck)	palmiers
Schweinsrippe	rib of pork
Schweinsschnitzel	escalope of pork, pork cutlet
Schweinsschopf	neck of prok
Schweizer Käse	Swiss cheese
schwenken (in heißem Fett)	to toss
Schwenkkartoffeln	sauté potatoes
schwer, üppig, vollmundig (Wein)	full-bodied, rich-bodied, heavy
Schwertfisch	swordfish
schwimmen, fließen	to float
Schwimmkrabben	velvet swim crabs
Schwimmweste	life vest
Scotch woodcock (Rührei auf Sardellentoast)	Scotch woodcock (scrambled egg on anchovy toast)
Seeforelle	lake trout
Seehecht	hake
Seeigel	sea urchin
Seelachs, Köhler	coalfish, coley, saithe
Seequappe	rockling, sea loach
Seespinne, Meerspinne	spider crab
Seeteufel, Lotte, Anglerfisch	angler-fish, monkfish, frogfish
Seezunge	sole
Seezunge auf Spinat	sole Florentine
Seezunge Colbert (paniert, gebacken und mit Kräuterbutter gefüllt)	sole Colbert (breaded, fried, filled with parsley butter)
Seezunge Orly (frittiert, mit Tomatensauce)	fillets of sole Orly (deep-fried, served with tomato sauce)
Sehne	sinew
Seife	soap
Seifenhalter	soap dish

German	English
Sektflöte	champagne flute
Sektkorken	champagne cork
Sektkübel	champagne bucket
Sektkühler	champagne cooler
Sekt-Orange	mimosa
Sekundarstufe (10 bis 14 Jahre)	secondary school
selbstbewusst	self-confident
Sellerie	celery
Sellerie(-knolle)	celeriac
Selterswasser	seltzer
Semmel, Brötchen	roll, French roll
Semmelknödel	white bread dumpling
senden, aussenden	to broadcast
Senf(körner)	mustard (grains/seeds)
Senfbutter	mustard butter
Senfsauce (Sauce Robert)	mustard sauce
Senfpulver	dry mustard
Senioren	elderly
sensibel, empfindlich	sensitive
September	September
servieren	to serve
Servierplatte	platter
Servierregel	service rule
Serviette	napkin, serviette
Serviettenknödel	dumpling in a napkin
Sesam	sesame
Sesamsauce	sesame sauce
Sessel, Fauteuil	armchair
Shaker	shaker
Sherry	sherry
Sherryglas	sherry glass
Sherrysauce	sherry sauce
Shiitake	shiitake
Sicherheitsbeamte/r	security officer
Sicherheitscheck	security check
Sicherheitshinweise	safety instructions
sicherlich (ja, gut)	certainly
Sieb, Filter, Passiermaschine	strainer
Sieb (Mehl)	sieve
Schüttelsieb	colander
sieben, durchsieben	to sift, to sieve
Siebschöpfer	skimmer
Siebtuch	straining cloth, muslin
sieden, langsam kochen	to simmer
Sieden	simmering
Siedepunkt	boiling point
Silberbesteck	silver cutlery
Silberfisch, Ukelei	bleak
Silbergeschirr	silverware

Simultanübersetzungsausrüstung	simultaneous translation equipment
Siphon	siphon, siphon bottle
Sirup	syrup
Sitz, Platz	seat
Sitzungssaal	boardroom
Sodawasser	(club) soda, sparkling water
sofort, umgehend	immediately, at once
Softeis	soft ice
Soja	soya
Sojabohnen	soyabeans
Sojabohnensprossen	soya-bean sprouts
Sojasauce	soya sauce
Sommelier	wine waiter
Sonderabfüllung, spezielle Auswahl	special selection
Sonnenaufgang	sunrise
Sonnenblumenkerne	sunflower seeds
Sonnenblumenöl	sunflower (seed) oil
Sonnenbrand	sunburn
Sonnenschirm	sun-shade
Sonnenschutzcreme	sunscreen
Sonnenschutzfaktor	protection factor
Sonnenstich	heatstroke, sunstroke
Sonnenuntergang	sunset, sundown
sonnige Abschnitte	sunny intervals
Sonntag	Sunday
Sorbet, Fruchteis	sorbet, sherbet
Sorge	concern
Sorgfalt	care
sorgfältig	carefully
sortieren	to sort
Soubise-Sauce (Zwiebelpüree mit Béchamel), Zwiebelsauce	soubise sauce (onion purée with béchamel)
Souvenirladen	gift shop
Spachtel	spatula
Spaghetti	spaghetti
Spaghettizange	spaghetti tongs
Spalte, Säule	column
spalten	to split
Spanferkel	suck(l)ing pig
Spargel	asparagus
Spargelspitzen	asparagus tips
– in Sauce vinaigrette	– in vinaigrette sauce
– mit Sauce hollandaise	– with hollandaise/Dutch sauce
Omelette mit Spargel	asparagus omelette
Spätlese	late vintage, late gathered
Speck	bacon
–, dünn geschnitten	rasher

German	English
Speckknödel	bacon dumpling
Specktörtchen	bacon tartlet
Tiroler Bauernspeck	speck (smoked raw ham)
Speckkuchen	quiche
Speisekammer	pantry
Speisekarte	menu
Spezialität	speciality
Spezialsuppe	special soup
spicken	to lard
Spicknadel	larding needle/pin
Spiegel	mirror
Spiegelkarpfen	mirror carp
Spiegelei	fried egg
– auf Spinat	fried egg on spinach
– auf einer Seite gebraten	egg sunny side up
– auf beiden Seiten gebraten	egg sunny side down
Spielecke	kid's corner
Spieß	skewer, brochette, spear
Spießchen, kleiner Spieß	small skewer, swizzle stick
am Spieß gebraten	spit-roast
Spinat	spinach
Spirituosen	spirits
Spitze, Punkt	point
Spitzer	pencil sharpener
Spritzsack	pastry bag
Spitzsieb	conical strainer
Sprachbox	mailbox
Sprachmitteilung	voice mail
Springform	spring mould
Spritzbeutel	piping bag
spritzen	to splash
Spritzer	dash
Spritzflasche	dash bottle
spritzig	spritzy
Spritzsack	pastry bag
Sprosse	sprout
Sprotte	sprat
Spucktüte	airsickness bag
spülen (Geschirr)	to wash up (crockery)
Spülbecken	sink
Spülung	flushing
Spülung (Wasserkasten)	cistern (flush)
Staatsbürger	citizen
Stäbchen	chopsticks
Stachelbeere(n)	gooseberry, -ies (pl)
Stachelbeersauce	gooseberry sauce
Stachelschnecken	murices
Stadtplan	street map

German	English
Stadtzentrum	city centre
ins Stadtzentrum	to the city centre
Stammgericht	standard dish
Stammkunden	regulars, regular customers
Stamperl	shot glass
Stangensellerie	stalk celery
Stapel	stack
stapeln	to stack
Stärke	starch
Stationskellner	station waiter
stauben, bestreuen	to powder
staubsaugen	to vacuum
Staubsauger	hoover (BE), vacuum cleaner (AE)
Staubtuch	duster
Staubwolke	dust cloud
Staubzucker	powdered sugar
Steak	steak
Steakmesser	steak knife
Steckdose	socket
Steckerlfisch, Stockfisch	salt cod
Steckrübe, Dotsche	swedes, Swedish turnips
stehen, ruhen	to stand
Stehlampe	floor/standard lamp
Stehpult	high desk
steil	steep
Stein	stone
Steinbeißer, Schmerle, Bartgrundel	loach
Steinbutt	turbot
Steinpilz	(yellow) boletus, cep, cèpe, porcini
Steinpilzsauce	cépe mushroom sauce
steirisches Masthuhn	Styrian fattened chicken (pullet)
steirisches Wurzelfleisch	boiled shoulder of pork with carrots, leeks, horseradish and celeriac
Stempel	stamp
Stempelkissen	ink pad
Stephanitag, 2. Weihnachtsfeiertag	Boxing Day
Sterlet	sterlet
Sternanis	star aniseed
sternförmig	star-shaped
Sternfrucht, Karambole	star fruit, carambola
Sterntülle	star-shaped nozzle
Steuer	tax
Stevia	stevia
Stiegenhaus	stairs, staircase
Stiel	stem
Stielpfanne	saucepan
Stieltopf	saucepan with a handle

German	English
Stift (für weiße Kunststofftafel)	(whiteboard) pen
Stint	smelt
Stirnband	headband
Stockbett	bunk bed
-stöckig	-storey
zweistöckig	two-storey
Stockschwämmchen	black popular mushrooms
stopfen	to stuff, to fill
Stoppuhr	stopwatch
Stör	sturgeon
stören	to disturb
„Bitte nicht stören"-Schild	"Do not disturb" sign
stören, sich einmischen	to interfere with
stornieren	to cancel
Stornierung	cancellation
Stornogebühr	cancellation charge/fee
Stoß, Stapel	pile
Stößel und Mörser	pestle and mortar
Straftat	offence
Strand	beach
Strandschnecken	winkles, periwinkles
Straßenbahn	cable car
Strauß	ostrich
streichen, bestreichen	to spread with
streichfähig	spreadable
Streichkäse	cheese spread, cream cheese
Streichwurst	sausage for spreading
Streichhölzer	matches
Streichholzkartoffeln, Pommes allumettes	shoestring potatoes, julienne potatoes
Streifen	strip, shred
Gemüsestreifen	vegetable strips
in Streifen schneiden	to cut into strips
Streik	strike
Streuer (Mehl)	dredger
(jegliche Art von) Streusel	hundreds and thousands
Streuselkuchen	crumble
Apfel mit Streuseln	apple crumble
Strohhalm	straw, drinking straw
Strohkartoffeln	straw potatoes, potato straws
Strohpilze	straw mushrooms
Strudel	strudel
Strunk, Stiel	stalk
Stubenküken	corn-fed chicks
Stück	piece
Stück Brot	chunk of bread
Stummschaltung	mic mute
stumpf	blunt
Sturm (Wein)	new wine

German	English
Sturm	storm
stürzen	to unmould, to turn out
süffig (Wein)	nice to drink, easy
Sultanine	sultana (BE), seedless white raisin (AE)
Sulz, Aspik	aspic
Suppe	soup, broth
–, gebunden	thick soup
–, klar	clear soup
Eintropfsuppe	soup with dropping pastry
Leberknödelsuppe	soup with liver dumpling
Fleischstrudelsuppe	soup with meat strudel
Milzschnittensuppe	soup with milt sippets/croutons
Frittatensuppe	soup with pancake stripes
Leberreissuppe	soup with rasped liver
Grießnockerlsuppe	soup with semolina dumplings
Schöberlsuppe	soup with sponge squares
Suppe mit Tiroler Knödeln	soup with Tyrolean dumplings
Suppen-/Fondtopf	stock pot
Suppenfleisch	meat for making soup
Suppenhuhn	boiling fowl
Suppenlöffel	soup/table spoon
Suppenschüssel, Suppenterrine	soup bowl, soup tureen
Suppentasse	soup cup
Suppenteller	soup plate
Suppentopf	stock pot
Suppenwürfel	stock cube, bouillon cube, meat cube
Surbraten	cured meat
Surfleisch	gammon steak
Surhaxe	*siehe Eisbein*
süß	sweet
Süßkartoffeln, Bataten	sweet potatoes
süßsauer	sweet-sour
süßsaure Sauce	sweet-and-sour sauce
Süßspeisen	sweets
Süßstoff (künstlich)	saccharin, sweetener (artificial)
Süßstofftablette	sweetener tablet
Süßwein	dessert wine, fortified wine
Süßwasserfisch	freshwater fish
Süßwasserschildkröte	terrapin
sympathisch, liebenswert, nett	likeable
Systemgastronom/in	system caterer
Systemgastronomie	system gastronomy
Szegediner Gulasch	goulash à la Széged (goulash with sauerkraut)

T

Tabak, nach Tabak	tobacco
Tabascosauce	Tabasco sauce
Tabelle	table
Tablett, Fach	tray
Taboulé (Salat aus Bulgur)	tabbouleh (bulgur salad)
Tafelspitz, gekochter	boiled round of beef
Tafelwein, Landwein	table wine
Tag der Arbeit, Staatsfeiertag	Labour Day
Tagesausflug	day trip
Tageskarte	travel card
Tageskarte (Menü)	specials of the day
Tagesordnung	agenda
Tagung	convention
talentiert	talented, in a talented way
Talg, Nierenfett	suet
Tannenzweig	fir twig
Tannin	tannin
Tapioka	tapioca
Tarif	fare
Normaltarif	normal fare
Sondertarif	special fare
Tarifart	fare type
Tasche, Beutel	sachet
Taschenrechner	calculator
Tastatur	keyboard
Taube	pigeon
Täublinge	russulas
Tauchschule	scuba diving centre
T-Bone-Steak	T-bone steak
Techniker	engineer
Tee	tea
Schwarztee	black tea
Früchtetee	fruit tea
Kräutertee	herbal tea
Kamillentee	camomile tea
Lindenblütentee	linden tea
Pfefferminztee	mint tea
Hibiskustee	hibiscus tea
Rooibostee	redbush tea
grüner Tee	green tea
Hagebuttentee	rosehip tea
– Natur	plain tea
– mit Zitrone	tea with lemon
– mit Milch	tea with milk
– mit Rum	tea with rum
–, teeinfrei	detanninated tea

German	English
Tasse Tee, am Bett serviert	early morning tea
Teebeutel	tea bag
Teeei	tea infuser
Teelöffel	tea/coffee spoon
Teelöffel voll	teaspoonful (tsp)
Teewagen	tea trolley
Teichhuhn, Wasserhuhn	moorhen, waterhen
Teig	dough
Teigkarte	rubber spatula
Teigwaren	pasta
Teildienst	split time shift
teilen	to share
Teilnehmer	participant
teilweise wolkig	partly cloudy
Teilzeit	part-time
Telefonbuch	telephone book
Telefonhörer	receiver
Tellerrand	plate edge
Tellerspiegel	plate mirror
Tellerwärmer	plate warmer
Temperatur	temperature
temperiert (Wein)	having the right temperature
Tennisplatz	tennis court
Teppich	carpet
Teppichläufer	rug
Terminplaner	appointment book, Filofax
Terrasse	terrace
Terrine	tureen
Teufelssauce (Demi-Glace, Weißwein oder Essig, Cayennepfeffer)	devil sauce (demi-glace, white wine or vinegar, cayenne)
Textverarbeitung	word processing
Thermalbad	thermal spa
Thermoskanne	thermos (flask)
Thunfisch	tunny, tuna
Thymian	thyme
Thymianbutter	thyme butter
Thymiansauce	thyme sauce
Tiefkühler	freezer
Tiefkühltruhe	deep freezer
Tier	animal
Timbale, Pastete	timbale
Tintenfisch	cuttlefish, octopus, poulp
Tintenfisch, Kalmar	squid
Tiroler Gröstl	tyrolean fried potatoes (fried potatoes with sliced beef, pork or bacon)
Tiroler Sauce (sauce tyrolienne)	Tyrolean sauce
Tisch decken	to lay the table
Tischdecke	tablecloth

Tischkarte	place card
Tischset	placemat
Tixo®, Klebeband	scotch tape, cellotape
Toast (mit ...)	toasted sandwich (with ...)
Toastbrot (Kastenbrot)	sandwich loaf
Toaster	griddle
toasten, rösten (Brot)	to toast
Toastständer	toast rack
Tofu	tofu
Toilettenpapier	toilet roll
Tomate	tomato
Tomatenmark	tomato puree
(rohe) Tomatensauce	(raw) tomato sauce
Tonic	tonic water
Topf	pot
Topflappen	pot holder
Topfen	curd/white cheese
Topfenknödel	curd/white cheese dumplings
Topfenstrudel	curd/white cheese strudel
Topinambur	Jerusalem artichoke
Torte (Obst, flach)	tart
Tortenheber	tart server, cake lifter/server/shovel/slice, pie server
Tortenschaufel	cake slice, pie server
Tortenteiler	cake divider
Törtchen	tartlet
Tortilla (Maisfladen)	tortilla (thin flat maize cake)
Totentrompeten	horns of plenty mushrooms
Tourist/in	tourist
Touristenklasse	economy class
Touristenmenü	tourist menu
tournieren	to turn into decorative shapes
Trafik	tobacconist
tranchieren	to carve
Tranchiergabel	carving fork
Tranchiermesser	carving knife
tränken mit etwas	to soak with sth
Treffen	appointment
Treibhausobst	hothouse fruit, forced fruit
Treibmittel, Backtreibmittel	raising agent
trennen	to divide, to separate
Trennung	separation
Treppe	stairway
Treppenlift	stair lift
Trichter	funnel
Trinkgeld	gratuity, tip
trocknen	to dry
trocken (Wein)	dry

Trockenerbse	dried pea
Trockenmasse	dry weight
tropfen	to drip
Tropfteil	batter (egg) drops, frying batter
Trüffel	truffle
–, schwarze	black truffle
Trüffelsauce (Sauce périgueux)	truffle sauce
Truthahn	turkey
Truthahnschnitzel	turkey fillets
Tülle	nozzle
Tumbler	tumbler
Türsteher	doorman

U

U-Bahn	underground, tube
überbucht	overbooked
Übergepäck	excess baggage
übergießen	to pour
überlappen	to overlap
übermorgen	day after tomorrow
übernachten	to stay overnight
Überraschung	surprise
überreif	overripe
Umberfisch	croaker, drumfish
umfangreich	extensive
umfassend	comprehensive
Umgebung	surrounding, setting
umhüllt vom Teigmantel	scrapped in pastry wrap
umkippen	to turn over
Umluft	recirculating heat
ummanteln, umhüllen	to coat
umranden	to surround
umrechnen	to convert
Umrechnungsrate	rate of exchange
Umrechnungstabelle	conversion chart
umrühren	to stir
Umsatz	turnover
umwickeln	wrap (a)round
Unannehmlichkeit	inconvenience
unbeaufsichtigt	unattended
Unfall	accident
ungefähr	approximate
ungesättigte Fettsäuren	unsaturated fatty acids
ungezuckert	unsweetened
unreif, grün	unripe
unruhig, hefig	yeasty, yeast-like

unter	below
unter Kontrolle haben	to stay in control
unterbreiten	to submit
untergärig (Bier)	bottom-fermented
unterschiedlich, verschieden	various
Unterschrift	signature
unterschreiben	to sign
Unterseite	underside, bottom side
Untersetzer	coaster, trivet
Unterstützung	support
unterteilen	to subdivide
unverdaulich, schwer verdaulich	indigestible
unverdünnt	undiluted
unzerbrechlich	unbreakable
Urlaubsort, Anlage	resort

V

Vacherin (Schichttorte aus Meringeböden und Schlagobers), Baisertorte	vacherin (rounds of meringue alternated with whipped cream), meringue cake
Vanille	vanilla
Vanillekipferl	vanilla crescents
Vanillesauce, -creme	custard
Vanilleschote	vanilla pod (BE), vanilla bean (AE)
Vanillezucker	vanilla sugar
variieren	to vary
Vase	vase
Vegetarier/in, vegetarisch	vegetarian
Veilchenblüte	violet
Velouté (weiße Grundsauce), Samtsauce	velouté (basic white sauce)
venezianische Sauce (Weißweinsauce mit Kräuterpüree)	Venetian sauce (white wine sauce with purée of herbs)
Venusmuschel	venus mussel, clam
verantwortlich	responsible
verantwortlich sein für	to be in charge of
verarbeiten	to process
Verbindungstür	connecting door
verbleibend, übrig	remaining
Verbot	prohibition
verdauen	to digest
verdaulich	digestible
verderben	to spoil
verderblich	perishable
verdorben	spoiled, spoilt, rotten, gone off
verdorrt, vertrocknet	withered
verdünnen	to dilute, to thin out

German	English
Vereinbarung, Vertrag	agreement
Verfallsdatum	expiration date
verfaulen	to rot
verfeinern, veredeln	to refine
verfügbar	available
Vergehen	wrongdoing
Vergnügen	pleasure
Vergrößerungsspiegel	magnifying mirror
verhandeln	to negotiate
Verhandlung	negotiation
verheiratet	married
verifizieren, nachprüfen	to verify
Verkaufstisch	counter
verkohlen	to char
Verlängerung	extension
Verlängerungskabel	extension cable/cord
verlängern (zeitlich)	to prolong
verlässlich	reliable
Verleih	rental
verlieren	to lose
verlobt	engaged
verlockend	enticing
Verlust	loss
Vermietung	rental facility
vermindern, verkleinern	to diminish
vermischen, schütteln	to toss
vermischter Salat	mixed salad
Vermittlung, Telefonist/in	operator, switchboard operator
vermuten	to suppose
vernünftig	sensible
verpacken	to wrap up
Verpackung	wrapping
verquirlen	to mix with a whisk, to whisk
verrechnen	to charge
verschieben	to postpone
Verschluss	fastener
verschmutzen	to contaminate
versichern, gewährleisten	to ensure
Versicherung	insurance
Versicherungspolizze	insurance policy
verständnisvoll	understanding
Verstärker	amplifier
verstopft	stopped up
Verstopfung	constipation
Verteiler	distributer
Dreifachverteiler	3-way distributer
Vertrag	contract
verwitwet	widowed

Verzeichnis (Telefon)	directory
Verzeichnis mit Hinweisen für den Hotelgast	hotel directory
verzinkt	galvanised
Vichyssoise (Kartoffel-Lauch-Suppe, kalt serviert)	vichyssoise (iced potato-leek cream soup)
Videorekorder	video recorder
Videoüberwachung	video surveillance
videoüberwacht	video-monitored
Vielfalt	diversity
Viertel	quarter
Villeroi-Sauce (weiße Sauce mit Champignonfond)	Villeroi sauce (white sauce with essence of mushrooms)
Vinaigrette (Essig-Kräutersauce)	vinaigrette, vinaigrette sauce, vinaigrette dressing
VIP-Etage	executive floor
Visitenkarte	business card
Vitrine	display case
Vogelbeere	rowanberry
Vogelbeerschnaps	rowanberry schnapps
Vogerlsalat, Feldsalat	corn salad, lamb's lettuce
Voisin-Kartoffeln (Kartoffeltörtchen mit Butter und Käse)	Voisin potatoes (cake of potato, butter and cheese)
Völker	peoples
Volksschule	primary school
voll, reichhaltig, schwer	rich
Vollkaskoversicherung mit Selbstbehalt	CDW (collision damage waiver)
Vollkaskoversicherung ohne Selbstbehalt	SCDW (super collision damage waiver)
Vollkonserven	full preserves
Vollkornbrot	wholemeal bread
Vollkornmehl	wholemeal flour
Vollpension	full board
Volumen, Inhalt	volume
Volumprozent	percentage by volume
vor (zeitlich)	ago, before
vor einer Woche	a week ago
vor (örtlich)	in front of
Vor-, Nachsaison, Nebensaison	low season
vorausgesetzt(, dass)	provided (that)
vorausplanen	to plan ahead
voraussichtlich	anticipated
vorbereiten, zubereiten	to prepare
vorbereitende Arbeiten	preparations
vorgebacken	prebaked
vorgegeben, zur Verfügung gestellt	provided (with)
Vorgehensweise	procedure
vorgekocht	precooked

vorgestern	day before yesterday
Vorhang	curtain
vorherig, vorhergehend	previous
Vorhersage	forecast
Vorlegebesteck	serving cutlery
vorlegen	to serve the food at the table
Vorort	suburb
Vorschlag	suggestion
vorschlagen	to suggest
Vorschrift	regulation
Vorschule	infant school, pre-school
Vorsichtsmaßnahme	precaution
Vorspeise, Appetitanreger	appetiser, starter
Vorspeisen	hors d'oeuvres
Vorstandssitzung einer Firma	company board meeting
Vortrag	lecture
Vortragende/r	lecturer
Vorwahl	area code

W

Waage	scales, weighing machine
waagrecht (Rätsel)	across
Wacholder(beeren)	juniper (berries)
Wacholderbutter	juniper berry butter
Wacholdersauce	juniper berry sauce
wachsam	vigilant
Wachsbohne	wax bean
Wachtel	quail
Waffel	wafer, waffle
Waffel-, Gitterkartoffeln	wafer potatoes
Waffeleisen	waffle iron
Wagen, Servierwagen	trolley
wählen, auswählen	to choose
während	during
wahrheitsliebend	truthful
wahrscheinlich	probably
Wahrzeichen	landmark
Waldchampignon, Portobellopilz	portobello
Walderdbeeren	wild strawberries
Waldmeister	woodruff
Waldorfsalat (Äpfel, Knollensellerie, Walnüsse, Mayonnaise)	Waldorf salad (apples, celeriac and walnuts, mayonnaise)
Waldpilze	wild mushrooms
Walnuss	walnut
Walnusskern	walnut kernel
Walnusssauce	walnut sauce, nut sauce
wandern	to hike

German	English
Wandschrank	built-in cupboard, wall cupboard
Wange	cheek
Ware	commodity
Wareneinsatz	food cost, cost of sales
warm	warm
warmes Getränk	warm beverage
warme Buttersaucen	warm butter sauces
warmer Pudding	warm pudding
warme Spezialsauce	special warm sauce
warme Vorspeise	hot appetiser
Wärmeplatte	chafing dish
Wärmepflaster	heatplaster
Wärmeschrank	heating cabinet
Warmhalteplatte	hot plate
Wärmetisch	hot food counter/table
Wartezeit	waiting period/time
Wartung, Haustechnik	maintenance
waschen	to wash
Waschbecken	washbasin, sink
Wäscherei	laundry
Wäscherin, Büglerin	laundry maid
Waschlappen	washcloth
Waschmittel	detergent, washing powder
Wasserglas	water glass
Wasserhahn	faucet, (water) tap
Wassermelone	water melon
wässern	to soak
wässrig	watery
WC-Papier	toilet paper
WC-Papier-Halter	toilet paper holder
Wechselgeld	change
Wechselkurs	exchange rate
Wechselstube	exchange office
Wecken, Gebäck	plaited rolls
Weckerl	bun
Weckruf	wake-up call, early morning call
wegwerfen	to throw away
weich werden	to become soft/tender
Weichkäse	soft cheese
Weichseln, Sauerkirschen	morellos, morello cherries
Weihnachtsabend	Christmas Eve
Weihnachtstag	Christmas Day
Wein	wine
Weingelee	wine jelly
Wein aus dem Ausland, ausländischer Wein	wine of foreign growth
Wein vom Fass	wine from the barrel/wood
Weinbau	viticulture
Weinberg	vineyard

Weinblatt, -blätter	vine leaf, leaves (pl)
Weinbrand, Branntwein	brandy
Weinbrandsauce	brandy sauce
Weinflaschen-Korb	wine cradle
Weinglas (Rot-/Weiß-)	(red/white) wine glass
Weingelee	wine jelly
Weinhefe	wine yeast
Weinkarte	wine list
Weinkeller	wine cellar
Weinkeller (Lokal)	wine tavern
Weinkellner	wine steward
Weinkühler	wine cooler
Weinprobe	wine tasting
Weinraute	rue
Weinstock	vine
Weintrauben (rot, weiß)	grapes (red, white)
Weißblech	tinplate
Weißbrot	white bread
weiße Bohnen	white beans
weißer Fond	white stock
weiße Rübe	turnip
weiße Sauce	white sauce
Weißfisch, Wittling, Merlan	whitefish, whiting
Weißwein	white wine
Weißweinsauce (Fischeinmachsauce)	white wine sauce (white fish stock)
Weißwurst	veal sausage
Weizen	wheat
Wellnessbereich	spa
Wellschliff (Messer), Sägemesser	serrated knife
Wels, Waller, Zwergwels	sheatfish, wels, catfish
Welsh Rabbit (geröstetes Brot, mit heißem Käse belegt)	welsh rabbit (dish of melted cheese on toast)
Werbung	advertisement
werben, inserieren, ankündigen	to advertise
Werkzeug, Gerät	tool
Wermut	vermouth
Wertsachen	valuables
Wetzstahl	sharpening steel
Wetzstein	whetstone
Whisk(e)y	whisk(e)y
irischer Whiskey	Irish whiskey
schottischer Whisky	Scotch whisky
kanadischer Whisky	Canadian whisky
amerikanischer Whiskey	American whiskey
– mit mind. 51 % Mais	bourbon
– mit mind. 51 % Roggen	rye
Whisky aus verschiedenen Getreidearten	grain whisky

Whisky nur aus Gerste	malt whisky
gemischter Whisky (malt und grain)	blended whisky
Whisk(e)yglas	rock glass, whisk(e)y glass, old-fashioned
Wickeltisch	baby change unit (BE), (diaper) changing table (AE)
Wickeltischauflage	changing table mat
widerwillig	unwilling
Wiedergutmachung	compensation
wiederverwerten	to recycle
wiegen	to scale, to weigh
Wiegen	weighing
Wiener Schnitzel (vom Kalb)	deep-fried breaded escalope of veal (veal cutlet)
Wild	game (animal)
Wildpüreesuppe	game (purée) soup
Wildgeflügel, Federwild	game birds
Wildkroketten	game croquettes
Wildpastete	game pâté
Wildsalat	game salad
Wildfond	game stock
Wild, Wildbret	venison
Wildente, Stockente	mallard, wild duck
Wildgans	wild goose
Wildgeflügel, Federwild	wild fowl
Wildhuhn	grouse
Wildlachs	wild salmon
Wildragout, Wildpfeffer	game stew
Wildreis	wild rice
Wildsauce	venison sauce
Wildschwein	(wild) boar
Wildsuppe mit Teighaube	game consommé in pastry crust
Wildtaube, Ringeltaube	ringdove
Williamsbirne	Williams pear, Bartlett pear (AE)
Windbeutel (gefüllt)	cream puff, chou bun
Windel	nappy (BE), diaper (AE)
Wintergemüse	winter vegetables
Winzer	wine-grower
Wirt/in (Vermieter/in)	landlord, landlady
Wochenmarkt	weekly market
Wohlergehen	well-being
wohlerzogen	well-bred
wohltuend	beneficial
Wohnsitz	domicile
Wok	wok
Wolke	cloud
wollend, bereit	willing
Worcestershire Sauce	Worcestershire sauce

German	English
Workshop	workshop
Wrackbarsch	stonebass, wreckfish
Wunde, wund	sore
wunderbar, großartig	marvellous
Wunsch	desire, wish
wünschen	to wish, to desire
Würfelzucker	lump sugar, cube sugar
Würstel im Schlafrock	sausage roll, toad-in-the-hole (sausages baked in batter)
Wurstsalat	sausage salad
Wurzel	root
Wurzelfleisch	boiled shoulder of pork with carrots, leeks, horseradish and celeriac
Wurzelkarpfen	carp with root vegetables
würzen	to flavour, to season
–, nach Geschmack	to season to taste
–, scharf	to spice
würzig	spicy
Würzmittel	aroma, flavourings, seasonings, spices

Z

German	English
Zabaione, Sabayon, Weinschaum (Chaudeau), (schaumige Creme aus Eigelb, Zucker und Wein)	sabayon (foamy wine sauce of egg yolk, sugar and wine), zabaglione
Zackenbarsch	grouper
zäh	tough
Zahlen	figures
Zahnbrasse	dentex
Zahnbürste	toothbrush
Zahnpaste	toothpaste
Zahnputzbecher	toothbrush cup
Zahnstocher	toothpick
Zander, Schill	pike-perch
Zange	tongs
Zapfanlage	drink dispensing equipment
zart, weich	tender
Zartbitterschokolade	dark/bittersweet/plain chocolate
Zeche prellen	to skip payment
Zeigestock	pointer
Zeile	line
Zeitschaltuhr	time switch
Zeitschrift	magazine
Zeitungsstand	newsstand
Zeitzonenuhr	time zones clock
Zentrum	downtown

German	English
zerbrechlich	fragile
zerdrücken	to crush
zerkleinern, schnetzeln, zerreißen	to shred
zerkochen	to overcook
zerreißen	to tear up
zerstoßen	to muddle
zerstoßen (im Mörser)	to pound
zerstoßenes Eis	crushed ice
Zestenreißer	zester
Zettelablage	stacking tray
Zeug, Ding	stuff
Zeugnis	certificate
Ziege	goat
Ziegenkäse	goat cheese, chèvre
Zielflughafen	point of destination
Zigeunerart	gipsy style
Zigeunersauce (Tomatensauce mit Paprika, Champignons, Zunge und Schinken)	gipsy sauce, zingara sauce (tomatoed sauce with strips of ham, ox-tongue, mushrooms)
ziehen lassen (in Marinade)	to steep
Zimmer	room
– mit 3 Mahlzeiten	American plan
– mit Frühstück und Abendessen	modified American plan
– mit Frühstück	B & B (bed and breakfast), continental plan
– ohne Frühstück	European plan
Zimmerkarte	key card
Zimmermädchen/Zimmerbursche, Raumpfleger/in	chambermaid, room maid/attendant
Zimmerpreis	room rate, tariff
Zimmerservice	room service
Zimmertemperatur	room temperature
Zimmerübersicht	room rack
Zimt	cinnamon
Zimtapfel	custard apple
Zirbe	Swiss (stone) pine
Zitrone	lemon
Zitronenbutter	lemon butter
Zitronenschale	lemon peel
Zitronenspirale	lemon twist
Zitronengras	lemon grass
Zitronengrassauce	lemon grass sauce
Zitronenmelisse	lemon balm
Zitronensauce	lemon sauce
Zitterrochen	electric ray, torpedo fish
Zoll	customs
Zollbeamter	customs officer
Zollerklärung	declaration form
zollfrei	duty-free

German	English
zu Fuß	on foot
zu Handen, wohnhaft bei	c/o (care of)
zu Ihrer Verfügung	at your disposal
zu stark gebraten	overdone
Zubereitung	preparation (of food)
Zubringerdienst	shuttle service
Zucchini	courgette, zucchini
Zucchiniblüten	squash blossoms
Zucht, Züchtung	cultivation
züchten	to breed
Zuchtforelle	farmed trout, trout from the fish-tank
Zucker	sugar
Zuckerdose, -schüssel	sugar bowl
Zuckermais	sweetcorn
Zuckermelone	cantaloupe
Zuckerschote	sugar snap
Zuckersirup, Melasse	molasses
Zuckerstreuer	sugar dredger/shifter
Zuckerwatte	candyfloss
zudecken	to cover
zufriedengestellt	satisfied
Zufriedenheit	satisfaction
zugänglich, erreichbar	accessible
zugunsten von	in favour of
Zündholzkartoffeln	matchstick chips/potatoes
zunehmend	increasing
Zunge	tongue
Zuppa pavese (Bouillon mit gerösteten Brotscheiben, darauf ein pochiertes Ei)	zuppa pavese (beef broth with slices of fried bread and a poached egg)
zuputzen, parieren, wegschneiden	to trim
zur Verfügung stellen	to provide
zurückführen auf	to trace to
zusammendrücken	to press together
zusammenfassen	to sum up
Zusammenfassung	summary
zusammenhalten	to stick together
Zusammenkommen, Treffen	gathering
Zusammensetzung	composition
zusammengesetzte Salate	compound salads
zusammenstellen	to compile, to put together
Zusammenstellung	putting together
zusätzlich	additional, supplementary
Zusatzstoff	additive
Zuschlag, Aufschlag	extra charge
Zustellbett	additional/extra bed
Zutaten	ingredients
zuvorkommend	obliging

zuweisen	to allocate
Zweck	purpose
Zweibettzimmer	twin(-bedded) room
Zweifel	doubt
Zweig, Stängel	sprig
Petersilienzweig	sprig of parsley
zweisprachig	bilingual
zweite Hausdame	assistant housekeeper
zweizinkige Gabel	two-pronged fork
Zwergdorsch	pout, pouting
Zwergkürbis	baby marrow
Zwetschkenfleck	plum cake
Zwetschkenröster	stewed plums
Zwieback	rusks, zwieback, biscuit rusks
Zwiebel	onion
Zwiebelsauce (Sauce soubise)	onion sauce, soubise sauce
Zwiebelrostbraten	braised fillet of beef/sirloin steak with onions
(überbackene) Zwiebelsuppe	(baked) onion soup
Zwischenrippenstück	sirloin steak
Zwischenstopp	stopover
Zwischensumme	subtotal

English – German

Englisch - Deutsch

A

à la polonaise	mit Butter und Bröseln (polnische Art)
abbreviation	Abkürzung
ability	Fähigkeit
abroad	im Ausland
to absorb	aufsaugen
to abstain from meat	kein Fleisch essen
acacia honey	Akazienhonig
accented by	betont durch
accessible	zugänglich, zu erreichen
accident	Unfall
accommodation	Beherbergung
to accompany	begleiten
accompanied by	begleitet von
accompanying person	Begleitperson
account	Rechnung
to settle the account	die Rechnung begleichen
account number	Kontonummer
accountancy	Buchhaltung
accuracy	Genauigkeit
accurate	genau
acid	sauer
acid, acidity	Säure
acidic	säuerlich
acidophilus/sour milk	Sauermilch
across	waagrecht (Rätsel)
adapter	Adapter
to add	hinzufügen
to add liquid to a roast	ablöschen (Braten, mit Wein oder Wasser)
additional	zusätzlich
additional charge	Aufpreis
additional/extra bed	Zustellbett
additions	Einlage, Zugaben
additive	Zusatzstoff
adhesive tape	Klebestreifen
adjoining	angrenzend
to admire	bewundern
to adore	begehren
to adorn	schmücken
adverse	negativ, ungünstig, nachteilig

to advertise	werben, inserieren, ankündigen
advertisement	Anzeige, Werbung
advice	Rat(schlag)
to give advice	einen Rat geben
to advise	beraten
aerophobia (fear of flying)	Flugangst
affordable	erschwinglich
aftertaste	Nachgeschmack, Abgang
to age	reifen
agenda	Tagesordnung
ago	vor (zeitlich)
a week ago	vor einer Woche
agreement	Vereinbarung, Vertrag
agricultural school	Landwirtschaftsschule
aioli sauce (garlic mayonnaise)	Aioli-Sauce (Knoblauch-Mayonnaise)
air	Luft
to air	lüften
air conditioning, AC	Klimaanlage
air-dried	luftgetrocknet
airline	Fluglinie
airline representative	Fluglinienangestellte/r
airplane	Flugzeug
airport shuttle (service)	Flughafenzubringer
airsickness bag	Spucktüte, Übelkeitstüte
aisle	Gang
aitchbone of beef	Hüferschwanzel, Rindsrose
alcohol	Alkohol
alcohol concentration	Alkoholgehalt
alcoholic	alkoholisch
alcoholic drink, liqueur	alkoholisches Getränk
ale, lager, pale ale	Bier, helles obergäriges Hefebier
alert	alarmieren, aufmerksam machen
alfresco dining	Abendessen im Freien
alive	lebendig
All Saints' Day	Allerheiligen
all-around view	Rundumblick
allergic (to)	allergisch (auf)
all-inclusive	alles inklusive
to allocate	zuweisen
allowance	erlaubte Menge
allspice, pimento	Piment
almond	Mandel
flaked almonds	Mandelsplitter
along	entlang, weiter, vorwärts
alternate	abwechseln
alternately	abwechselnd
although	obwohl
aluminium foil, tinfoil	Alufolie

English	German
amandine	mit Mandeln
amaranth	Amarant
amaretto (almond-flavoured liqueur)	Amaretto (Mandellikör)
ambitious	ehrgeizig
amendment	Änderung
American plan	Zimmer mit drei Mahlzeiten
modified American plan	Zimmer, Frühstück und Abendessen
amount	Menge, Betrag
amplifier	Verstärker
anchovy, -ies (pl)	Anchovis, Sardellen
anchovy butter	Sardellenbutter
anchovy sauce	Sardellensauce
Andalusian sauce (tomato-based mayonnaise)	Andalusische Sauce (tomatisierte Mayonnaise)
angler-fish, monkfish, frogfish	Seeteufel, Lotte, Anglerfisch
animal	Tier
aniseed	Anis
aniseed brandy	Anisschnaps
ankle	Knöchel
to twist the ankle	umknicken
annual holiday	Jahresurlaub
answering machine	Anrufbeantworter
anticipated	voraussichtlich
anxious	begierig, bestrebt
aperitif, before dinner drink	Aperitif
appearance	Erscheinung(sbild)
appetiser, starter	Vorspeise, Appetitanreger
appetising	appetitlich
apple	Apfel
apple fritters	gebackene Apfelspalten, Apfelringerln
apple purée/sauce	Apfelmus
apple strudel	Apfelstrudel
apple turnover	Apfeltasche
apple/Asian pear	Nashi-Birne
appliance	Gerät
application	Anwendung, Bewerbung
application form	Antragsformular
to apply for (a job)	bewerben für (einen Job)
appointment	Treffen
apprentice	Lehrling, Auszubildende/r
apprenticeship	Lehre
approximate	ungefähr
apricot	Marille
apricot soufflé	Marillenauflauf
apricot dumplings	Marillenknödel
apricot brandy	Marillenbrand

April	April
apron	Schürze
area code	Vorwahl
armchair	Sessel, Fauteuil
aroma	Aroma
aromatic	aromatisch
to arrange	einteilen, arrangieren
arrival	Ankunft
arrowroot	Pfeilwurz
artichoke	Artischocke
artichoke base/bottom	Artischockenboden
artichoke heart	Artischockenherz
artificial	künstlich
arugula	Rucola
Ascension Day	Christi Himmelfahrt
ashtray	Aschenbecher
asparagus	Spargel
– tips	Spargelspitzen
– (tips) in vinaigrette sauce	Spargel(spitzen) in Sauce vinaigrette
– with hollandaise/Dutch sauce	– mit Sauce hollandaise
asparagus omelette	Omelette mit Spargel
aspic	Sulz, Aspik
assembly point	Sammelplatz
to assess	schätzen, beurteilen
assessment	Einschätzung, Beurteilung
assistant chef/cook	Hilfskoch, Küchenhilfe
assistant housekeeper	zweite Hausdame
assistant waiter	Hilfskellner
associate	Partner/in
assorted	gemischt
assorted raw vegetables (crudités)	Rohkost(platte)
assorted salad	gemischter Salat, Beilagensalat
assorted sliced/cold meats/cuts	Aufschnitt, kalte Platte
Assumption	Mariä Himmelfahrt
at once	sofort
at pleasure, as much as you like	nach Belieben, so viel man will
at the cashier's office, at the reception	an der Kassa, am Empfang
at the latest, by	bis spätestens
at the rear	hinten
at your disposal	zu Ihrer Verfügung
ATM (automated teller machine)	Bankomat
to attach	befestigen
attention	Aufmerksamkeit
au bleu	blau gekocht
aubergine	Aubergine, Melanzani
auditor	Prüfer
August	August

English	German
Aurore sauce	Aurorasauce
Austrian	österreichisch
Austrian doughnut, krapfen	Krapfen, Faschingskrapfen, Berliner
available	verfügbar
aviation	Luftfahrt
avocado	Avocado
awful	schrecklich, furchtbar

B

English	German
basic brown sauce	Sauce Demi-Glace, braune Grundsauce
boeuf bourguignon (beef stew in red wine), Burgundy beef stew	Burgunderbraten (Rinderragout in Rotwein)
B & B (bed and breakfast)	Zimmer mit Frühstück
baba, rum baba (small yeast-raised cake soaked in rum syrup)	Baba mit Rum, Rum-Baba
baby change unit	Wickeltisch
baby cot	Babybett
baby marrow	Zwergkürbis
babysitting service	Babysittervermittlung
background music	Hintergrundmusik
backpack	Rucksack
backside	Rückseite
bacon	Speck
bacon dumpling	Speckknödel
bacon tartlet	Specktörtchen
bacteria	Bakterien
bag	Beutel
bagel (round roll with a hole in the middle)	Bagel
baggage	Gepäck
baggage allowance	Freigepäck
baggage claim	Gepäckausgabe
baggage claim area	Gepäckabholbereich
baguette	Baguette
to bake	backen
baked apple	Bratapfel
baked jacket potatoes (baked in their skin)	Ofenkartoffeln (in der Schale gebacken)
baked noodles	Nudelgratin
baked potatoes	Folienkartoffeln
baking dishes	Backgeschirr
baking paper	Backpapier
baking powder	Backpulver
potatoes en papillote	Folienkartoffeln
balance due	Rechnungsbetrag

balanced	ausgeglichen
ballpoint pen	Kugelschreiber
ballroom	Festsaal
bamboo shoots	Bambussprossen
banana	Banane
banana fritters	gebackene Bananen
band-aid	Pflaster
bank account	Bankkonto
bank connection	Bankverbindung
banquet	Bankett, Festessen
bar	Bar
bar menu	Barkarte
bar spoon	Messlöffel
bar stool	Barhocker
bar strainer	Barsieb
bar towel	Bartuch
barman, barkeeper	Barkeeper
barbecue, BBQ	Griller
to barbecue	grillen
barbell	Barbe
barber's shop	Herrenfriseur
barley	Gerste
barley soup	Gerstensuppe
barley coffee	Malzkaffee
barrel	Fass
barrique	Fass
basement	Keller, Untergeschoß
basil	Basilikum
to baste	aufgießen (z. B. den Braten)
bath	Badewanne
bath mat	Badematte
bath towel	Badetuch
batter (egg) drops, frying batter	Backteig, Tropfteig
to batter	eintauchen in Backteig
Bavarian cream	bayerische Creme
bay	Lorbeer
bay leaf	Lorbeerblatt
beach	Strand
beans	Bohnen
to bear in mind	berücksichtigen, beachten
béarnaise sauce (hollandaise sauce with tarragon)	Sauce béarnaise (Sauce hollandaise mit Estragon)
to beat	schlagen, klopfen
to beat egg whites	Eischnee schlagen
to beat into a foam	schaumig schlagen
beautician	Schönheitspfleger/in
beauty salon	Schönheitssalon
béchamel sauce (basic white sauce)	Béchamelsauce (weiße Grundsauce)

B English – German

to become	werden
– detached	ablösen
– hard/tough	hart werden
– lukewarm	lauwarm werden
– soft/tender	weich werden
bed	Bett
bedside lamp	Nachttischlampe
bedside table	Nachttisch
bedspread	Bettüberwurf
beef	Rindfleisch
beef carbonade	Rindskarbonade
beef roulades	Rindsrouladen
beef salad/vinaigrette	Rindfleischsalat
beef stew, stewed beef, ragout of beef	Rindsragout
beef broth/tea	Rindssuppe
beef carpaccio (thin slices of raw beef seasoned with oil and Parmesan)	Carpaccio (rohe Filetscheiben mit Öl und Parmesan), Rindercarpaccio
beer	Bier
draught beer	Bier vom Fass
beer jug/mug	Bierkrug
beer mat	Bierdeckel
beer sauce	Biersauce
beer tumbler	Bierglas (groß)
beet sugar	Rübenzucker
beetroot (BE), red beet (AE)	Rote Rübe, Rote Beete
beetroot sauce	Rote-Rüben-Sauce, Rote-Beete-Sauce
before	vor (zeitlich)
before-dinner drink	Aperitif
beignet, fritter	Beignet, Krapfen
bell	Glocke
bellboy	Page
belly	Bauch
below	unter
beneficial	wohltuend
Bercy sauce (butter, shallots, white wine), shallot sauce	Bercy-Sauce (Butter, Schalotten, Weißwein), Schalottensauce
berries	Beeren
beside	neben
best before/by date	Mindesthaltbarkeitsdatum
best end neck of veal (loin of veal)	Kalbskarree
beverage	Getränk
to beware of	sich hüten vor
bicarbonate of soda	Natron
bigarade sauce (flavoured with bitter oranges)	Bigarade-Sauce (mit Saft von Bitterorangen)

bilberry, -ies (pl) (BE), blueberry, -ies (pl) (AE)	Blaubeere(n), Heidelbeere(n)
bilingual	zweisprachig
bill	Rechnung
to bind	binden (z. B. mit Mehl oder Stärke), eindicken, legieren
to bind with string	mit Bindfaden umwickeln
biodegradable	biologisch abbaubar
biological bread	Bio-Brot
bird's nest soup	Schwalbennestersuppe
biscuit	Keks
Bismarck herring (marinated herring fillet)	Bismarckhering
bisque	Cremesuppe
bisque of crayfish	Krebssuppe
bite-sized	mundgerecht
Bitoke (kind of Hamburg steak)	Bitok (russisches Hacksteak)
bitter	bitter
bitterness	Herbe
black bass	Forellenbarsch
black butter	schwarze Butter
Black Forest cake (with morello cherries)	Schwarzwälder-Kirsch-Torte
black popular mushrooms	Stockschwämmchen
black pudding, blood sausage	Blutwurst
blackberry, -ies (pl)	Brombeere(n)
blackbird	Amsel
blackcurrant	Johannisbeere
blacklist	schwarze Liste
bladder	Blase
blade	Schneide, Klinge
to blanch	blanchieren
blanket	Decke
blanquette of veal	Kalbsragout in weißer Sauce
bleak	Silberfisch, Ukeleie
to blend	mischen
blender	Mixer
blini (small buckwheat pancake)	Blini (Buchweizenpfannkuchen)
bloater	Bückling
blossom	Blüte
blow	Schlag
to blow the nose	schnäuzen
blue cheese	Blauschimmelkäse
blunt	stumpf
boar	Wildschwein
board	Brett
to board	einsteigen
boarding area	Abflugsbereich
boarding house/school	Internat

English	German
boarding pass	Bordkarte, Einstiegskarte
boardroom	Sitzungssaal
body	Körper
to boil	kochen
boiled potatoes	Salzkartoffeln
boiled ribs of beef	Beinfleisch
boiled round of beef	gekochter Tafelspitz
boiled shoulder of pork with carrots, leeks, horseradish and celeriac	steirisches Wurzelfleisch
boiled/cooked ham	gekochter Schinken
boiling fowl	Suppenhuhn
boiling point	Siedepunkt
boletus	Steinpilz
bone	Knochen
to bone	auslösen, entgräten
bone marrow	Knochenmark
boneless	ausgelöst
boning knife	Ausbeinmesser
booking	Buchung
booking form	Buchungsformular
bookshelf	Bücherregal
bookshop	Buchladen
borage	Borretsch
bordelaise sauce (wine sauce with beef marrow)	Bordelaise-Sauce (Weinsauce mit Rindermark)
to bother with	sich beschäftigen mit
bottle	Flasche
bottle opener	Flaschenöffner
bottled beer	Flaschenbier
bottled sodas	Limonaden
bottled wine	Flaschenwein
bottom-fermented	untergärig (Bier)
bouchée	Pastetchen
bouillon	Rindssuppe
bouillon potatoes	Bouillonkartoffeln
boulangère potatoes (baked with onions)	Bäckerin-Kartoffeln (mit Zwiebel überbacken)
bouquet	Bouquet
bouquet of herbs	Kräutersträußchen
bowl	Schüssel
bowtie	Fliege, Mascherl
box	Kiste
Boxing Day	Stephanitag, 2. Weihnachtsfeiertag
bracket	Klammer
brain	Gehirn
to braise	schmoren, im Ganzen (braun) dünsten
braised beef	Rinderschmorbraten

braised fillet of beef/ sirloin steak with onions	Zwiebelrostbraten
braised stuffed green peppers	gefüllte Paprika
brambleberry, -ies (pl),	Brombeere(n)
bran	Kleie
brand	Marke
brandy	Weinbrand, Branntwein
brandy sauce	Weinbrandsauce
brandy snifter	Cognacschwenker
brat, bratwurst	Bratwurst
brawn (in aspic jelly)	Schweinskopfsülze
brawn of pig's trotters	Schweinshaxelsulz
brawn chopped pig's head	Presskopf
Brazil nut	Paranuss
bread (brown, white)	Brot (schwarzes, weißes)
to bread	panieren
bread basket	Brotkorb
bread cubes	Brotwürfel
bread sauce	Brotsauce
bread sauce	Brotsauce
breadcrumbs	Brösel, Paniermehl
breadsticks	Knabbergebäck
to break	aufschlagen
breakfast	Frühstück
breakfast buffet	Frühstücksbuffet
breakfast menu	Frühstückskarte
bream	Brasse
breast of ...	...brust
roast stuffed breast of veal	gefüllte Kalbsbrust
to breath	atmen, belüften von Wein
to breed	züchten
to brew	brauen, kochen (Tee)
brewer's yeast	Bierhefe
brewery	Brauerei
bridal suite	Hochzeitssuite
brief	kurz
in brief	in Kürze
brightly-coloured	leuchtend bunt
brightness	Glanz
brill	Glattbutt
brine, souse, pickle	Salzlake, Pökel
to bring to the boil	aufkochen
brioche	Brioche
brisket	Bruststück
brittle	Krokant
broad beans	Saubohnen, dicke Bohnen
to broadcast	senden, aussenden

English	German
broccoli	Brokkoli, Spargelkohl
– with breadcrumbs and butter	– mit Butterbröseln
broccoli florets	Brokkoliröschen
brochette	Spieß
to broil	grillen, schmoren, braten
broth	Kraftbrühe, Suppe
beef tea/broth	Rinderkraftsuppe
brown (black) butter	braune Butter, Nussbutter
to brown	bräunen
brown/black butter	braune Butter, Nussbutter
brown rice	brauner Reis, Vollreis
brown sauce	braune Sauce
brown soup	Einbrennsuppe
brown stock	brauner Fond
brown sugar	Rohzucker
brown/black bread	Schwarzbrot
brown loaf	Laib Schwarzbrot
brown/brook trout	Bachforelle
brunch (BReakfast + lUNCH)	Brunch
bruschetta (toasted garlic bread)	Bruschetta (geröstetes Knoblauchbrot)
brush	Bürste
to brush	einstreichen
Brussels sprouts	Kohlsprossen, Rosenkohl
brut	Schaumwein mit weniger als 15 g Restzuckergehalt
bucket	Eimer
buckling	Bückling
buckwheat	Buchweizen
buckwheat pancake	Buchweizenpfann-kuchen
buffalo mozzarella	Büffel-Mozzarella
to build in glass	im Glas zubereiten
built-in cupboard	Wandschrank
bull	Stier
bun	Weckerl
bunk bed	Stockbett
burbot	Quappe, Trüsche
burgundy (red, white)	Burgunder (rot, weiß)
burgundy sauce (red wine sauce)	Burgundersauce (Rotweinsauce)
burnet	Bibernelle, Pimpinelle
to burst	platzen
busecca (tripe and bean soup)	Busecca (Kuttelsuppe mit weißen Bohnen)
business card	Visitenkarte
business class	erste Klasse
business lunch/meal	Geschäftsessen
business school	Handelsakademie
butter	Butter
to butter	in Butter schwenken

butter biscuit	Butterkeks
butter fish	Butterfisch
butter sauce	Buttersauce
buttermilk	Buttermilch
buttermilk dough	Sauerteig
by	mit, (spätestens) bis
by car/bus/plane ...	mit dem Auto/Bus/Flugzeug...
by credit card	mit Kreditkarte
by debit card	mit Bankkarte

C

c/o (care of)	zu Handen, wohnhaft bei
cabbage	Kraut, Kohl
(stuffed) cabbage rolls	Krautwickler, Krautrouladen
cabbage salad	Krautsalat
cabbage strudel	Krautstrudel
cable car	Straßenbahn
cake	Kuchen, Torte
cake divider	Tortenteiler
cake slice, pie server	Tortenschaufel
cake tin	Backblech
calamaries, squids	Kalmare
calculator	Taschenrechner
calf	Kalb
calf's brain	Kalbshirn
calf's cheeks	Kalbsbackerln
calf's head	Kalbskopf
calf's heart	Kalbsherz
calf's kidneys	Kalbsnieren
calf's liver	Kalbsleber
calf's sweetbread	Kalbsbries
calf's tongue	Kalbszunge
calf's brain with egg	Hirn mit Ei
calf's liver sausage	Kalbsleberwurst
calf's liver with apple	Berliner Leber
call	Anruf
local call	Ortsgespräch
long-distance call	Ferngespräch
calvados (apple brandy)	Calvados (Apfelschnaps)
camomile	Kamille
camomile tea	Kamillentee
campsite	Campingplatz
canapé	Canapé, belegtes Brötchen
to cancel	stornieren
cancellation	Stornierung
cancellation charge/fee	Stornogebühr
candelabrum	Kerzenleuchter

candied orange peel	Aranzini
candle	Kerze
candleholder, candlestick	Kerzenhalter
candyfloss	Zuckerwatte
cane sugar	Rohrzucker
cannelloni (stuffed rolls of noodle dough)	Cannelloni (gefüllte Nudelteigrollen)
cantaloupe	Zuckermelone
capacity	Kapazität, Volumen
caper	Kaper
caper sauce	Kapernsauce
capercaillie	Auerhahn
capon	Kapaun
car parking	Parkplatz
car rental	Autovermietung
carafe	Karaffe
in carafe	offen (Wein)
carambola, starfruit	Karambole, Sternfrucht
caramel sugar	Karamellzucker
caraway seed	Kümmel
carbon dioxide	Kohlensäure
cardamom	Kardamom
cardinal sauce (bechamel and lobster butter)	Kardinalsauce (Béchamel und Hummerbutter)
cardoon	Kardone, Gemüseartischocke
care	Sorgfalt
carefully	sorgfältig
career-minded	karrierebewusst
car-hire company	Autovermietung
caring	mitfühlend, sozial, liebevoll
Carinthian pasta	Kärntner Kasnudeln
Carmen soup (cream of rice coloured with tomato purée)	Carmen-Suppe (passierte Reissuppe, mit Tomatenmark gefärbt)
carob	Johannisbrot
carousel	Karussell
carp	Karpfen
carp with root vegetables	Wurzelkarpfen
carpaccio, beef carpaccio (thin slices of raw beef seasoned with oil and Parmesan)	Carpaccio, Rindercarpaccio (rohe Filetscheiben mit Öl und Parmesan)
carpet	Teppich
carrot	Karotte, Gelbe Rübe
carrot sauce	Karottensauce
carry-on bag	Handgepäck
cartilage	Knorpel
to carve	tranchieren
carving fork	Tranchiergabel
carving knife	Tranchiermesser

English	German
cash	bar
cash desk, cashier's office	Kassa
cash machine/dispenser	Bankomat
cashew (nut)	Cashewnuss
cassata (slice of ice cream with candied fruit)	Cassata (Sahneeisschnitte mit kandierten Früchten)
casserole	Kasserolle
cassis (liqueur made from blackcurrants)	Cassis (Schwarzer-Johannisbeer-Likör)
cast iron	Gusseisen
castor sugar	Kristallzucker
casual clothes	Freizeitkleidung
catch of the day	Fisch, fangfrisch
to catch the bus	Bus erreichen
catfish	Wels, Waller, Zwergwels
cattle	Rind
cauliflower	Karfiol, Blumenkohl
–, deep-fried breaded	–, gebacken
cauliflower cheese	–, gratiniert
cauliflower mould/pudding	Karfiolauflauf
caviar	Kaviar
caviar butter	Kaviarbutter
caviar sauce	Kaviarsauce
cayenne (pepper)	Cayenne(pfeffer)
CDW (collision damage waiver)	Vollkaskoversicherung mit Selbstbehalt
celery	Sellerie
celeriac	Sellerie(-knolle)
cell phone	Mobiltelefon
cellotape	Klebeband, Tixo®
central stove	Herd (freistehend)
to centrifuge	schleudern
cèpe mushroom sauce	Steinpilzsauce
cereals	Getreide
cereal bowl	Müslischüssel
certainly	sicherlich, mit Sicherheit, allerdings
certificate	Zeugnis
certificate of apprenticeship	LAP-Zeugnis
chafing dish	Wärmeplatte
chambermaid	Zimmermädchen
chamois	Gämse
jugged chamois	Gämsenpfeffer
champagne	Champagner
champagne bucket	Sektkübel
champagne cooler	Sektkühler
champagne cork	Sektkorken
champagne flute	Sektflöte
champagne sauce	Champagnersauce
champagne tulip	Champagnertulpe

English	German
champignon sauce	Champignonsauce
to change	ändern, wechseln
change	Wechselgeld
changing table	Wickeltisch
changing table mat	Wickeltischauflage
chanterelles	Eierschwammerln, Pfifferlinge
chanterelles sauce	Eierschwammerl/Pfifferlingsauce
Chantilly sauce	Chantilly-Sauce
char(r)	Saibling
to char	verkohlen
to charcoal broil	grillen (Holzkohle)
characteristic	Eigenschaft
(Swiss) chard	Mangold
to charge	verrechnen
to be in charge of	verantwortlich sein für
charming	charmant
chartreuse (with mixed vegetables cooked in moulds)	Kartäuser-Art (mit verschiedenem Gemüse, in Becherform gekocht)
chasseur	Jägerart
chateau/castle potatoes (olive-shaped fried potatoes)	Schlosskartoffeln (olivenförmig geschnitten und in Butter gebraten)
Chateaubriand sauce (meat glaze enriched with butter and parsley)	Sauce Chateaubriand (Fleischglace, Butter, Petersilie)
check	Scheck, Rechnung
to check out	auschecken
check-in	Anreise
early check-in	frühe Anreise
late check-in	späte Anreise
check-in counter	Eincheckschalter, Abfertigungsschalter
cheddar cheese	Cheddarkäse
cheek	Wange
cheerful	gut aufgelegt
cheese	Käse
cheese cover	Käseglocke
cheese cutter	Käseschneider
cheese grater	Käsereibe
cheese knife	Käsemesser
cheese kransky	Käsekrainer
cheese puffs, chou buns with cheese	Käsewindbeutel
cheese slicer	Käsehobel
cheese spaetzle	Käsespätzle
cheese spread	Streichkäse
cheese straw (with puff pastry)	Käsestange (mit Blätterteig)
cheese tartlets	Käsetörtchen, Ramequins
chef's kerchief	Halstuch (Koch)
chef's recommendation	Empfehlung des Hauses/Küchenchefs

chef's salad	Chefsalat
cherry, -ies (pl)	Kirsche(n)
cherry tomatoes	Kirschtomaten
chervil	Kerbel
chervil butter	Kerbelbutter
chest of drawers	Kommode, Schubladenschrank
chester straws	Chesterstangen
chestnut	Maroni, Kastanie
chicken	Huhn
chicken broth	Hühnerkraftsuppe
chicken croquettes	Geflügelkroketten
chicken curry	Hühnercurry
chicken galantine	Hühnergalantine
chicken giblets (and trimmings)	Hühnerklein
chicken liver	Hühnerleber
chicken liver omelette	Omelette mit Hühnerleber
chicken pâté	Hühnerpastete
chicken salad	Geflügelsalat
chicken soufflé	Geflügelauflauf
chicken stew	Geflügelragout
chicken stock	Geflügelfond
chicken thigh/drumsticks	Hühnerkeule
chicken wings/winglets	Hühnerflügel
spring chicken	Huhn, Junghuhn
chickpeas	Kichererbsen
chicory	Chicorée, Brüsseler Spitzen
child, children (pl)	Kind, Kinder
childcare	Kinderbetreuung
to chill	abkühlen
chilled/iced	geeist
chilli, chili	Chili
chilli con carne (chili-stew of minced beans and beef)	Chili con Carne
chilli pepper	Pfefferoni, Chilischote
chilli powder	Chili(pulver)
chilli sauce	Chilisauce
Chinese cabbage	Chinakohl
Chinese noodles	Glasnudeln
to chip off	absplittern
chips	Pommes frites, Kartoffelstäbchen
chives	Schnittlauch
chive butter	Schnittlauchbutter
chive potatoes	Schnittlauchkar-toffeln
chive sauce	Schnittlauchsauce
chocolate bar	Schokoladenriegel
chocolate cake "Sacher"	Sachertorte
chocolate glaze	Schokoladenglasur
chocolate soufflé	Schokoladenauflauf
choice of	Auswahl an

English	German
to choose	wählen, auswählen
chop	Kotelett (mit Knochen)
to chop up	hacken, klein hacken
chopped pork	Schweinsfaschiertes
chopper, cleaver	Hackbeil
chopping block	Hackstock
chopping board	Hack-/Schneidebrett
chopping knife	Hackmesser, Wiegemesser
chopsticks	Stäbchen
Choron sauce (Béarnaise sauce with tomato purée)	Choron-Sauce (Sauce béarnaise mit Tomatenmark)
choux pastry	Brandteig
Christmas Day	Weihnachtstag
Christmas Eve	Weihnachtsabend
chunk (of bread/cheese/meat ...)	Stück (Brot/Käse/Fleisch ...)
chutney	Gewürzfruchtpastete
(hard) cider	Most, Apfelwein
cinnamon	Zimt
cioppino (stew of fish and shellfish in tomato sauce)	Cioppino (Fischragout in Tomatensauce)
cistern (flush)	Spülung, Wasserkasten
citizen	Staatsbürger
city centre	Stadtzentrum
to the city centre	ins Stadtzentrum
to claim	behaupten
clam	Venusmuschel
clam chowder	Muschelsuppe (mit Venus-muscheln)
clam fritters	Muschelbeignets
to clarify	klären
clarified butter	geklärte Butter
to clean	putzen, reinigen
cleaning agent	Putzmittel
cleanliness	Sauberkeit
clear roux	helle Einmach
clear soup	klare Suppe
– with dropping pastry	Eintropfsuppe
– with pancake stripes	– mit Fritatten
– with liver dumpling	– mit Leberknödel
– with meat strudel	– mit Fleischstrudel
– with milt sippets/croutons	– mit Milzschnitten
– with semolina dumplings	– mit Grießnockerln
– with sponge squares	– mit Schöberln
– with Tyrolean dumplings	– mit Tiroler Knödel
– with rasped liver	Leberreissuppe
cleaver	Hackbeil
clementine	Clementine
clerk	Angestellte/r
to click on	anklicken

English	German
clipboard	Klemmbrett
cloakroom	Garderobe
cloakroom attendant	Garderobenfrau
closet	Schrank
to clot	dick werden lassen (Milch)
cloud	Wolke
clove	Nelke, Gewürznelke
clove of garlic	Knoblauchzehe
club sandwich	Clubsandwich
club soda	Sodawasser
to coagulate	gerinnen
coalfish, coley	Seelachs, Köhler
coarse	grob
coarse salt	grobkörniges Salz
coaster	Untersetzer
coat	Mantel
to coat	bedecken, ummanteln, nappieren
coathanger	Kleiderbügel
coating	Belag
cobbler	Cocktail mit Früchten
cock	Hahn
cock-a-leekie (soup of chicken and leeks)	schottische Hühnersuppe mit Lauch
cockerel	junger Hahn
cockscomb	Hahnenkamm
cockle	Herzmuschel
cockpit	Cockpit
cocktail	Cocktail
cocktail glass	Cocktailschale
cocktail list	Cocktailkarte
cocoa	Kakao
coconut	Kokosnuss
coconut cream	Kokosnusscreme
coconut fat	Kokosfett
coconut sauce	Kokossauce
cod, codling, codfish	Dorsch, Kabeljau
coffee	Kaffee
black coffee	–, schwarz
coffee with cream	– mit Sahne (Obers)
coffee with milk	– mit Milch
coffee mug	Kaffeebecher
coffee pot	Kaffeekanne
coffee/tea cup	Kaffee-/Teetasse
cognac	Cognac
coin	Münze
colander	Sieb, Schüttelsieb
Colbert sauce (maître d'hôtel butter blended with meat jelly)	Colbert-Sauce (Kräuterbutter mit Fleischsulz vermischt)

English	German
cold	kalt
cold appetisers (starters)	kalte Vorspeisen
cold pudding	Pudding, kalt
cold rice pudding	Reispudding
cold roast meat	Braten, kalter
cold sauce	kalte Sauce
cold cuts	Aufschnitt
cold store	Kühlraum
cold-pressed	kaltgepresst
college for home economies	HBLA
Collins glass	Collinsglas
colouring	Färbung
colt	Fohlen (Fleisch)
column	Spalte, Säule
comb	Kamm
to combine	mischen, vermengen, zusammengeben
commercial college	Handelsschule, Handelsakademie
commis-chef	Jungkoch
commodity	Ware
company board meeting	Vorstandssitzung einer Firma
company dinner	Geschäftsessen
compensation	Wiedergutmachung
to compile	zusammenstellen
to complain	(sich) beschweren
complaint	Beschwerde
complemented by	abgerundet mit
complex	komplex
complimentary	frei, auf Haus
composition	Zusammensetzung
compound salads	zusammengesetzte Salate
comprehensive	umfassend, ausführlich
comprehensive school	Gesamtschule
concentrate	Konzentrat
concern	Sorge
condensed milk	Kondensmilch
confectionary	Konditoreiware
confectioner	Konditor, Zuckerbäcker
conference room	Konferenz-, Besprechungsraum
confirmation	Bestätigung
confit of goose (goose preserved in fat)	Gänseconfit (eingemachtes Gänsefleisch)
conger eel	Meeraal
conical strainer	Spitzsieb
connecting door	Verbindungstür
to conserve	konservieren
consideration	Betrachtung, Rücksicht
consistent	konsequent, beständig

English	German
consommé	Consommé, Kraftsuppe
consommé Célestine (with shredded pancake)	Frittatensuppe, Kraftbrühe Célestine (mit Pfannkuchenstreifen)
consommé madrilène (chicken broth with tomatoes)	Geflügelsuppe mit Tomaten, Madrider Suppe
constipation	Verstopfung
to contain	beinhalten
container	Behälter, Container
to contaminate	verschmutzen
contamination	Kontamination, Verschmutzung
contemplative	nachdenklich
content	Inhalt, Gehalt
continental plan	Zimmer mit Frühstück
contract	Vertrag
to control	kontrollieren, überwachen
to have under control	unter Kontrolle haben
control panel	Bedienungsfeld
control tower	Kontrollturm
convection oven	Konvektomat
convention	Tagung
conversion chart	Umrechnungstabelle
convert	umrechnen
converted rice	parboiled Reis
convertible sofa	Ausziehcouch
conveyor belt	Fließband
cook	Koch/Köchin
cook's fork	Fleischgabel
cook's knife	großes Messer, Kochmesser
cooked au bleu	blau gekocht
cookery book	Kochbuch
cooking method	Garmethode
cooking utensils	Küchengeräte
cookie	Keks
cookie sheet	Backpapier
to cool	kühlen
cool counter	Kühlvitrine
cooler	Cocktail mit Gingerale
coot	Blesshuhn
copy	Kopie
to copy	kopieren
cord	Kabel
cordless	schnurlos
cordial glass	Likörglas
to core	entkernen
coriander	Koriander
coriander sauce	Koriandersauce
corkscrew	Korkenzieher
corky	korkig

corn, sweetcorn	Mais, Zuckermais
corn oil	Maisöl
corn on the cob	Maiskolben
corn salad, lamb's lettuce	Vogerlsalat, Feldsalat
corn-fed chicks	Stubenküken
cornflakes	Cornflakes
cornflour, cornstarch	Maismehl
corned beef	gepökeltes Rindfleisch
(at/on the) corner	(an der) Ecke
cornets of raw ham	Schinkenrolle
cornichon	Essiggurke
Cornish pasty	Fleischpastete
Corpus Christi	Fronleichnam
corresponding drinks	dazupassende Getränke
corrosive, acidly	ätzend
cost saving	Kostenersparnis
cosy	gemütlich
cottage	Ferienhaus
cottage cheese	Hüttenkäse
cough reliever	Hustenstiller
counter	Bar, Verkaufstisch, Schalter
country code	Landesvorwahl (Telefon)
country omelette (bacon and potatoes)	Bauernomelette (Speck und Kartoffeln)
country/farmhouse loaf	Bauernbrot
couple	Paar
courgette, zucchini	Zucchini
course (first, second ...)	Gang (erster, zweiter)
3-course dinner	3-gängiges Abendessen
courtesy	Höflichkeit
by courtesy	aus Höflichkeit
courtesy of	mit freundlicher Genehmigung
courteous	höflich
couscous	Couscous
to cover	bedecken, zudecken, verschließen
cover plate	Platzteller
cover service	Gedeck, Kosten
cowberry, mountain cranberry	Preiselbeere
crab	Krabbe
crabmeat cocktail	Krabbencocktail
crackling	Grammel
cracknel	Krokant
cranberry, -ies (pl)	Preiselbeere(n)
cranberry sauce	Preiselbeersauce
crawfish	Languste
crayfish	Krebs
crayfish (crab) butter	Krebsbutter
crayfish sauce	Krebssauce
crayfish stew	Ragout von Flusskrebsen

cream	Obers
to cream	schaumig rühren, legieren, abrühren
cream cheese	Streichkäse
cream of ...	Cremesuppe (von)
cream puff, chou bun	Windbeutel (gefüllt)
cream sauce	Rahmsauce, Sahnesauce
cream slice	Cremeschnitte
cream strudel	Rahmstrudel
creamed	legiert, schaumig gerührt
creamed cakes	Rührteigkuchen
creamed horseradish	Oberskren
creamed potatoes	Rahmkartoffeln
creamed veal escalope, veal escalope in cream sauce	Rahmschnitzel, Kalbsschnitzel in Sahnesauce
creamer	Milchkännchen
creamy	cremig
cream soup, cream of ...	Cremesuppe
cream of asparagus	Spargelcremesuppe
cream of cauliflower	Karfiolcremesuppe, Blumenkohlsuppe
cream of chicken	Geflügel-/Hühnercremesuppe
cream of leek	Lauchcremesuppe
cream of mushroom	Champignon-/Pilzcremesuppe
cream of pea	Erbsencremesuppe
cream of potato	Kartoffelcremesuppe
cream of vegetable	Gemüsecremesuppe
cream of venison	Wildcremesuppe
credit card	Kreditkarte
crème brûlée, burnt cream	Crème brûlée
creole	kreolische Art (mit Reis, Tomaten, Paprikaschoten)
creole sauce	Kreolensauce
crêpe suzette (with flaming orange liqueur)	Crêpe Suzette (mit Orangenlikör flambiert)
crescent, croissant	Kipferl
cress	Kresse
cress butter	Kressebutter
crib	Gitterbett
crispbread (Swedish wholemeal crackers)	Knäckebrot
crisps	Chips, Kartoffelscheiben
croaker, drumfish	Umberfisch
crockery, china	Geschirr
croquettes	Kroketten
croquette potatoes amandine	Mandelkroketten (Kartoffelkroketten mit Mandeln paniert), Berny-Kartoffeln
to cross out	durchstreichen

croutes, toast	Crostini (belegtes, geröstetes Brot)
croutons	Croûtons (geröstete Brotwürfel)
crudities, assorted raw vegetables	Rohkost(platte)
cruet stands	Menagen, Gewürzständer
cruise	Kreuzfahrt
crumble	Streuselkuchen
apple crumble	Apfel mit Streuseln
crunchy	knusprig
to crush	zerdrücken
crushed ice	zerstoßenes Eis
crustacean	Krustentier
crustas	Cocktails mit Zuckerrand
to crystallise	kandieren
to cube/dice	in Würfel schneiden
cube sugar	Würfelzucker
cucumber	Gurke
cucumber sauce	Gurkensauce
culinary	kulinarisch
cultivation	Zucht, Züchtung
Cumberland sauce (redcurrant jelly, mustard, orange juice and port)	Cumberlandsauce (Johannisbeergelee, Senf, Orangensaft, Portwein)
cumin	Kreuzkümmel
cup (chilled drink of wine and fruits)	Bowle (kaltes Getränk aus Wein und Früchten)
curd/white cheese	Topfen
curd/white cheese dumplings	Topfenknödel
curd/white cheese strudel	Topfenstrudel
curdled milk	Dickmilch
to cure	beizen
cured	gepökelt
cured meat	Surbraten
currant (red, black)	Johannisbeere (rot, schwarz)
currant juice	Johannisbeersaft
currants	Korinthen, Rosinen
currency exchange	Geldwechsel
curry (powder)	Curry(pulver)
curry sauce	Currysauce, indische Sauce
curtain	Vorhang
custard	Vanillesauce, Vanillecreme
custard apple	Zimtapfel
customers	Kundschaft
custom-made	auf Wunsch des Kunden
customs	Zoll
customs officer	Zollbeamter
to cut	schneiden
to cut to size	zuschneiden
cut up pancake	Kaiserschmarren
cutting board	Schneidebrett

cutlery	Besteck
cutlet	Kotelett (ohne Knochen)
cuttlefish	Tintenfisch
CV (curriculum vitae)	Lebenslauf

D

dauphine potatoes (potato croquettes)	Dauphine-Kartoffeln, Kartoffelkroketten
dab	Limande, Kliesche (Fisch)
dairy	Molkerei
dairy foods/products	Milchprodukte
dallop	Klecks
damp	feucht
dandelion salad	Löwenzahnsalat
Danish pastry	Plundergebäck
Darblay soup (potato soup with shredded vegetables)	Darblay-Suppe (Kartoffelsuppe mit Gemüsestreifen)
dark beer	dunkles Bier
dark roux	Einbrenn, dunkle Mehlschwitze
dark/bittersweet chocolate	Zartbitterschokolade
dash	Spritzer
dash bottle	Spritzflasche
date	Dattel
date-shells	Meer-, Steindatteln
date	Datum
date of arrival	Anreisedatum
date of departure	Abreisedatum
day after tomorrow	übermorgen
day before yesterday	vorgestern
day trip	Tagesausflug
debreziner (sausage)	Debreziner
decaffeinated coffee, caffeine-free coffee	koffeinfreier Kaffee
to decalcify	entkalken
to decant	dekantieren
December	Dezember
declaration form	Zollerklärung
to decorate	dekorieren
deep freezer	Tiefkühltruhe
to deep-fry	frittieren
deep-fried breaded escalope of veal (veal cutlet)	Wiener Schnitzel (vom Kalb)
deep-fried breaded mushrooms	gebackene Champignons
deep fryer	Fritteuse
deer/stag	Hirsch
deer chop	Hirschkotelett
deer steak	Hirschsteak

English	German
deer stew, ragout of deer	Hirschragout
leg of deer	Hirschkeule, -schlegel
to defrost	abtauen, enteisen
degree	Grad
demi-glace sauce	Sauce Demi-Glace
to denote	kennzeichnen
denoted are required fields	gekennzeichnete Felder sind verpflichtend
dentex	Zahnbrasse
department store	Kaufhaus
departure	Abflug, Abreise
dependent	abhängig
deposit	Anzahlung
to describe	beschreiben
description	Beschreibung
desire	Wunsch
to desire	wünschen, begehren
desk	Schreibtisch
desk pad	Schreibunterlage
dessert/sweets	Dessert, Nachspeise
dessert knife	Dessertmesser
dessert pastry	Dessertgebäck
dessert spoon	Dessertlöffel
dessert wine, fortified wine	Süßwein
dessert/salad/pudding fork	Dessertgabel
to destalk	entstielen
detanninated tea	Tee, teinfrei
detergent, washing powder	Waschmittel
detrimental	nachteilig, schädlich
devil sauce (demi-glace, white wine or vinegar, cayenne)	Teufelssauce (Demi-Glace, Weißwein oder Essig, Cayennepfeffer)
diaper	Windel
diarrhoea	Durchfall
to dice	in Würfel schneiden
diced bread dumpling	böhmischer Knödel
diced potatoes	gewürfelte Kartoffeln
diet	Diät
dietary restrictions	Diäteinschränkungen
to digest	verdauen
digestible	verdaulich
digital camera	Digitalkamera
diligent	fleißig
dill	Dill
dill butter	Dillbutter
dill sauce	Dillsauce
to dilute	verdünnen
diminish	vermindern, verkleinern
dining room	Restaurant
dining room manager/maître d'	Restaurantleiter

dinner	Abendessen
dinner dance	Abendessen mit Tanz
dinner fork	Fleischgabel
dinner knife	Fleischmesser
to dip	eintauchen
directory	Verzeichnis (Telefon)
disabled	behindert
disabled access	behindertengerechter Zugang
disabled person	behinderte Person
discount	Rabatt, Abzug
discretion	Diskretion
dishwasher	Geschirrspüler
to disinfect	desinfizieren
disorder	Krankheit
to dispense (drinks)	ausgeben (Getränke)
display case	Vitrine
to dissolve	auflösen
to distend	ausdehnen
distributer	Verteiler
3-way distributer	Dreifachverteiler
to disturb	stören
"Do not disturb" sign	„Bitte nicht stören"-Schild
diversity	Vielfalt
to divide	trennen
divorced	geschieden
dogfish	Katzenhai
domestic	heimisch
domicile	Wohnsitz
doorman	Türsteher
dorado	Goldbarsch, Goldmakrele
dormitory	Schlafsaal
double fillet steak	Chateaubriand
double room	Doppelzimmer
double Scotch	doppelter Scotch
double sirloin steak	doppeltes Zwischenrippenstück
double tenderloin steak	doppelte Lendenschnitte
double-decker	Doppeldecker
doubt	Zweifel
dough	Teig
doughnut	Donut
Austrian doughnut	Krapfen
downstairs	hinunter
to go downstairs	hinuntergehen
downtown	im Zentrum
dozen (of)	Dutzend
drain	Abfluss
to drain	abseihen, abtropfen, trocknen
draught beer	Bier vom Fass
drawer	Schublade

to dredge	bestäuben, bestreuen
dredger	Streuer (Mehl)
to dress	anrichten
dressed in	angerichtet in
dresser	Kommode
dressing gown/bathrobe	Bademantel
drink	Getränk
fancy drink	Kreation des Barkeepers
drink dispensing equipment	Zapfanlage
drink list	Getränkekarte
to drip	tropfen
dripping	Bratenfett, Schmalz
driver	Chauffeur
driving licence	Führerschein
to drizzle	besprühen, träufeln
drop action pencil	Druckbleistift
drumstick	Hühnerkeule
dry	herb, trocken
to dry	trocknen
dry cleaner	Reiniger (chemische Reinigung)
dry mustard	Senfpulver
dry weight	Trockenmasse
dried fruits	getrocknete Früchte
dried pea	Trockenerbse
Du Barry soup, cream of cauliflower soup	Karfiol-/Blumenkohlcremesuppe
duchess potatoes (potato croquettes browned in the oven)	Duchesse-/Herzoginkartoffeln (überbackene Kartoffelkroketten)
duck	Ente
duckling	Entenküken
duckboards, slatted frame	Lattenrost
dumpling	Knödel, Nockerl
dumpling in a napkin	Serviettenknödel
dumplings with pork cracklings	Grammelknödel
during	während
durum wheat	Hartweizen
to dust	bestäuben, abstauben
dust cloud	Staubwolke
dustbin, garbage bin	Mülltonne
duster	Staubtuch
Dutch cheese	holländischer Käse, Edamer
Dutch sauce	Sauce hollandaise
duty	Pflicht
duty roster	Dienstplan
duty-free	zollfrei
DVD player	DVD-Spieler
to dye	färben

E

English	German
early morning call, wake-up call	Weckruf
early morning tea	Tasse Tee, am Bett serviert
early vegetables	Frühgemüse
earphones	Kopfhörer
earthenware pot	Römertopf
earthy	erdig
Easter Monday	Ostermontag
easy	süffig
éclairs (small cakes of choux pastry filled with cream and chocolate glazing)	Éclairs (längliches Brandteiggebäck mit Cremefüllung und Schokoladenglasur)
economy class	Touristenklasse
Edam	Edamer Käse
education	Ausbildung
educated	gebildet
eel	Aal
eel in jelly (aspic)	– in Aspik
smoked eel	–, geräuchert
eel on the spit	Aal vom Spieß
eel stew, matelote of eel	Aalragout
eelpout	Quappe, Trüsche
egg	Ei
poached egg in jelly	Ei in Aspik
egg in mayonnaise	Ei in Mayonnaise
stuffed egg, egg mimosa	gefülltes Ei
soft-boiled egg	weich gekochtes Ei
hard-boiled egg	hart gekochtes Ei
medium-boiled egg	wachsweiches Ei (5 min)
en cocotte	in Cocotte (pochiert)
egg sunny side up	Spiegelei (auf einer Seite gebraten)
egg sunny side down	Spiegelei (auf beiden Seiten gebraten)
fried egg	Spiegelei
fried egg on spinach	Spiegelei auf Spinat
scrambled egg	Eierspeise
poached egg	pochiertes Ei
stuffed egg	gefülltes Ei
stuffed eggs, Russian style	russische Eier
egg noodles	Eiernudeln
egg sauce	Eiersauce
egg slicer	Eierschneider
egg white	Eiweiß
egg yolk	Eidotter
egg/kitchen timer	Eieruhr
eggplant	Aubergine, Eierfrucht, Melanzani

English	German
eggs any style	Eier nach Wunsch
eggs Benedict (poached egg with ham and hollandaise sauce)	Eier Benedikt (pochiertes Ei auf Toast mit Schinken und Sauce hollandaise)
eggs Bercy, fried (with grilled sausage and tomato sauce)	Eier Bercy (Spiegeleier mit Bratwürstel und Tomatensauce)
eggs Chimay, stuffed (eggs au gratin with mushroom stuffing)	Eier Chimay (überbackene Eier mit Champignonfüllung)
eggs cooked to order	Eier nach Wunsch
eggs Florentine, poached (eggs on bed of leaf-spinach)	Eier florentinisch (pochiertes Ei auf Blattspinat)
eggs Mornay, poached (au gratin)	Eier Mornay (pochierte Eier, gratiniert)
eggs Turbigo, fried (with sausage)	Eier Turbigo (Spiegeleier mit Bratwürstel)
eggshell	Eierschale
elastic	elastisch, dehnbar
elbow macaroni	Hörnchen
elderberry, -ies (pl)	Holler, Holunder
elderberry blossom syrup	Holunderblütensirup
elderberry sauce	Holundersauce
elderly	Senioren
electric ray, torpedo fish	Zitterrochen
electrician	Elektriker/in
elegant	fein
elevator, lift	Lift
elk	Elch
elver, silver eel	Glasaal
embarrassing	peinlich
emergency	Notfall
emergency call	Notruf
emergency exit	Notausgang, Fluchtweg
emery board	Nagelfeile
employer	Arbeitgeber/in
employment	Anstellung
to emulsify	emulgieren
en papillote (in paper casing)	in Folie, in Papier
en suite bath	mit Bad
end piece	Endstück
endive	Endivie
engaged	besetzt, verlobt
engineer	Techniker/in
English muffin	Muffin (sauer), Art Bagel
enhanced	angereichert, verstärkt
to ensure	versichern, gewährleisten
to enter	eintragen, eingeben (Tastatur)
enthusiastic	begeistert, enthusiastisch
enticing	verlockend

English	German
entrance	Eingang
entrance hall	Eingangshalle
entrecôte	Beiried
entry date	Eintrittsdatum
envelope	Kuvert
Epiphany	Dreikönig
equipment	Geschirr, Ausrüstung
equipped	ausgestattet
eraser	Radiergummi
escalope	Schnitzel
– of deer, fillet of deer	Hirschschnitzel, Hirschfilet
– of pork, pork cutlet	Schweinsschnitzel
– of veal cordon bleu (filled with ham and cheese)	Cordon bleu (Kalbsschnitzel, gefüllt mit Käse und Schinken)
– of veal, Parisienne (dipped in beaten egg and fried)	Pariser Schnitzel (in verquirltes Ei getaucht und gebacken)
– of veal, veal cutlet	Kalbsschnitzel
espresso	Espresso
estimate	Kostenvoranschlag
to estimate	schätzen
European plan	Zimmer ohne Frühstück
to evaluate	beurteilen, einschätzen
evaporated milk	Kondensmilch
even	glatt
ewe's milk	Schafmilch
excess baggage	Übergepäck
exchange office	Wechselstube
exchange rate	Wechselkurs
excited	aufgeregt, begeistert
executive chef	Chefkoch, -köchin
executive floor	VIP-Etage
executive housekeeper	Hausdame
exhausted	erschöpft
exhaustible	erschöpflich
exhibition	Ausstellung
experience	Erfahrung
expiration/expiry date	Verfallsdatum, Ablaufdatum
explanation	Erklärung
extension	Durchwahl, Klappe, Verlängerung
extension cable/cord	Verlängerungskabel
extensive	ausgiebig, umfangreich
exterior	Außenseite
external	betriebsfremd
extra charge	Zuschlag, Aufschlag

F

fish soup (French style, French fish soup with saffron)	Bouillabaisse (Fischsuppe mit Safran)
face	Gesicht
to face a challenge	sich einer Herausforderung stellen
facility	Einrichtung
facsimile transmitter	Faxgerät
fallow deer	Damhirsch
family plan	Familienprogramm
fancy	fantastisch, kunstvoll
fancy salad	bunter Salat
fare	Tarif
normal fare	Normaltarif
special fare	Sondertarif
fare type	Tarifart
farewell	Abschied
fashion show	Modenschau
fastener	Verschluss
fat content	Fettgehalt
fat separator	Fettabscheider
to fatten	mästen
fattened chicken	Masthuhn
fattening	dick machend
faucet	Wasserhahn
favourite	Lieblings...
fawn	Hirschkalb
fax machine	Faxgerät
feather	Feder
February	Februar, Feber
fee	Gebühr
fennel	Fenchel
fennel sauce	Fenchelsauce
fenugreek	Bockshornklee
fera blue	Reinanke
fermentation	Fermentation, Gärung
fever	Fieber
fibre	Ballaststoff
fifty-fifty	halbe-halbe
fig	Feige
figures	Zahlen
filbert soufflé	Haselnussauflauf
file cabinet	Ordnerablage
to fill	füllen
to fill in	ausfüllen
to fill up	auffüllen

English	German
to fillet	filetieren
fillet of ...	Filet, Lungenbraten, auch Schnitzel
fillet steak, prime steak	Filetsteak, Lendenschnitte
filleting knife	Filetiermesser
filling, stuffing	Fülle
Filofax	Terminplaner
filter paper	Filterpapier
filtered coffee	Filterkaffee
fin	Flosse
final examination	LAP (Lehrabschlussprüfung)
to finalise	festlegen, beschließen
finger bowl, finger glass	Fingerschale
finger food, snacks	Appetithäppchen
finishing touches	Abschlussarbeiten
Finnish rye	Finnenbrot
fir twig	Tannenzweig
fire alarm	Feueralarm, Feuermelder
fire brigade	Feuerwehr
fire escape	Feuerleiter
fire extinguisher	Feuerlöscher
fireplace	Kamin
fireproof	feuerfest
firm reservation	feste Reservierung
firmness	Festigkeit
first aid	Erste Hilfe
first aid kit	Erste-Hilfe-Kasten
fish	Fisch
fish dish	Fischgericht, -geschirr
fish finger	Fischstäbchen
fish fork	Fischgabel
fish kettle	Fischkochtopf
fish knife	Fischmesser
fish scaler	Entschuppungsgerät
fisher sauce	Fischersauce (à la pecheur)
fishmonger	Fischhändler
fishstock, court-bouillon	Fischfond
fitted sheet	Leintuch
fittings	Ausstattung
fixed price meal	Mahlzeit zu einem festen Preis
flakes	Flocken
to flambé	flambieren
flan	Obsttorte
flanring	Obsttortenring
flanky/puff pastry	Blätterteig
to flap	zappeln
flat	flach, geschmacklos
flat baking tin	flache Backform
flat rate	Pauschale

flavour	Geschmack
to flavour	würzen
flavour enhancer	Geschmacksverstärker
flavourings	Aroma, Würzstoffe
flesh	Fleisch
flexitime	Gleitzeit
flight	Flug
domestic flight	Inlandsflug
international flight	Auslandsflug
flight attendant	Flugbegleiter/in
flip	Cocktail mit Sahne
flip chart	Flipchart
to float	schwimmen, fließen
floor maid/attendant	Hausmädchen, Hausbursche
floor plan	Grundriss
floor/standard lamp	Stehlampe
floral decoration	Blumenschmuck
flounder	Flunder
flour	Mehl
flour sifter, bolter	Mehlsieb
flower bouquet	Blumenstrauß
flower shop	Blumengeschäft
flower vase	Blumenvase
flowery/floral	blumig
fluffy	flaumig
flummery	Flammeri
flummery of semolina	Grießflammeri
flushing	Spülen, Spülung
foam bath	Schaumbad
foamed	aufgeschäumt
foamed milk	geschäumte Milch
focaccia, flat bread	Fladenbrot
fog	Nebel
fogas	Fogosch (Zander)
to fold	falten, zusammenlegen
to fold in	darunterziehen (z. B. Eischnee unter die Masse ziehen)
folded-over pizza	Pizzatasche
to follow	folgen
fondant potatoes	Schmelzkartoffeln
font size	Schriftgröße
font type	Schriftart
food colourant	Lebensmittelfarbe
food cost, cost of sales	Wareneinsatz
food processor	Küchenmaschine
food supplies	Lagerbestände
foot	Fuß
on foot	zu Fuß
football pitch	Fußballfeld

foothills of the Alps	Alpenvorland
forecast	Vorhersage
foreign currency, in a	Fremdwährung, in einer
foreignness	Fremdartigkeit
fork	Gabel
former	ehemalig
fortified wine, dessert wine	Süßwein
fortnight	14 Tage
fowl	Geflügel
fragile	zerbrechlich
framework	Rahmenprogramm
Frankfurters, frankfurter sausage, Wieners	Frankfurter Würstel
free of charge	gebührenfrei
free-range eggs	Eier aus Freilandhaltung
to freeze	einfrieren
freezer	Tiefkühler, Gefrierschrank
French bread	Baguette
French fries	Pommes frites, Kartoffelstäbchen
French onion soup	französische Zwiebelsuppe
French toast	Armer Ritter, Pofese
fresh	frisch
fresh cheese	Frischkäse
fresh fruit	frisches Obst
freshness	Frische
freshwater fish	Süßwasserfisch
fricassee	Frikassee
Friday	Freitag
frittata	italienisches/offenes Omelette
fritter, beignet	Krapfen, Beignet
frizzy mint	Krauseminze
frog legs	Froschschenkel
from the cask	offen (Wein)
front	Vorderseite, Front
in front of	vor (örtlich)
front office	Rezeption
froth	Schaum
to froth	schäumen
frothy	schaumig
fruit, fruits	Frucht, Früchte, Obst
fruits in batter	Früchte in Backteig
fruit cocktail	Fruchtcocktail
fruit dumpling	Obstknödel
fruit jelly, -ies (pl)	Früchtegelee(s)
fruit juice	Fruchtsaft
fruit knife	Obstmesser
fruit pie	Obstkuchen
fruit salad	Früchte-/Obstsalat
fruit purée	Fruchtmark

English	German
fruit coulis	Früchtespiegel
fruit flesh, pulp	Fruchtfleisch
fruit juice	Fruchtsaft
fruit knife	Obstmesser
fruit loaf	Kletzenbrot
fruit schnapps	Obstler
fruit-flavoured brandy	Fruchtlikör
fruity	fruchtig
fruity finish	fruchtiger Abgang (Wein)
to fry	braten
to fry/deep-fry	frittieren
fryer	Fritteuse
frying pan	Bratpfanne
fried batter drops (pea-sized balls of choux pastry)	Backerbsen
fried chicken	Backhuhn
fried pork sausage with sauerkraut	Bratwurst mit Sauerkraut
fried potatoes with sliced beef, pork or bacon	Tiroler Gröstl
full board	Vollpension
full preserves	Vollkonserven
full-bodied/rich-bodied	schwer, üppig, vollmundig, gehaltvoll (Wein)
fully booked	ausgebucht
fun-loving	lebenslustig
funnel	Trichter
furrow	Rille

G

English	German
galangal	Galgant
galantine	Galantine
galette (potato)	Kartoffelfladen, Kartoffellaibchen
gall bladder	Galle
gallon	Maßeinheit: ca. 4 l
galvanised	verzinkt
game	Wild
game (purée) soup	Wildpüreesuppe
game birds	Wildgeflügel, Federwild
game croquettes	Wildkroketten
game pâté	Wildpastete
game salad	Wildsalat
game stock	Wildfond
game consommé in pastry crust	Wildsuppe mit Teighaube
game stew	Wildragout, Wildpfeffer
gammon	gesurt
gammon steak	Surfleisch
garbanzo	Kichererbsen

English	German
garden cress	Gartenkresse
garlic	Knoblauch
garlic (clove)	Knoblauch(zehe)
garlic butter	Knoblauchbutter
garlic press	Knoblauchpresse
garlic sauce	Knoblauchsauce
garlic sausage	Knoblauchwurst
garment	Bekleidung
garnish	Garnitur
to garnish	garnieren
gas cooker	Gasherd
gate	Flugsteig
gathering	Zusammenkommen, Treffen
gauze bandage	Mullbinde
Gazpacho (soup of uncooked vegetables with vinegar and oil)	Gazpacho (kalte Suppe aus rohem Gemüse mit Essig und Öl)
gear	Ausrüstung, Gang (Auto)
gelling agent	Geliermittel
generous	großzügig
genevoise sauce (red wine sauce with anchovy butter)	Genfer Sauce (Rotwein mit Sardellenbutter)
gentian	Enzianschnaps
gentian sauce	Enziansauce
gents (toilet)	Herrentoilette
genuinely	grundsätzlich
germ	Keim
German mustard	Gewürzsenf
German sauce (with veal stock)	Deutsche Sauce (Sauce allemande)
germiny soup (sorrel soup bound with egg yolks and cream)	Germiny-Suppe (Sauerampfersuppe, stark mit Eigelb und Obers legiert)
to get up	aufstehen
gherkins	Essiggurken
giant, jumbo	riesen...
giblets	Geflügelklein
gift shop	Souvenirladen
gilthead	Goldbrasse, Dorade
ginger	Ingwer
ginger sauce	Ingwersauce
gingerbread	Lebkuchen, Pfefferkuchen
gipsy sauce	Zigeunersauce
gipsy style	Zigeunerart
gizzard	Geflügelmagen
glaze	Glace
to glaze	glacieren
glazing, icing, frosting	Glasur
glove	Handschuh
glue	Kleber, Uhu

to go with	passen zu
goes well with	passt gut zu
goat	Ziege
goat cheese, chèvre	Ziegenkäse
goblet	Kelchglas
goby	Meergrundel
golf course	Golfplatz
gone off	verdorben (Essen)
Good Friday	Karfreitag
good-humoured	gut gelaunt
goose, geese (pl)	Gans, Gänse
goose liver, foie gras	Gänseleber
goose liver pâté	Gänseleberpastete
goose paste	Gänsefleischpastete
gooseberry, -ies (pl)	Stachelbeere(n)
gooseberry sauce	Stachelbeersauce
gossip	Klatsch, Tratsch
goulash	Gulasch
goulash á la széged	Szegediner Gulasch
goulash soup (highly seasoned soup of beef and potatoes)	Gulaschsuppe
gourmet	Feinschmecker
for gourmets	Feinschmeckerart
Graham bread	Grahambrot
grain	Korn, Getreide
grammar school	Gymnasium
granola	Müsli
granola bar	Müsliriegel
granulated sugar	Kristallzucker
grapefruit	Grapefruit, Pampelmuse
grapes (blue, white)	Weintrauben (blau, weiß)
grassy	grasig
to grate	reiben (mit Reibeisen)
grated cheese	geriebener Käse
grater	Reibe, Reibeisen
to gratinate	gratinieren, überbacken
gratuity, tip	Trinkgeld
graved	gebeizt
gravy	Bratensaft, Fleischfond
gravy boat	Saucenschüssel
grayling	Äsche (Fisch)
to grease	einfetten, schmieren
greasy	schmierig, fettig
greaves	Grammeln
green cabbage	Grünkohl, Blattkohl
green butter	grüne Butter
green mayonnaise (with purée of herbs)	grüne Mayonnaise (mit Kräuterpüree)
green pea purée soup	Erbsenpüreesuppe

green sauce	grüne Sauce (sauce verte)
green/French/string beans	Fisolen (grüne Bohnen)
greengage	Ringlotte
grenadine	Granatapfel
grey mullet	Meeräsche
gribiche sauce (tartare sauce with capers)	Gribiche-Sauce (Sauce tartare mit Kapern)
griddle	Grill, Rost, Toaster
to grill	grillen
grills, grilled meats/dishes	Grillgerichte, Grilladen
to grind	faschieren, klein hacken
Grisons air-dried beef	Bündner Fleisch
grissini (crisp bread in long thin sticks)	Grissini (knuspriges Stangenbrot)
grits	Haferschrot, Hafergrütze
to groom	pflegen
gross	brutto
to ground	mahlen, gemahlen
group leader	Gruppenleiter
group rate	Gruppentarif
grouper	Zackenbarsch
grouping	Gliederung
grouse	Wildhuhn
guarantee	Gewährleistung
gudgeons	Gründling
guest	Gast
guest room	Gästezimmer
gugelhupf	Gugelhupf
guideline	Richtlinie
guinea fowl/hen	Perlhuhn
guitar cutter	Harfe (zum Schneiden von Käse, Pasteten ...)
gunard	Knurrhahn
to gut	ausnehmen
guts	Eingeweide
gym	Fitnessraum, Turnsaal

H

headcheese	Presskopf
habit	Gewohnheit
haddock	Schellfisch
haggis (sheep's offal boiled in the animal's stomach)	Haggis (Innereien vom Schaf, im Schafsmagen gekocht)
hail	Hagel
hairdresser	Friseur
hairdryer	Fön
hake	Seehecht

half	Maßeinheit: 1/4 l
half/part board, demi pension	Halbpension
halibut	Heilbutt
hall porter	Chefportier
ham	Schinken
boiled ham	gekochter Schinken
smoked ham	geräucherter Schinken
raw ham	Rohschinken
ham cornets/ham rolls	Schinkenröllchen
ham dumpling	Schinkenknödel
ham mousse	Schinkenmousse
ham sausage	Schinkenwurst
ham soufflé	Schinkenauflauf
hamburger	Fleischlaibchen
hand luggage	Handgepäck
hand mill	Handmühle
hand towel	Handtuch
handicap accessible rooms	behindertengerechte Zimmer
handle	Klinke, Griff
to handle	handhaben
handrail	Handlauf
handy	praktisch, nützlich
to hang up	auflegen
hard cheese	Hartkäse
hare	Hase
harissa (chilli sauce)	Harissa (Chilisauce)
harmful	schädlich
hashed brown potatoes	Röstkartoffeln
haul	Strecke, Transportweg
–, long/short	–, lang/kurz
haunch	Keule
hay fever	Heuschnupfen
hazelnut, filbert	Haselnuss
hazelnut cream	Haselnusscreme
head chef	Küchenchef
head of wine cellar	Kellermeister
headache	Kopfschmerzen
headband	Stirnband
headset	Kopfhörer
health insurance	Krankenversicherung
to heap	anhäufen
heart	Herz
hearty	herzhaft
to heat	erhitzen
heating	Heizung
heating cabinet	Wärmeschrank
heatplaster	ABC-Pflaster, Wärmepflaster
heat-proof	hitzebeständig
heavy	schwer, üppig, vollmundig (Wein)

hemp seed	Hanfsamen
hemp seed oil	Hanföl
hen night	Junggesellinnenabschied
herbs, aromatic herbs	Kräuter, Gewürzkräuter
herb butter	Kräuterbutter
herbaceous	nach Kräutern
herb sauce	Kräutersauce
herring	Hering
smoked herring	–, geräuchert
marinated herring	–, mariniert
herring salad	Heringssalat
high chair	Kinderstuhl
high desk	Stehpult
high season	Hochsaison
highball glass	Longdrinkglas
to hike	wandern
hindquarters	hinteres Viertel
to hire	mieten
hole puncher	Locher
holiday	Feiertag, Urlaub
public holiday	staatlicher Feiertag
religious holiday	religiöser Feiertag
plant holidays	Betriebsurlaub
hollandaise sauce (yolks of egg, melted butter, lemon juice)	Hollandaise (Eigelb, geschmolzene Butter, Zitronensaft), holländische Sauce
home-baked bread	selbst gebackenes Brot
homefries	selbst gemachte Pommes frites
homemade	hausgemacht
home-marinated	hausgebeizt
hominy (crushed maize cooked with water or milk)	Maisgrießbrei (in Wasser oder Milch gekocht)
honey	Honig
honeydew melon	Honigmelone
honeyed	nach Honig schmeckend
honeymoon	Flitterwochen
hood	Kapuze
hop	Hopfen
horns of plenty mushrooms	Totentrompeten
hors d'oeuvres	Vorspeisen
hors d'oeuvres of fish	Fischvorspeisen
horse meat	Pferdefleisch
horseradish	Kren, Meerrettich
horseradish sauce	Krensauce, Semmelkren
creamed horseradish	Oberskren
hospitality	Gastfreundschaft
host family	Gastfamilie
hot appetisers	warme Vorspeisen
hot chocolate	heiße Schokolade

hot food counter/table	Wärmtisch
hot plate	Warmhalteplatte
hotel chain	Hotelkette
hotel directory	Verzeichnis mit Hinweisen für den Hotelgast
hotel register	Gästebuch
hotel stationery	Schreibpapier des Hotels
hothouse fruit	Treibhausobst
hotpot, hotchpotch	Eintopf, Eintopfgericht
hourglass	Sanduhr
house wine	Schankwein
housekeeper	Hausdame, Haushälter/in
huchen, Danube salmon	Huchen, Donaulachs
hundreds and thousands	(jegliche Art von) Streusel
hungry	hungrig
hunter sauce	Jägersauce (Sauce chasseur)
hurricane glass	Cocktailtulpe
husk	Schote
to husk	schälen (Hülsenfrüchte)

I

ice bucket	Eiskübel
ice cream	Eiscreme
ice cream maker	Eismaschine
ice cream tub	Eisbecher
ice cube	Eiswürfel
ice machine	Eismaschine
ice omelette, baked Alaska (icecream covered with meringue)	Eisomelette (Omelette surprise), Eis mit Baiserhaube
ice scoop	Eisschaufel
ice tongs (pl)	Eiszange
ice wine	Eiswein
iceberg lettuce	Eisbergsalat
iced/chilled	geeist, eisgekühlt
iced water	Eiswasser
identity card	Ausweis, Personalausweis
Immaculate Conception	Mariä Empfängnis
immediately	sofort, umgehend
immigration	Einwanderung
imperial mushrooms	Kaiserpilze, Kaiserlinge
inch	Zoll (Längenmaß: 2,54 cm)
inconvenience	Unannehmlichkeit
to incorporate	einarbeiten
increasing	zunehmend
Indian cress, nasturtium	Kapuzinerkresse
indication	Hinweis
indigestible	unverdaulich, schwer verdaulich

indoor pool	Hallenbad
induction cooktop	Induktionsplatte
infant school/preschool	Vorschule
inflammable	entzündlich
information (desk)	Information
information rack	Informationsständer
ingredient	Zutat
ink pad	Stempelkissen
inn, country-inn	Gasthaus
inquiry	Anfrage
insipid	geschmacklos
to inspect	kontrollieren
instant broth	Instantbrühe
instant meal/food	Fertiggerichte
instruction,	Anleitung
insurance	Versicherung
insurance policy	Versicherungspolizze
to interfere with	stören, sich einmischen
interior	Inneneinrichtung
internet	Internet
intestine	Darm
invoice	Rechnung
Irish coffee glass	Irish-Coffee-Glas
Irish stew (mutton stew with onions and potatoes)	Irish Stew (Hammelfleischeintopf)
iron	Glätteisen, Bügeleisen
iron service	Bügelservice
issued	ausgestellt
Italian pasta	italienische Teigwaren
Italian sauce	italienische Sauce
Italian vegetable soup	Minestrone
item	Gegenstand

J

jacket	Jacke
jacket potatoes, potatoes in their jackets	Pellkartoffeln, Kartoffeln in der Schale
jam	Marmelade
January	Jänner
Japanese artichoke	Knollenkartoffel, Knollenziest
jar	Glas
jelly, -ies (pl)	Gelee(s)
fruit jellies	Früchtegelees
wine jelly	Weingelee
in jelly/aspic	in Aspik
jellyfish	Qualle
Jerusalem artichoke	Topinambur

English	German
jeweller's shop	Juweliergeschäft
jigger	Messbecher in der Bar
John Dory, Dory	Petersfisch, Heringskönig
Joinville sauce (fish sauce with shrimp butter)	Joinville-Sauce (Fischsauce mit Garnelenbutter)
jugged hare	Hasenpfeffer
juice extractor	Saftpresse
juice groove	Saftrinne
July	Juöi
junction	Kreuzung
June	Juni
juniper (berries)	Wacholder(beeren)
juniper berry butter	Wacholderbutter
juniper berry sauce	Wacholdersauce
junior high school	Hauptschule
junior suite	kleine Suite in einem Raum

K

English	German
kale	Grünkohl, Blattkohl
kamut	Kamut
keen	eifrig
to be keen on	auf etwas versessen sein
kettle	Kessel
key card	Zimmerkarte
to key in	eingeben (Tastatur)
keyboard	Tastatur
keyword	Schlüsselwort
kid	Kitz, Zicklein (Fleisch)
kid's corner	Spielecke
kidney	Niere
kidney beans, red beans	Kidneybohnen, rote Bohnen
kind	freundlich
king prawn	Riesengarnele, Hummerkrabbe
kipper (kippered herring)	Salzhering, Bückling, Räucherhering
–, dried or smoked	–, getrocknet oder geräuchert
kir (white wine and cassis)	Kir (Weißwein und Cassis)
kir royal (champagne and cassis)	Kir Royal (Champagner und Cassis)
kirsch, kirschwasser	Kirschwasser
kitchen assistant	Küchengehilfe
kitchen counter	Arbeitsplatz
kitchen paper	Küchenkrepp
kitchen personnel	Küchenbrigade
kitchen range	Herd, Kochplatz
kitchenette	Kochnische
kiwi	Kiwi

English	German
to knead	kneten
kneaded butter	Mehlbutter
knife, knives (pl)	Messer
knife block	Messerblock
chef's knife	Küchenmesser
knowledgeable	belesen
knuckle of veal (braised)	Kalbsvögerl
kohlrabi	Kohlrabi
kosher	koscher
kosher butchering	Schächten
kumquat	Kumquat, Zwergorange

L

English	German
Liptauer (soft, white cheese of ewe's milk with paprika and caraway seeds)	Liptauer (Frischkäse aus Schafmilch mit Paprika und Kümmel)
label	Etikette
labelled	beschriftet, etikettiert
Labour Day	Tag der Arbeit, Staatsfeiertag
ladies (toilet)	Damentoilette
ladle	Schöpfer
to ladle	schöpfen
lager (beer)	Lagerbier
laid down	festgehalten, niedergeschrieben
lamb	Lammfleisch, Lamm
quarter of lamb	Lammviertel
spring/baby lamb	Milchlamm
lamb pluck	Beuschel vom Lamm, Lamminnereien
lamb's lettuce	Vogerlsalat, Feldsalat
lamp	Lampe
lamprey	Neunauge
to land	landen
landlord, landlady	Wirt/in, Vermieter/in
landmark	Wahrzeichen
langouste	Languste
laptop	Laptop
lard	Schweineschmalz, weißer Speck
to lard	spicken
larding needle/pin	Spicknadel
larder	Gardemanger
lasagne	Lasagne
laser pointer	Laserpointer
late vintage, late gathered	Spätlese
laundry	Wäscherei
laundry maid	Wäscherin, Büglerin
lavender	Lavendel

English	German
law	Gesetz
to lay the table	Tisch decken
layer	Schicht
layer salad	Schichtsalat
layout	Entwurf
leaf	Blatt
lean	mager
leap year	Schaltjahr
lecture	Vortrag
lecturer	Vortragende/r
lectern	Rednerpult
leek	Lauch, Porree
leek sauce	Lauchsauce
leg of ...	Stelze
leg of pork (pickled)	Eisbein
legible	leserlich
legitimate	rechtmäßig, legitim
leisure	Freizeit
lemon	Zitrone
lemon butter	Zitronenbutter
lemon peel	Zitronenschale
lemon twist	Zitronenspirale
lemon balm	Zitronenmelisse
lemon grass	Zitronengras
lemon grass sauce	Zitronengrassauce
lemon sauce	Zitronensauce
lemon sole	Rotzunge
(aerated) lemonade	Limonade
lengthways	längs, der Länge nach
Lenten dish	Fastenspeise, Fastenkost
Lenten soup, soup maigre	Fastensuppe
lentils	Linsen
lentil (purée) soup	Linsenpüreesuppe
letterhead paper	Briefpapier (vorgedruckt)
lettuce	Häuptelsalat, Kopfsalat
lettuce leaves	Salatblätter
lever	Hebel
library	Bibliothek
licence plate number	Kfz-Kennzeichen
lid	Deckel
life vest	Schwimmweste
to lift the receiver	(Hörer) abheben
lift, elevator	Lift
liftboy	Fahrstuhlführer
light	leicht
light (pale) beer	helles Bier
light bulb	Glühbirne
light/heavy shower	leichter/schwerer Regenschauer
lightening	Blitz

lighter	Feuerzeug
likeable	sympathisch, liebenswert, nett
Lima beans	Limabohnen, Mondbohnen
lime	Limette
lime blossom	Lindenblüten
lime butter	Limettenbutter
lime sauce	Limettensauce
limpet	Napfschnecke
line	Zeile
linen sheets	Leintücher
liner	Passagierschiff
ling	Leng, Lengfisch
linseed oil	Leinöl
liqueur	Likör
liqueur-like	likörartig
liquid	Flüssigkeit
litter	Abfall
lively	lebendig
liver	Leber
liver dumpling	Leberknödel
liver pie in pig's caul	Leberschädel
liver sausage, liverwurst	Leberwurst
loach	Steinbeißer, Schmerle, Bartgrundel
loaf	Laib
lobby	Hotelhalle
lobster	Hummer
stuffed lobster	–, gefüllt
lobster butter	Hummerbutter
lobster cocktail	Hummercocktail
lobster mayonnaise	Hummermayonnaise
lobster salad	Hummersalat
lobster bisque	Hummerbisque (-cremesuppe)
lobster sauce	Hummersauce
lobster pick	Hummergabel
lobster cracker	Hummerzange
American style lobster (in rich tomato sauce)	Hummer auf amerikanische Art (in Tomatensauce)
lobster flambé	flambierter Hummer
thermidor (lobster meat baked in the lobster shell)	Thermidor (Hummerfleisch, in der Schale überbacken)
local	Einheimische/r
local wine	Landwein
location	Lage, Standort
lock	Schloss
loin of ...	Karree, Lende
loin of pork	Schweinskarree
long drink	Longdrink
long grain rice	Langkornreis
long-life milk	H-Milch

to look after	betreuen
to look into sth	auf den Grund gehen
to loosen	lockern, sich ablösen
loquat, Japanese medlar	japanische Mispel
lorette potatoes (cheesy potato croquettes)	Lorette-Kartoffeln (Käsekroketten)
to lose	verlieren
loss	Verlust
lost and found	Fundbüro
lost property	Fundsache
lounge	Foyer, Aufenthaltsraum
lovage	Liebstöckl
low season	Vor-, Nach-, Nebensaison
low-calorie	kalorienarm
low-fat	fettarm
lucrative	lukrativ, einträglich
luggage	Gepäck
luggage carrier	Gepäckswagen
luggage tag	Gepäcksschild
lukewarm	lauwarm
lump	Klumpen
lump sugar, cube sugar	Würfelzucker
lumpy	klumpig
lunch	Mittagessen
buffet lunch	Mittagessen vom Buffet
lung, lights	Lunge
luxury hotel	Luxushotel
lychee	Litschi
lyonnaise potatoes (fried with onions)	Lyoner Kartoffeln (mit Zwiebeln gebraten)
lyonnaise sauce (onion sauce)	Lyoner Sauce (Zwiebelsauce)

M

macadamia nut	Macadamianuss
macaire potatoes (potato cake fried in butter)	Macaire-Kartoffeln (Kartoffelkuchen, in der Pfanne gebraten)
macaroni	Makkaroni
macaroons	Amaretti, Mandelmakronen
mace	Muskatblüte
mackerel	Makrele
smoked mackerel	–, geräuchert
Madeira	Madeira
Madeira sauce	Madeirasauce
magazine	Zeitschrift, Magazin
magnifying mirror	Vergrößerungsspiegel
magnum	bottle equal to two regular 750 ml bottles

maiden name	Mädchenname
mailbox	Sprachbox
main course	Hauptgang
main dish	Hauptgericht
maintenance	Wartung, Haustechnik
maître d'hôtel butter	Kräuterbutter
maître d'hôtel potatoes (with parsley butter)	Maître-d'hôtel-Kartoffeln (mit Petersilbutter)
maître d'hôtel sauce (butter, parsley and lemon juice)	Maître-d'hôtel-Sauce (Butter, Petersilie, Zitronensaft)
major	gängig
major credit cards	gängige Kreditkarten
mallard, wild duck	Wildente, Stockente
mallet	Fleischklopfer
malt	Malz
Maltese sauce (hollandaise with orange juice)	Malteser Sauce (Hollandaise mit Orangensaft)
manager/boss	Chef
manager on duty	Manager im Dienst
mandarin	Mandarine
mango, -es (pl)	Mango(s)
manufacturer	Hersteller
manufacturing date	Herstellungsdatum
map	Landkarte
maple syrup	Ahornsirup
maraschino (liqueur from sour cherries)	Maraschino (Sauerkirschenlikör)
maraschino cherries	Cocktailkirschen, Maraschino Kirschen
marble	Marmor
marble cake	Marmorkuchen
marbled	durchwachsen (Fleisch)
marbled gugelhupf	Marmorgugelhupf
March	März
marengo (with tomato and white wine)	Marengo (mit Tomaten und Weißwein)
margarine	Margarine
Margarita glass	Margaritaschale
marigold	Ringelblume
marinade	Marinade
to marinate	marinieren, beizen
marital status	Familienstand
marjoram	Majoran
mark of origin	Herkunftsbezeichnung
marmalade	Orangenmarmelade
married	verheiratet
marrow	Knochenmark, Kürbis
marrow dumpling	Markknödel
marrow sauce	Marksauce

English – German M

English	German
Martini glass	Martiniglas
marvellous	wunderbar, großartig
marzipan	Marzipan
to mash	pürieren, zerstampfen
mashed potatoes	Kartoffelpüree, Kartoffelbrei
matches	Streichhölzer
matchstick chips/potatoes	Zündholzkartoffeln
matelote sauce	Matrosensauce
matie herring	Matjeshering
mattress	Matratze
mature	reif, reifen
May	Mai
mayonnaise (sauce)	Mayonnaise(sauce)
meal	Gericht
mealy	mehlig
mean	Mittel, Möglichkeit
mean of identification	Ausweis, Identifikationsnachweis
measure pourer	Flaschenportionierer
measurement	Maßeinheit
measuring cup/jug	Messbecher
meat dish	Fleischgericht
meat for making soup	Suppenfleisch
meat knife	Fleischmesser
meat loaf	Leberkäse,
meat mincer/grinder	Fleischwolf
meat scraps	Fleischabfälle
meatballs	Fleischlaibchen, Buletten, Fleischklöße
meatballs in savoury sauce	Königsberger Klopse
meat-filled cabbage rolls	Kohlrouladen
meatless	fleischlos
medallion	Medaillon
medium	mittel
medium dry	halbtrocken
medium sweet	halbsüß
medlar	Mispel
mellow	mild (Wein), ausgereift
melon	Melone
to melt	schmelzen
melted butter	geschmolzene Butter
memo pad	Notizzettel
menu	Speisekarte
meringue	Schaumgebäck, spanischer Wind, Baiser
meringue mixture	Baisermasse
meringue pie	Baisertorte
mesclun salad	Blattsalat, Mischung aus jungen Blattsalattrieben
metal spatula	Palette

English	German
mic mute	Stummschaltung
microwave oven	Mikrowelle
middle	Mitte, mittel
mild	mild
milk	Milch
long-life milk	Haltbarmilch
milk and cream strudel	Milchrahmstrudel
milk jug	Milchkännchen
milk powder	Milchpulver
milk roll	Milchbrötchen
milk sauce/béchamel sauce	Béchamelsauce
mill	Mühle
millet	Hirse
milt on toast	Milzschnitten
mimosa	Sekt-Orange
to mince	faschieren, klein hacken
minced meat	Faschiertes
mincer	Fleischwolf
mineral water	Mineralwasser
mini-pizza	Minipizza
mint	Minze
mint sauce	Minzsauce
mint tea	Pfefferminztee
minute rice	parboiled Reis
minutes	Protokoll
Mirabelle, yellow plum	Mirabelle
mirror	Spiegel
mirror carp	Spiegelkarpfen
to be mistaken	irren, sich irren
to mix	mischen
– thoroughly	gut verrühren, abtreiben
– a cocktail	Cocktail mischen
– with a whisk	verquirlen
mixed salad	vermischter Salat
mixer	Mixer
mixing bowl	Rührschüssel
mixing glass	Rührglas
mobile phone	Mobiltelefon, Handy
mock turtle soup	falsche Schildkrötensuppe
molasses	Zuckersirup, Melasse
Monday	Monatg
monitor	Bildschirm
monkfish, angler-fish	Seeteufel, Anglerfisch
montblanc (mashed chestnuts with cream)	Montblanc (Kastanienpüree mit Schlagobers)
moorhen, waterhen	Teichhuhn, Wasserhuhn
moose	Elch
moray eel	Muräne

English	German
morel	Morchel
morel tartlet	Morcheltörtchen
morel sauce	Morchelsauce
morellos, morello cherries	Weichseln, Sauerkirschen
Mornay sauce, cheese sauce	Sauce Mornay, Käsesauce (Béchamel mit Käse)
mortadella	Mortadella
mortar	Mörser
moselle	Moselwein
mother tongue	Muttersprache
mould	Form, Becherform
mouldy	schimmelig
to go mouldy	schimmeln
mountain cock	Auerhahn
mouse	Maus
mousse (frozen whipped cream mixture)	Mousse (gefrorenes aromatisiertes Schlagobers)
mousseline potatoes (mashed potatoes with whipped cream)	Schaumkartoffeln (Kartoffelpüree mit Schlagobers)
mousseline sauce (hollandaise sauce with whipped cream)	Mousseline-Sauce (Hollandaise mit geschlagenem Schlagobers), Schaumsauce
mouthful	Bissen, Mund voll
muddle	zerstoßen
muesli (flakes of cereals with nuts and dried fruit)	Müsli (Getreideflocken mit Nüssen und Früchten)
muffin	Muffin
muffin tray	Muffinform, Muffinblech
mufflon, mouflon	Mufflon (Fleisch)
mug	Becher
mugwort	Beifuß
mulberry, -ies (pl)	Maulbeere
mule	Maultier
mulled cider	Glühmost
mulled wine	Glühwein
mullet	Barbe
mulligatawny (soup) (curry soup with chicken)	Mulligatawny-Suppe (Currysuppe mit Huhn)
multi-grain/multi-cereals bread	Mehrkornbrot
murices	Stachelschnecken
muscatel, muscat grapes	Muskateller
mushroom sauce	Pilzsauce
mushroom, white mushroom	Champignon
mushy	matschig
musk duck	Barbarie-Ente
muslin	Siebtuch
mussels	Muscheln
gratinated mussels	–, überbacken
mussel salad	Miesmuschelsalat

mussel-bed	Muschelgarten
farmed mussels	Zuchtmuscheln
mustard (grains/seeds)	Senf(körner)
mustard butter	Senfbutter
mustard sauce	Senfsauce (Sauce Robert)
mutton	Hammel-, Lamm-, Schaffleisch, Schöpsernes
breast of mutton	Lammbrust
leg of mutton/lamb	Lammkeule
loin of mutton	Lammkarree
mutton/lamb chop	Lammkotelette
mutton/lamb stew	Lammragout
rack/loin of mutton	Lammkarree
rib of mutton	Lammrippenstück
roast mutton/lamb	Lammbraten
saddle of mutton	Lammrücken
shoulder of mutton	Lammschulter
mutton trotters	Hammelfüße

N

nail clipper	Nagelzwicker
nail file	Nagelfeile
nail scissors	Nagelschere
name tag	Namensschild
Nantua sauce (béchamel with crayfish butter)	Nantua-Sauce (Béchamel mit Krebsbutter)
napfkuchen (yeast cake with raisins)	Napfkuchen, Gugelhupf
napkin	Serviette
nappy	Windel
narrow	eng
nasal spray	Nasenspray
National Day	Nationalfeiertag
nationality	Nationalität
native, local	einheimisch
near to	in der Nähe von
neat	ordentlich, sauber, hübsch, pur
necessity	Notwendigkeit
neck of pork	Schweinsschopf
nectar	Nektar
nectarine	Nektarine
need	Bedarf
needs	Bedürfnisse
needlefish, garfish	Hornhecht
to negotiate	verhandeln
negotiation	Verhandlung
nest	Nest

net	netto
nettle	Brennnessel
new potatoes	Heurige (Kartoffeln)
new secondary school	Mittelschule, neu
newsstand	Zeitungsstand
new wine	Sturm
New Year's Day	Neujahrstag
next to	neben
nice to drink	süffig (Wein)
night table	Nachttisch
nightmare	Alptraum
no show	Gast, der nicht erscheint
noble	edel
noisette	Haselnuss, Nüsschen
lamb noisette	Lammnüsschen
noisette potatoes (nut-shaped fried potatoes)	Nusskartoffeln (haselnussgroße Bratkartoffeln)
non-alcoholic	alkoholfrei
non-returnable bottle	Einwegflasche
noodles	Nudeln
Norwegian sauce	Norweger-Sauce
notepad	Notizblock
notes	Notiz
notice	Kündigung, Bekanntmachung
give notice	kündigen
nouveau	jung, neu
November	November
nozzle	Düse, Tülle
nut	Nuss
nutcracker	Nussknacker
nutmeg	Muskatnuss
nutmeg grater	Muskatnussreibe
nutritial science	Ernährungslehre

O

oak barrel	Eichenfass
oats	Hafer
oat flakes, rolled oats	Haferflocken
oat cakes	Hafergebäck
oatmeal soup	Haferflockensuppe
obliging	zuvorkommend
occasion	Gelegenheit, Anlass
occupation	Belegung
to occur	auftreten (Problem)
October	Oktober
octopus, poulp	Tintenfisch
offals	Innereien

English	German
off-dry	lieblich
offence	Straftat
offer	Angebot
to offer	anbieten
oil	Öl
to oil	– mit Öl einstreichen
oil and vinegar cruet set	Essig- und Ölkaraffen
okra pods, gumbos	Okraschoten, Gombos
olive	Olive
green olive	grüne Olive
black olive, ripe olive	schwarze Olive
olive paste	Olivenpaste
stuffed olives	gefüllte Oliven
olive potatoes, chateau potatoes (olive-shaped fried potatoes)	Olivenkartoffeln, Schlosskartoffeln (olivenförmig geschnitten und in Butter gebraten
omelette	Omelette
cheese and potato omelette	– auf savoyische Art (mit Kartoffeln und Käse)
Spanish omelette (flat omelette with onions, pimiento and tomatoes)	– auf spanische Art (Eierkuchen mit Tomaten, Zwiebeln und Paprika)
herb/savoury omelette	– mit Kräutern
Florentine/spinach omelette	– mit Spinat
peasant's omelette (omelette with sorrel, potatoes and bacon, not folded)	– nach Bauernart (mit Speckwürfeln, Kartoffeln und Sauerampfer)
wild mushroom omelette	– nach Försterinart (mit Waldpilzen)
plain omelette	– Natur
omentum	Netz
one-way street	Einbahn(straße)
onion	Zwiebel
onion sauce, soubise sauce	Zwiebelsauce (Sauce soubise)
(baked) onion soup	(überbackene) Zwiebelsuppe
open sandwich	belegtes Brot
opening hours	Öffnungszeiten
operator, switchboard operator	Vermittlung, Telefonist/in
opposite of	gegenüber
orange	Orange
orange squash	Orangensaft, frisch gepresst
orange butter	Orangenbutter
orange sauce	Orangensauce
orange segment	Orangenspalte
orangeade	Orangenlimonade
orchid	Orchidee
order	Bestellung
to order	bestellen
oregano, wild marjoram	Oregano

organic, organically	bio, biologisch
organisation chart	Organigramm
organisation file	Konferenzmappe
organiser	Terminplaner
origin	Herkunft
Orlov (browned in hot oven with onion purée), saddle of veal Orlov	Orlow (braisiert und mit Zwiebelmus glaciert), Kalbsrücken Orlow
ossobuco (braised slice of veal shank)	Ossobuco (Kalbshaxe, in Scheiben gedünstet)
ostrich	Strauß
outbreak	Ausbruch
outdoor pool	Freibad
oval eared dish	Anrichteplatte
oven	Backrohr
oven temperature	Back(ofen)temperatur
ovenproof	feuerfest
oven-ready	bratfertig
overbooked	überbucht
to overcook	zerkochen
overdone	zu stark gebraten
overhead compartment	Handgepäcksablage
overhead projector	Overheadprojektor
to overlap	überlappen
overripe	überreif
owner	Besitzer/in
ox	Ochse
ox' heart	Rindsherz
ox-cheek/muzzle salad	Ochsenmaulsalat
oxtail	Ochsenschwanz
(clear) oxtail soup	(klare) Ochsenschwanzsuppe
ox-tongue	Ochsenzunge
oxygen mask	Sauerstoffmaske
oyster	Auster
oyster boats	Austernschiffchen
oyster knife	Austernmesser
oyster mushroom	Austernpilz
oyster sauce	Austernsauce

P

p.a. (per adult)	pro Erwachsenem
PA (public address) system	Lautsprecheranlage
package	Pauschale, Paket
package tour	Pauschalreise
pageboy	Hausbote
PAI (personal accident insurance)	Insassenversicherung

pain	Schmerz
pain killer	Schmerztabletten
pain reliever	Schmerzmittel
pale	blass
palmiers	Schweinsohren (Gebäck)
pan	Pfanne
pancake	Pfannkuchen, Palatschinke
pan-fried potatoes	Bratkartoffeln
to pan-fry	in der Pfanne braten
pantry	Speisekammer
papaya	Papaya
paper clip	Büroklammer
paper cutter	Papierschneider, Schneidemaschine
paper money	Papiergeld, Geldschein
paper shredder	Aktenvernichter
paper-frill	Kotelettmanschette
paprika	Paprika (Gewürz)
paprika chicken	Paprikahuhn
paprika sauce, sweet pepper sauce	Paprikasauce
parasol mushroom	Parasolpilz, Schirmpilz
to pare	schälen
parfait	Parfait, Halbgefrorenes
paring knife	Schälmesser
parisienne potatoes (noisette potatoes rolled in meat-glaze)	Pariser Kartoffeln (Nusskartoffeln, in Fleischglace glasiert)
parking area/lot	Parkplatz
parking space/spot	–, einzeln
Parma ham	Parmaschinken
parmentier potatoes (cube-shaped and fried)	Parmentier-Kartoffeln (gebratene Kartoffelwürfel)
parmesan en brochettes	Parmesanspießchen
parsley	Petersilie
parsley potatoes	Petersilienkartoffeln
parsley root	Petersilwurzel
parsley sauce	Petersiliensauce
parsnip	Pastinake
parson's nose	Bürzel
participant	Teilnehmer/in
partly cloudy	teilweise wolkig
partridge	Rebhuhn
part-time	Teilzeit
passenger	Passagier/in
passion	Leidenschaft
passion fruit	Passionsfrucht
passionate	leidenschaftlich
passport	Reisepass
pasta	Teigwaren
pasta squares	Fleckerl

English	German
– with cabbage	Krautfleckerl
– with ham (au gratin)	Schinkenfleckerl (überbacken)
paste	Paste
pasteurised milk	Milch, pasteurisiert
pastry	Backwerk, Gebäck
pastry bag	Spritzsack
pastry brush	Backpinsel
pâté	Pastete
patience	Geduld
patty, -ies (pl)	Pastetchen
patties filled with fine (veal, chicken, game, ham ...) stew	Blätterteigpastetchen mit feinem Ragout (Kalbs-, Hühner-, Wild-, Schinken- ...)
pay phone	Münztelefon
pay TV	kostenpflichtiges Fernsehen
pea purée	Erbsenpüree
peach	Pfirsich
peach Alexandra (on vanilla ice cream with strawberry purée)	Pfirsich Alexandra (auf Vanilleeis mit Erdbeermus)
peak period	Hauptsaison
peanut	Erdnuss
peanut butter	Erdnussbutter
peanut sauce	Erdnusssauce
pear	Birne
pear Alma (stewed in port wine, decorated with whipped cream)	Birne Alma (in Portwein pochiert, mit Schlagobers garniert)
pear Helena (pear on vanilla icecream with hot chocolate sauce)	Birne Helene (mit Vanilleeis und heißer Schokoladensauce)
pears in red wine	Rotweinbirnen
pearl barley	Graupen
pearl onion, pickled onions	Perlzwiebel, Silberzwiebeln
peas (fresh, dried, green)	Erbsen (frisch, getrocknet, grün)
peasant-style soup (vegetable soup)	Bauernsuppe (Gemüsesuppe)
pecan nut	Pekannuss
pectin	Pektin
pedestrian crossing	Fußgängerübergang
pedestrian zone	Fußgängerzone
to peel	schälen
peeler	Schäler
peeling knife	Schälmesser
pencil	Bleistift
pencil lead	Bleistiftmine
pencil sharpener	Spitzer
penthouse	Penthouse, Luxussuite im obersten Stockwerk
people	Leute
peoples	Völker

pepper (whole, crushed, ground)	Pfeffer (ganz, geschrotet, gemahlen)
pepper mill	Pfeffermühle
pepper pod	Paprikaschote
pepper sauce	Pfeffersauce
peppercorn	Pfefferkorn
peppermint	Pfefferminze
to pepper	pfeffern
peppery	peffrig
pepper (green, red, yellow), bell pepper	Paprika (grün, rot, gelb)
per glass, in carafe, from the cask	offen (Wein)
per serving	pro Portion
percentage	Prozent
percentage by volume	Volumsprozent
perch	Barsch, Flussbarsch
percolated coffee,	Filterkaffee
perfectionist	perfektionistisch, Perfektionist/in
perishable	verderblich
persimmon	Kaki, Kakipflaume
pesto sauce (basil paste in olive oil)	Pestosauce (Basilikumpaste in Olivenöl)
pet's supplement	Aufpreis für Haustier
petal	petal
petits fours, fancy biscuits	Petits fours, Teegebäck
pheasant	Fasan
photocopier, photocopying machine	Kopierer
physalis	Physalis
piccatta (slice of veal fried in butter with parsley and lemon)	Piccata (kleines Naturschnitzel mit Petersilie und Zitrone)
pickled	eingelegt
pickled herring	Matjeshering
pickled leg of pork	Eisbein, Surhaxe
pickles	Essiggurken
pickling	Pökeln
piddocks	Dattelmuscheln
piece	Stück
pies	Pasteten
pig	Schwein
pig's heart	Schweinsherz
pig's kidneys	Schweinsnieren
pig's liver	Schweinsleber
pig's tongue	Schweinszunge
pig's trotter	Schweinsfuß
pigeon	Taube
pike	Hecht
pike-perch	Zander, Schill
pilaw/pilaf/pilau rice	Pilawreis
pile	Stoß, Stapel

English	German
pillow	Kopfpolster
pillow case	Kissenüberzug
pilot	Pilot
pilot light	Kontrolllampe
Pilsner glass	Biertulpe
pin board	Pinnwand
pinch	Prise
pine nut	Pinienkern
pine nut sauce	Pinienkernsauce
pineapple	Ananas
pineapple fritters	–, gebacken
pint	Pint(e) (Maßeinheit: ca. 1/2 l)
pint glass	Pintglas
piping bag	Spritzbeutel
piquant sauce (with vinegar, gherkins, parsley)	pikante Sauce (mit Essig, Essiggurkerln, Petersilie)
pistachio	Pistazie
pitcher	Krug
pitted, sconed	entsteint, entkernt
pizza	Pizza
to place	legen, geben, platzieren
place card	Tischkarte
place charges on	auf die Rechnung setzen lassen
place mat	Tischset
place setting	Gedeck
plaice	Scholle
plain	pur
plain cooking/food	Hausmannskost, bürgerliche Kost
plain potatoes	Salzkartoffeln
plain salad	einfacher Salat
plain/dark chocolate	Zartbitterschokolade
plaited roll	Weckerl, Gebäck
to plan ahead	vorausplanen
planning	Planung
plant holidays	Betriebsurlaub
plastic container	Plastikbehälter
plastic wrap/cling film	Frischhaltefolie
plate	Platte, Teller
plate edge	Tellerrand
plate mirror	Tellerspiegel
plate of raw vegetables/crudities	Rohkostplatte
plate warmer	Tellerwärmer
platter	Servierplatte
pleasure	Freude, Vergnügen
pleasant	angenehm
plonk	billiger Wein
ploughman's lunch	kalte Jause (mit großen Stücken Brot, Käse, Speck ...)

English	German
pluck	Innereien
to pluck	rupfen
plum	Pflaume, Zwetschke
plumber	Installateur/in
PO Box	Postfach
to poach	pochieren
to pod	enthülsen
(pea) pod	(Erbsen-)Schote
point	Spitze, Punkt
point of destination	Zielflughafen
point of origin	Herkunft
pointer	Zeigestock
laser pointer	Laserpointer
poivrade sauce (with vinegar and pepper), pepper sauce	Pfeffersauce (mit Essig und Pfefferkörnern)
polenta (maize porridge)	Polenta, Sterz, Maisbrei
policy	Polizze
polite	höflich
politeness	Höflichkeit
Pollack, green cod	Pollack
polytechnical school	Poly(technische Schule)
pomegranate	Granatapfel
pomegranate sauce	Granatapfelsauce
pompano	Gabelmakrele
poppyseeds	Mohn
poppy seed noodles	Mohnnudeln
porbeagle, mackerel shark	Heringshai
porcelain	Porzellan
porcini	Steinpilze
pork	Schweinefleisch
pork chop	Schweinskotelett
pork stew, stewed pork, ragout of pork	Schweinsragout
pork knuckle, leg of pork	Schweinshaxe, -stelze
pork with root vegetables	Wurzelfleisch
porridge	Haferbrei
port (wine)	Portwein
port wine sauce	Portweinsauce
porter	Portier, Gepäckträger
porterhouse steak	Porterhouse-Steak
portobello	Waldchampignon, Portobellopilz
Portuguese sauce	portugiesische Sauce
Portuguese soup (tomato soup)	portugiesische Suppe (Tomatensuppe)
postal scales	Briefwaage
post-it notes	Haftnotizzettel
postpone	verschieben
pot	Topf
pot holder	Topflappen

English	German
to pot roast	in der Kasserolle dünsten
potted	eingemacht
potato	Kartoffel/Erdapfel
potato balls	Kartoffelbällchen
potato croquettes	Kartoffelkroketten
potato dishes	Kartoffelgerichte
potato dumpling	Kartoffelknödel
potato fritters	Kartoffelpuffer
potato goulash	Kartoffelgulasch
potato noodles	Kartoffelnudeln
potatoes en papillote	Folienkartoffeln
potato chipper	Pommes-frites-Schneider
potato gnocchi	Kartoffelgnocchi
potato nests	Kartoffelnester
potato salad	Kartoffelsalat
potatoes Anna (potato cake)	Anna-Kartoffeln (Kartoffelfladen)
pot-au-feu (broth with meat and vegetables)	Suppentopf, Potaufeu (Fleisch- und Gemüseeintopf)
pottery	Keramik
poultry	Geflügel
poultry liver	Geflügelleber
poultry shears	Geflügelschere
to pound	zerstoßen (im Mörser)
to pour	(aus)gießen, (aus)leeren
to pour in	einschenken
to pour on	begießen
to pour onto	aufgießen
to pour over	begießen
to pour over with sth	mit etwas übergießen
pouring	Übergießen
poussin	Poularde
pout, pouting	Zwergdorsch
to powder	stauben, bestreuen
powdered sugar	Staubzucker
powerful	kräftig
prawn	Garnele, Krevette
prawn cocktail	Garnelencocktail
prawn sauce	Garnelensauce
prebaked	vorgebacken
precaution	Vorsichtsmaßnahme
precise	präzise, exakt, genau
precision	Genauigkeit
pre-cooked	vorgekocht
to prefer	bevorzugen
premise	Räumlichkeit
to prepare	vorbereiten, zubereiten
to prepare for cooking	parieren, zuputzen
preparations	vorbereitende Arbeiten
preparation (of food)	Zubereitung

English	German
to present	präsentieren
presenter's case	Moderatorenkoffer
preserves	Konserven
preservative	Konservierungsmittel
preserved meat	Büchsenfleisch
preserving jar	Einmachglas
preserving sugar	Gelierzucker
to press	pressen, drücken
cold-pressed	kaltgepresst
hot-pressed	heißgepresst
to press together	zusammendrücken
pressed ham	Presschinken
pressure	Druck
pressure cooker	Schnellkochtopf
press conference	Pressekonferenz
pretzel (crispy knot-shaped biscuit), bretzel	Brezel
previous	vorherig, vorhergehend
price tag	Preisschild
prickly	prickelnd
prickly pear	Kaktusfeige
primary school	Volksschule
prime rib of beef	Hochrippe
princess soup (cream of chicken soup with asparagus tips)	Prinzessin-Suppe (Geflügelcremesuppe mit Spargelspitzen)
printer	Drucker
print cartridge	Druckerpatrone
probably	wahrscheinlich
procedure	Ablauf, Vorgangsweise
to process	verarbeiten
to produce	herstellen
profession, job	Beruf
profit	Gewinn
profit margin	Gewinnspanne
profiteroles	Brandteigkrapferln, Backerbsen
progressively	nach und nach
prohibition	Verbot
projector	Beamer
to prolong	verlängern (zeitlich)
proof of origin	Herkunftsnachweis
prosecco	Prosecco
to protect	schützen
protective clothing	Schutzkleidung
protection factor	Sonnenschutzfaktor
to prove	gehen lassen (Teig)
provençale sauce	provenzalische Sauce

to provide	zur Verfügung stellen
provided (that)	vorausgesetzt, (dass)
provided (with)	vorgegeben, zur Verfügung gestellt
province	Bundesland, Region
prune	Dörrpflaume
public announcement	Durchsage
puff pastry	Blätterteig
puffed rice	Knusperreis, Müslireis
pullet, fattened chicken	Masthuhn
pulses	Hülsenfrüchte
pumpernickel (wholemeal ryebread)	Pumpernickel
pumpkin	Kürbis
pumpkin seed	Kürbiskern
pumpkin seed oil	Kürbiskernöl
punch	Punsch
pupil	Schüler
purchase	Einkauf
to purchase	einkaufen
purée soup	Püreesuppe
purpose	Zweck
purslane	Portulak
to push	schieben, stoßen
pushpin	Reißzwecke
to put	legen, setzen, quellen, stellen
to put ... down	notieren
to put together	zusammenstellen
putting together	Zusammenstellung

Q

qaint	reizend, entzückend
quail	Wachtel
quality	Qualität
quality wine	Qualitätswein
quantity	Quantität
quarter	Viertel
queen scallops	Kammmuscheln
quenelles	Nockerln
query	Anfrage
questionnaire	Fragebogen
queue	(Menschen-)Schlange
to queue up	anstellen
quiche	Speckkuchen
quiche Lorraine (flan with bacon and cream)	Quiche Lorraine (Lothringer Specktorte)
to quick-freeze	schockgefrieren
quince	Quitte

quinoa	Quinoa
quoted	genannt, zitiert

R

rabbit	Kaninchen
rack (of …)	Rücken, …-rücken
racy	rassig
radicchio (red-leaved chicory)	Radicchio
radicchio sauce	Radicchiosauce
radish (white, black)	Rettich (weiß, schwarz)
ragout of veal	Kalbsragout
rain	Regen
rainbow trout	Regenbogenforelle
raisin	Rosine
raising agent	Treibmittel, Backtreibmittel
rancid	ranzig
range	Herd
rape (seed) oil	Rapsöl
rare	blutig
rasher	dünne Scheibe Speck oder Schinken
rasher of bacon	Speckscheibe
to rasp	raspeln, grob reiben
raspberry, -ies (pl)	Himbeere(n)
rate of exchange	Umrechnungsrate
ravigote sauce (vinaigrette with capers and fine herbs)	Ravigote-Sauce (Vinaigrette mit Kapern und feinen Kräutern), Kräutersauce
ravioli	Ravioli
raw	roh, blau
raw fruit and vegetables	Rohkost
raw ham	Rohschinken
raw sausage	Rohwurst
ray	Rochen
razor	Rasierer
razor shells, razor clams	Messer-, Scheidenmuscheln
reading lamp	Leselampe
ready to cook	kochfertig
to reallocate	neu zuweisen
receipt	Empfang, Erhalt, Quittung, Rechnung
to receive	erhalten
to receive guests	Gäste empfangen, begrüßen
receiver	Empfänger/Telefonhörer
reception (desk)	Empfang, Rezeption
receptionist	Empfangschef, Empfangsdame
recipe	Rezept
recipient	Empfänger

R English – German

recirculating heat	Umluft
to recommend	empfehlen
recommendation	Empfehlung
recreation	Erholung
recreation facilities	Freizeiteinrichtungen
to recycle	wiederverwerten
red beans	rote Bohnen
red beet	Rote Rübe
red cabbage	Blau-, (Rot)kraut
red mullet	Rotbarbe
red perch, redfish	Goldbarsch, Rotbarsch
red prawns	Hummerkrabben
red radish	Radieschen
red sea-bram	Rotbrasse
red snapper	roter Schnapper
red wine	Rotwein
red wine sauce	Rotweinsauce
red/white wine glass	Rot-/Weißweinglas
redcurrant	Ribisel
redcurrant sauce	Johannisbeersauce
to reduce	reduzieren
reduction	Ermäßigung, Reduktion
to refer to	beziehen auf
reference	Referenz
to refine	verfeinern, veredeln
refined	raffiniert
refined sugar (crystals)	Kristallzucker
refreshing	erfrischend, leicht säuerlich (Wein)
refreshment	Erfrischung
refreshment room	Erfrischungsraum
to refrigerate	kühlen
refrigeration	Kühlung, Kühlverfahren
refrigerator/fridge	Kühlschrank
refund	Rückerstattung
regard	Gruß
to register	anmelden
registration form	Gästeblatt, Meldeblatt
regular/filter coffee	Filterkaffee
regulars, regular customers	Stammkunden
regulation	Vorschrift
reimbursement	Erstattung
reindeer	Rentier
reliable	verlässlich
remaining	verbleibend, übrig
remote control	Fernbedienung
remoulade sauce (mayonnaise with mustard, capers and gherkins)	Remoulade-Sauce (Mayonnaise mit Senf, Kapern und Essiggurkerln)

English	German
to remove	entfernen, weggeben
to remove fat from	entfetten
to remove rind	abschwarten
to remove the froth	entschäumen
removable	abnehmbar
to render down	auslassen (Speck)
rental	Verleih
rental facility	Vermietung
to replace	ersetzen
to replenish	auffüllen, wieder auffüllen
representative	Angestellter, Vertreter
reputation	Ruf
request	Wunsch, Anfrage
on request	auf Anfrage, auf Wunsch
to require	brauchen, benötigen
requirements	Anforderungen
reservation	Reservierung, Bestellung
reservation rack	Reservierungsübersicht
to reserve	reservieren
resident	Einwohner/in
resort	Urlaubsort, Anlage
responsible	verantwortlich
restaurant car	Speisewagen
to restock	auffüllen
resume	Lebenslauf
retail	Einzelhandel
return call	Rückruf
revolting	ekelhaft, widerlich
revolving door	Drehtür
Rhine salmon	Rheinsalm
Rhine wine, hock	Rheinwein
rhubarb	Rhabarber
rib of pork	Schweinsrippe
ribbon	Band, Schleife
ribbon noodles	Bandnudeln
rice	Reis
curried rice	Curryreis
basmati rice	Basmatireis
rice crispies	Knusperreis, Müslireis
rice pudding	Milchreis
rice soufflé	Reisauflauf
rice with meat	Reisfleisch
rice with peas	Risipisi
rich	voll, reichhaltig, schwer
rim/edge	Rand
salt rim/edge	Salzrand
sugar rim/edge	Zuckerrand
rind	Schwarte
rind (of fruit)	Schale

English	German
ring	Kranz, Ring
ring cake	Kranzkuchen
ringdove	Wildtaube, Ringeltaube
to rinse	abspülen, waschen
to rinse with cold water	abschrecken
ripe	reif
ripeness	Reife
to rise	aufgehen
risotto (Italian rice dish)	Risotto
rissoles (fried cakes with meat or fish stuffing)	Rissolen (frittierte Blätterteigtaschen)
roach	Rotauge
to roast	rösten, braten (im Ofen)
roast ...	...braten
(cold) roast beef	(kalter) Rindsbraten, (kaltes) Roastbeef
roast (rolled) loin of veal with kidneys	(gerollter) Kalbsnierenbraten
roast neck of pork	Schopfbraten
roast pork	Schweinsbraten
roast pork sausage	Bratwurst
roast veal	Kalbsbraten
roasting dish	Bräter
roasting pan	Bratenpfanne
roasting rack	Bratengitter
roasting spit	Bratenwender
Robert sauce (onion, white wine, mustard)	Robert-Sauce (Zwiebel, Weißwein, Senf)
rock	Fels, Stein
rock candy	Kandiszucker
rock glass	Whisk(e)yglas
rock lobster	Langustine
on the rocks	auf Eis
rocket	Rukola, Rauke
rocket pesto	Rukola-/Raukepesto
rockling, sea loach	Seequappe
roe	Rogen (vom Fisch)
roe lumpfish	deutscher Kaviar (vom Seehasen), Lumpfischrogen
roe, roebuck (male)	Reh
(French) roll	Semmel, Brötchen
rolled	ausgerollt
– and boned roast beef	Rollbraten
– boned ham	Rollschinken
– pastry	ausgerollter Teig
– pickled herring	Rollmops
– sponge cake, Swiss roll	Biskuitroulade
– stuffed veal cutlet	Kalbsroulade
rolling pin	Nudelholz

rollmops (rolled herring)	Rollmops
romaine lettuce	Römersalat
room	Zimmer
room maid/attendant	Zimmermädchen, Zimmerbursche, Raumpfleger/in
room rack	Zimmerübersicht
room rate, tariff	Zimmerpreis
room service	Zimmerservice
room temperature	Zimmertemperatur
root	Wurzel
Roquefort sauce	Roquefortsauce
rosé wine	Roséwein
rosefish	Goldbarsch, Rotbarsch
rosehip	Hagebutte
rosemary	Rosmarin
rosemary sauce	Rosmarinsauce
Rösti (fried pancake of grated potatoes)	Rösti (geraspelte Bratkartoffeln)
to rot	verfaulen
rotten	verdorben
round	rund
routing	Flugstrecke
roux	Einbrenn
rowanberry	Vogelbeere
rowanberry schnapps	Vogelbeerschnaps
royale soup (with egg custard)	Kraftsuppe mit Eierstich
to rub	reiben
to rub in	einreiben
to rub oil into sth	einölen
rubber mat	Gummimatte
rubber spatula	Teigkarte
rudd	Rotfeder
rue	Weinraute
rug	Teppichläufer
rum	Rum
rumen	Pansen
rump steak	Rumpsteak
to run the business/hotel	das Geschäft/Hotel leiten
runway	Rollbahn, Piste, Start-/Landebahn
rusks, zwieback, biscuit rusks	Zwieback
Russian eggs, eggs à la russe	russische Eier
russulas	Täublinge
rustic	ländlich
rye	Roggen
rye bread	Roggenbrot
rye crisps	Knäckebrot

S

sabayon (foamy wine sauce of egg yolk, sugar and wine), zabaglione	Zabaione/Sabayon/Weinschaum (Chaudeau), (schaumige Creme aus Eigelb, Zucker und Wein)
saccharin	Süßstoff
sachet	Tasche, Beutel
saddle (of)	Rücken, ...-rücken
safe	Safe
safe deposit box	Schließfach
safety instructions	Sicherheitshinweise
safety rail	Absturzsicherung
saffron	Safran
saffron sauce	Safransauce
saffron stigmas	Safranfäden
sage	Salbei
sage butter	Salbeibutter
sage sauce	Salbeisauce
salad	Salat
salad plate	Salatteller
salad spinner	Salatschleuder
salamander	Salamander, Grill mit Oberhitze
salami	Salami
salary	Gehalt
salmi of guineahen	Perlhuhnragout
salmon	Lachs
–, boiled	–, gekocht
salmon in pastry	– in Blätterteig
dill marinated salmon	– in Dillmarinade
salmon in salt crust	– in Salzkruste
salmon butter	Lachsbutter
salmon cornets	Lachsröllchen
salmon of the Baltic Sea	Ostseelachs
salmon tartare	Lachstatar
salmon trout	Lachsforelle
salsify	Schwarzwurzel
salt	Salz
to salt	salzen
salt and pepper shaker	Salz- und Pfefferstreuer
salt cod	Steckerlfisch, Stockfisch
salt crust	Salzkruste
salt(ed) (pickled) pork	Pökelfleisch
salted butter	gesalzene Butter
saltimbocca (escalope with sage and ham)	Saltimbocca (Schnitzel mit Salbei und Schinken)
saltwater/sea fish	Salzwasserfisch
salutation	Begrüßung
sample	Muster

English	German
sandwich	Sandwich
sandwich loaf	Toastbrot, Kastenbrot
sandwich toast (toasted ham and cheese sandwich)	Schinken-Käse-Toast, Croque-monsieur
sanitary facilities	sanitäre Anlagen
sardine, pilchard	Sardine
sardines in oil	Sardinen in Öl
satisfaction	Zufriedenheit
satisfied	zufriedengestellt
saturated	gesättigt
saturated fatty acids	gesättigte Fettsäuren
saturation	Sättigung
Saturday	Samstag
sauce	Sauce
sauce chasseur (mushrooms, white wine, tomato sauce)	Jägersauce (Champignons, Weißwein, Tomatensauce
sauce financière (Madeira sauce flavoured with truffle)	Finanzmannsauce (Madeirasauce mit Trüffelfond)
sauce grand-veneur (poivrade sauce with game extract and redcurrant jelly), venison sauce	Grand-veneur-Sauce (Pfeffersauce mit Wildextrakt und Johannisbeergelee), Wildsauce
sauce normand (white wine sauce with fishstock)	normannische Sauce (Weißweinsauce mit Fischfond)
sauce poulette (white sauce with egg yolk)	Poulette-Sauce (weiße Sauce mit Eigelb)
saucepan	Stielpfanne
saucepan with a handle	Stieltopf
saucer, sauce boat	Sauciere
sauerbraten (braised beef, previously marinated in vinegar)	Sauerbraten (in Essigbeize vorbehandelter Schmorbraten)
sauerkraut	Sauerkraut
sauna	Sauna
sausage for spreading	Streichwurst
sausage roll, toad-in-the-hole (sausages baked in batter)	Würstel im Schlafrock
sausage salad	Wurstsalat
to sauté	sautieren, schwingend rösten
sauté pan	Sautierpfanne
sauté potatoes	Schwenkkartoffeln
sautéed liver	geröstete Leber
savory	Bohnenkraut
savoury	herzhaft, würzig
savoury butters	Buttermischungen
savoy cabbage	Kohl, Wirsing
savoy potatoes (potatoes gratinated with broth and cheese)	Savoyer Kartoffelgratin (mit Bouillon und Käse überbacken)
sawfish	Sägefisch
scald	erhitzen, abbrühen

to scale	wiegen, entschuppen (Fisch)
scales	Waage
scallion	Frühlingszwiebel
scallop	Jakobsmuschel
scallop brochettes	Jakobsmuschel-spießchen
to scallop	im Rohr, in einer Sauce dünsten
scalloped fish	Fisch in Muschelschalen
scampi, Dublin Bay prawns	Scampi, Kaisergranat
scarf	Halstuch
SCDW (super collision damage waiver)	Vollkaskoversicherung ohne Selbstbehalt
scent/smell	Geruch
schnapps	Korn(schnaps)
scissors	Schere
scorpion fish	Drachenkopf
Scotch broth (soup of mutton or beef and pearlbarley)	schottische Suppe (Hammel- oder Rindssuppe mit Graupen)
Scotch® tape	Tixo®, Klebeband
Scotch woodcock (scrambled egg on anchovy toast)	Scotch woodcock (Rührei auf Sardellentoast)
scrambled egg	Rührei
to scrape	schaben
scraper	Schaber
scrapped in pastry wrap	umhüllt vom Teigmantel
scrumptious	lecker
scuba diving centre	Tauchschule
sea bass	Meerbrasse, Wolfsbarsch, Loup
sea buckthorn	Sanddorn
sea ears, ormers, abalones	Meerohren
sea fish	Salzwasserfisch
sea perch	Rotbarsch
sea salt	Meersalz
sea urchin	Seeigel
sea view	Meerblick
sea-bram	Meerbrasse
seafood sauce	Meeresfrüchtesauce
seafood, shellfish	Meeresfrüchte
seal of quality	Gütesiegel, Gütezeichen
to sear	scharf anbraten
to season	würzen
to season to taste	abschmecken, nach Geschmack würzen
seasonings (spices)	Würzmittel (Gewürze)
seasonal, in season	gemäß den Jahreszeiten
seat	Sitz, Platz
seat belt	Gurt
seaweed	Alge, Meeresalge
second helping/serving	Nachschlag

secondary (modern) school	Hauptschule, Sekundarstufe (10 bis 14 Jahre)
security check	Sicherheitscheck
security officer	Sicherheitsbeamter
sediment	Bodensatz, Ablagerung
seed	Kern
seed roll	Mohnbrötchen
seedless	kernlos
seedlings	Keimlinge
to seem	scheinen
self-confident	selbstbewusst
sell-by date	Haltbarkeitsdatum
seltzer	Selterswasser
semi-hard	halbfest
semi-soft	schnittfest
semi-sweet	halbsüß
semolina	Grieß
semolina dumpling	Grießknödel, -nockerl
semolina pudding	Grießbrei, Grießpudding
senior high school	höhere Schule
sensible	vernünftig
sensitive	sensibel, empfindlich
to separate	trennen
separation	Trennung
September	September
serrated knife	Wellschliff (Messer), Sägemesser
to serve	servieren
to serve the food at the table	vorlegen
server's manual	Bedienungsanleitung
service	Bedienung
service (not) included	Bedienungsgeld (nicht) inbegriffen
service charge	Bedienungsgeld, -zuschlag
service rule	Servierregel
serviette	Serviette
serving	Ausgabe
serving cutlery	Vorlegebesteck
serving hatch	Durchreiche
sesame	Sesam
sesame sauce	Sesamsauce
set dinner	Abendmenü
set lunch	Mittagsmenü
set meal	Menü
setting	Umgebung, Lage
historic setting	historische Lage
to settle	begleichen, ausgleichen, bezahlen
to settle an account	bezahlen, Konto ausgleichen
shad roe	Maifischrogen
shad, allice shad	Maifisch, Alse

English	German
to shake (well)	(gut) schütteln
shaker	Shaker
shallot	Schalotte
shallot butter	Schalottenbutter
shallow-fried	Müllerinnen-Art
shandy	Radler (Bier mit Limonade), Alsterwasser
shank	Keule, Unterschenkel
shape	Form
to shape	in Form bringen
to share	teilen
shark	Hai
sharp-edged	scharfkantig
sharpening steel	Wetzstahl
shashliks (meat on skewers), kebabs	Schaschliks
shaver	Rasierapparat
shaving foam	Rasierschaum
sheatfish, wels, catfish	Wels, Waller
sheep's cheese	Schafskäse
shelf, shelves (pl)	Regal
shelf life	Haltbarkeit
shell	Schale
to shell	schälen (Eier, Nüsse)
shellfish	Krustentier
shellfish sauce	Krustentiersauce
shelter	Schutzhütte
shepherd's pie (minced meat topped with mashed potato)	Hirtenpastete (Kartoffelpüree auf Faschiertem, überbacken)
sherbet/sorbet	Sorbet
sherry	Sherry
sherry glass	Sherryglas
sherry sauce	Sherrysauce
shift	Schicht (Job)
shiitake	Shiitake
shiny	glänzend
shoestring potatoes	Streichholzkartoffeln, Pommes allumettes
shoot	Sprosse
short cake	Mürbteigkuchen
short circuit	Kurzschluss
short crust pastry	Mürbteig
short drink	kurzes Getränk
short grain rice	Rundkornreis, Perlreis
short-staffed	knapp an Personal
shot glass	Stamperl
shoulder of ...	...schulter
shovel	Schaufel
shower cubicle	Duschkabine

shower curtain	Duschvorhang
shower head	Duschkopf
shower hose	Duschschlauch
shred	Streifen
shred, coarsely ground wholemeal	Schrot, grobes Mehl
to shred	zerkleinern, schnetzeln, zerreißen
shredded liver	Leberreis
shrimp	Garnele, Krevette
shrimp (prawn) cocktail	Garnelencocktail
shrimp butter	Garnelen-/Krevettenbutter
shrimp sauce	Garnelensauce
shuttle service	Zubringerdienst
siblings	Geschwister
sick leave	Krankenstand
side dish	Beilage
side plate, bread and butter plate	Couvertteller, Butterteller
side knife	Buttermesser
sieve	Sieb
to sieve/sift	sieben, durchsieben
to sign	unterschreiben
signature	Unterschrift
silver cutlery	Silberbesteck
silverware	Silbergeschirr
similar	ähnlich
to simmer	sieden, langsam kochen
simmering	Sieden
simple	einfach
simple sugar syrup	Läuterzucker
simultaneous	gleichzeitig
simultaneous translation	Simultanübersetzung
sincere	aufrichtig
sincerely	mit freundlichen Grüßen
sinew	Sehne
single	ledig, einzeln
single room	Einzelzimmer
single supplement	Aufschlag für Einzelzimmer
single use	Einzelnutzung
sink	Abwasch, Spülbecken
siphon, siphon bottle	Siphon
sirloin	Beiried
sirloin steak	Zwischenrippenstück
sirloin steak lyonnais (with fried onions)	Entrecote nach Lyoner Art (mit Zwiebeln)
sirloin steak Mirabeau (with anchovy fillets and olives)	Entrecote Mirabeau (mit Sardellenfilets und Oliven)
sirloin tips	Rinderfiletspitzen
size of portion/serving	Portionsgröße

skewer	Spieß
small skewer	Spießchen, kleiner Spieß
to skewer	aufspießen
skills	Fähigkeiten
to be skilled	ein Könner sein
skim	abschäumen
skim(med) milk	Magermilch
skimmer	Siebschöpfer
skin	Haut
to skin	abhäuten, schälen
to skip payment	Zeche prellen
slatted frame	Lattenrost
to slaughter	schlachten
sleek	elegant
sleet	Schneeregen, Graupel
to slice	in Scheiben, Streifen schneiden
slice of ...	Scheibe/Schnitte von ...
sliced pancakes	Frittaten
slicer	Aufschnittmaschine, Hobel
to slide	rutschen
slide projector	Diaprojektor
sliding door	Schiebetür
slightly	ein wenig
to slip	ausrutschen
slip, slippage	Rutschen
slipcloth	Napron
slippery	rutschig
sloping	schräg
smell	Geruch
to smell	riechen
smelt	Stint
to smoke	räuchern, selchen, rauchen
smoke detector	Rauchmelder
smoked pork	Geselchtes
smoked raw ham	geräucherter Rohschinken
smoking area/zone	Raucherbereich
smooth hound, dogfish	Glatthai
smoothing iron	Glätteisen
to smother	dünsten
snack	Imbiss, Jause
snack on a wooden platter	Brettljause
snail	Schnecke, Weinbergschnecke
snail butter	Schneckenbutter
snail with herb butter	Schnecke mit Kräuterbutter
snail pan	Schneckenpfanne
snail tongs	Schneckenzange
snapper	Schnapper
snipe	Schnepfe
to snorkel	schnorcheln

snow	Schnee
snow/white grouse	Schneehuhn
to soak	einweichen
to soak with sth	tränken mit etwas
soaking	Wässern
soap	Seife
soap dish	Seifenhalter
sober	nüchtern
socket	Steckdose
soda/sparkling water	Sodawasser
soft	mild
soft cheese	Weichkäse
soft drink	alkoholfreies Getränk, Limonade
soft ice	Softeis
softly lit	leicht beleuchtet
soigné	gepflegt
soil	Boden
sole	Seezunge
sole Florentine	Seezunge auf Spinat
sole Colbert (breaded, fried, filled with parsley butter)	Seezunge Colbert (paniert, gebacken und mit Kräuterbutter gefüllt)
fillets of sole Orly (deep-fried, served with tomato sauce)	Seezunge Orly (frittiert, mit Tomatensauce)
sommelier	Sommelier
sorbet/sherbet	Sorbet, Fruchteis
sore	Wunde, wund
sorrel	Sauerampfer
sorrel sauce	Sauerampfersauce
to sort	sortieren
soubise sauce (onion purée with béchamel)	Soubise-Sauce (Zwiebelpüree mit Béchamel), Zwiebelsauce
soufflé	Auflauf
soufflé potatoes	Auflaufkartoffeln
soufflé dish	Auflaufform
soufflé of white bread and stewed apples	Scheiterhaufen
soufflé Stephanie (with strawberries)	Omelette Stephanie (mit Erdbeeren)
soundproof	schalldicht
soup	Suppe
soup bowl	Suppenschüssel
soup cup	Suppentasse
soup plate	Suppenteller
soup tureen	Suppenschüssel, Suppenterrine
soup/table spoon	Suppenlöffel
sour	sauer, säuerlich
sour cherry, -ies (pl)	Sauerkirsche(n)
sour cream	Sauerrahm

sour cream dip	Sauerrahmdip
sour cream sauce	Sauerrahmsauce, Smitane
sour cream soup	Rahmsuppe
sourdough	Sauerteig
to souse	einlegen, marinieren
soya	Soja
soya bean	Sojabohne
soya bean sprout	Sojabohnensprosse
soya sauce	Sojasauce
spa	Wellnessbereich
spaghetti	Spaghetti
spaghetti tongs	Spaghettizange
spare ribs	Ripperln
spare time	Freizeit
sparkling	mit Kohlensäure
sparkling water	Sodawasser
sparkling wine	Schaumwein, Sekt
spatula	Spachtel
speaker	Lautsprecher
spear	Spieß
to spear	aufspießen
special cold sauces	kalte Spezialsaucen
special selection	Sonderabfüllung, spezielle Auswahl
special soup	Spezialsuppe
special warm sauces	warme Spezialsaucen
speciality	Spezialität
specials of the day	Tageskarte
speck (smoked raw ham)	Speck, Tiroler Bauernspeck
spelt	Dinkel
spelt noodles	Dinkelnudeln
spice	Gewürz
to spice	scharf würzen
spicy	würzig
spider crab	Seespinne, Meerspinne
spinach	Spinat
spinal marrow	Rückenmark
spiny lobster, rock lobster, crawfish	Languste
– en Bellevue (lobster meat in jelly)	Bellevue (Schwanzscheiben in Gelee)
– in jelly	Bellevue in Aspik
– Catalan style	–, katalanisch
spiny lobster mayonnaise	–, mit Mayonnaise
spirit	Branntwein, Schnaps
spirits	Spirituosen
spit	Bratenspieß
spit-roast	auf dem Spieß gebraten
to splash	spritzen
spleen	Milz

to split	spalten
split time shift	Teildienst
to spoil	verderben
spoiled, spoilt	verdorben
sponge	Schwamm
sponge biscuits, sponge finger	Biskotte, Löffelbiskuits
sponge cake	Biskuittorte
sponge square	Schöberl
spoon	Löffel
(wooden) spoon	Kochlöffel
spotlight	Scheinwerfer
sprat	Sprotte
sprayed	gespritzt (Obst, Gemüse)
spread	Aufstrich
to spread (with)	streichen, (mit etwas) bestreichen
to spread out (a tablecloth)	ausbreiten (Tischtuch)
spreadable	streichfähig
spreader	Buttermesser
sprig	Zweig, Stängel
sprig of parsley	Petersilienzweig
spring mould	Springform
spring onion	Frühlingszwiebel
spring roll, egg roll	Frühlingsrolle
spring vegetables	Frühlingsgemüse
sprinkle	Prise
to sprinkle	bestreuen
to sprinkle with flour	mehlieren, mit Mehl bestreuen
sprinkled with ...	bestreut mit ...
spritzy	spritzig
sprout	Sprosse
square	Platz, viereckig
squash	Kürbis
squash blossoms	Zucchiniblüten
to squeeze	auspressen
squid	Tintenfisch, Kalmar
squiggle	Schnörkel
stack	Stapel
to stack	stapeln
stacking tray	Zettelablage
staff	Personal
stag night	Junggesellenabend
stage	Bühne
stainless steel	Edelstahl
stairs, staircase	Stiegenhaus
stair lift	Treppenlift
stairway	Treppe
stale	abgestanden, altbacken (Brot)
stalk	Strunk, Stiel
stalk celery	Stangensellerie

stamp	Stempel
to stand	stehen, ruhen
standard dish	Stammgericht
to staple	klammern
stapler	Klammermaschine
star aniseed	Sternanis
star fruit, carambola	Sternfrucht, Karambole
starch	Stärke
star-shaped	sternförmig
star-shaped nozzle	Sterntülle
state of health	Gesundheitszustand
station waiter	Stationskellner
stationery	Schreibwaren
stay	Aufenthalt
pleasant stay	angenehmer Aufenthalt
to stay in control	unter Kontrolle haben
to stay overnight	übernachten
steak	Steak
steak knife	Steakmesser
steak tartare/tartar steak	Beefsteak tatare
to steam	dämpfen
steamed potatoes	Dampfkartoffeln
steamed rice	Reis, gedünstet
to steam up	beschlagen (Dampf)
steamed chocolate pudding with whipped cream (and vanilla ice cream)	Mohr im Hemd
steamer	Dämpfer
to steep	eintauchen, ziehen lassen (in Marinade)
steep	steil
stein	Bier-, Maßkrug
stem	Stiel
sterlet	Sterlet
stevia	Stevia
stew	Ragout, Eintopf
to stew	schmoren, dünsten
stewed beef or veal in paprika sauce	Gulasch (Rinds-, Kalbsgulasch)
stewed calf's heart and lights	Beuschel, Kalbsbeuschel
stewed fruit, compote	Früchtekompott
stewed plums	Zwetschkenröster
stewed potatoes	Schmorkartoffeln
to stick	kleben
to stick together	zusammenhalten
sticky tape	Klebeband
still mineral water	Minerlwasser ohne Kohlensäure
stingray	Rochen
to stipulate	fordern, verlangen

to stir	(um)rühren
stirring continually	unter ständigem Rühren
stirrer	Rührstab
stir-fry	Gemüsepfanne
to stir-fry	kurz anbraten
stock	Fond
stock cube	Suppenwürfel
stock pot	Suppen-/Fondtopf
stomach	Magen
stone	Stein
to stone	entsteinen, entkernen
stoned	entkernt
stonebass, wreckfish	Wrackbarsch
stopover	Zwischenstopp
stopped up	verstopft
storage	Lager
storage room, storeroom	Lager, Vorratsraum
storage volume	Nutzinhalt
to store	lagern
-storey	-stöckig
two-storey	zweistöckig
storm	Sturm
stout	dick
stout beer	dunkles Bier
stove	Herd
straight	Pur, gerade
a "straight" whiskey	Whiskey pur
straight ahead	geradeaus
to strain	passieren, filtern, abseihen
strainer	Sieb, Filter, Passiermaschine
straining cloth	Siebtuch
straw, drinking straw	Strohhalm
straw mushrooms	Strohpilze
straw potatoes, potato straws	Strohkartoffeln
strawberry, -ies (pl)	Erdbeere(n)
strawberry ice cream	Erdbeereis
streaky	durchwachsen
streaky bacon	Bauchspeck
street map	Stadtplan
strike	Streik
string	Bindfaden
string beans	Fisolen
strip	Streifen
vegetable strips	Gemüsestreifen
to cut into strips	in Streifen schneiden
to strip off	abstreifen
strudel	Strudel
stuff	Zeug, Ding
to stuff	fest füllen, stopfen

English	German
stuffed egg, Russian style	russische Eier
stuffing	Füllung
sturgeon	Stör
Styrian fattened chicken (pullet)	steirisches Masthuhn
to subdivide	unterteilen
to submit	unterbreiten
substantial	deftig, nahrhaft
substitute	Ersatz
to substitute	ersetzen
subtotal	Zwischensumme
suburb	Vorort
succulence	Saftigkeit
succulent	saftig
to suck	lutschen, saugen
suck(l)ing pig	Spanferkel
suet	Talg, Nierenfett
to suffer	leiden
sufficient	genügend, ausreichend
sugar	Zucker
sugar bowl	Zuckerdose, -schüssel
sugar crystals	Hagelzucker
sugar cubes	Würfelzucker
sugar dredger/shifter	Zuckerstreuer
sugar lump	Würfelzucker
sugar peas, mangetout peas	Erbsenschoten
sugar snap	Zuckerschote
to suggest	vorschlagen
suggestion	Vorschlag
suitable	geeignet
suitcase	Koffer
sultanas	Sultaninen
to sum up	zusammenfassen
summary	Zusammenfassung
sunburn	Sonnenbrand
(coupe) Sundae	Eisbecher
Sunday	Sonntag
sun	Sonne
sunburn	Sonnenbrand
sunflower (seed) oil	Sonnenblumenöl
sunflower seeds	Sonnenblumenkerne
sunny intervals	sonnige Abschnitte
sunrise	Sonnenaufgang
sunset, sundown	Sonnenuntergang
sunscreen	Sonnemilch
sunstroke	Sonnenstich
sun-shade	Sonnenschirm
supervise	beaufsichtigen
supper	(spätes) Abendessen

English	German
supplement	Aufschlag, Ergänzung
supplementary	zusätzlich
supply	Lieferung
to supply	liefern, beliefern
supply cabinet	Bürolager
supplier	Liferant/in
support	Unterstützung
to suppose	vermuten
supreme of ...	Hühnerbrust
suprême sauce (chicken stock with cream)	Sauce suprême (Geflügeleinmachsauce)
surface	Oberfläche
surname, last name	Nachname
surprise	Überraschung
to surround	umranden
surrounding	Umgebung
Swedes, Swedish turnips	Steckrübe, Dotsche
Swedish platter (marinated and smoked fish specialities)	Schwedenplatte (marinierte und geräucherte Fischspezialitäten)
to sweep	Kehren, aufwischen
sweet	süß
sweet pepper	Gemüsepaprika
sweet potatoes	Süßkartoffeln, Bataten
sweet rolls	Golatschen
sweetbread	Bries
sweetcorn	Zuckermais
sweetened	gezuckert
sweetener (artificial)	Süßstoff (künstlich)
sweetener tablet	Süßstofftablette
sweets	Süßspeisen
sweet-sour	süßsauer
sweet-and-sour sauce	süßsaure Sauce
to swell	quellen (lassen)
Swiss (stone) pine	Zirbe
Swiss chard	Mangold
Swiss cheese, emmenthal	Schweizer Käse, Emmentaler
switch	Schalter
to switch on	einschalten (Licht)
swivel chair	Drehstuhl
swordfish	Schwertfisch
sympathy	Mitgefühl, Verständnis, Be leid
syrup	Sirup
system caterer	Systemgastronom/in
system gastronomy	Systemgastronomie

T

Tabasco sauce	Tabascosauce
tabbouleh (bulgur salad)	Taboulé (Salat aus Bulgur)
table	Tisch, Tabelle
table d'hôte meal	Menü (gesetzt)
table wine	Tafelwein, Landwein
tablecloth	Tischdecke
tablespoonful (tbs)	Esslöffel voll
tail	Schwanz
to take away	entfernen, mitnehmen
to take off	abheben, starten (Flugzeug)
talented, in a talented way	talentiert
tangerine, mandarin	Mandarine
tannin	Tannin
tap	Wasserhahn
tapioca	Tapioka
tariff	Preisliste, Tarif
tarragon	Estragon
tarragon butter	Estragonbutter
tarragon sauce	Estragonsauce
tart	Torte (Obst, flach)
tart server	Tortenheber
tartlet	Törtchen
tartar steak, steak tartare	Beefsteak tartare
tartare sauce (mayonnaise with chopped pickles)	Sauce tartare (Mayonnaise aus hart gekochtem Eigelb mit Schnittlauch)
taste	Geschmack
to taste	schmecken, kosten, probieren, abschmecken
to taste of	schmecken nach
tasty	geschmackvoll
tax	Steuer
T-bone steak	T-Bone-Steak
tea	Tee
–, plain	– Natur
– with lemon	– mit Zitrone
– with milk	– mit Milch
– with rum	– mit Rum
black tea	Schwarztee
fruit tea	Früchtetee
herbal tea	Kräutertee
camomile tea	Kamillentee
linden tea	Lindenblütentee
mint tea	Pfefferminztee
hibiscus tea	Hibiskustee
redbush tea	Rooibostee

English	German
green tea	grüner Tee
rosehip tea	Hagebuttentee
tea cloth/towel	Geschirrtuch
tea infuser	Teeei
tea trolley	Teewagen
teabag	Teebeutel
tea/coffee spoon	Teelöffel
teaspoonful (tsp)	Teelöffel voll
to tear up	zerreißen
technical college	HTL
teetotaller	Antialkoholiker/in, Abstinenzler/in
telephone book	Telefonbuch
temperature	Temperatur
to have the right temperature	temperiert sein (Wein)
tench	Schleie
tender	zart, weich
tender finish	sanfter Abgang (Wein)
tenderloin	Lungenbraten, Rinderfilet
double tenderloin steak	doppelte Lendenschnitte (Chateaubriand)
tenderloin/fillet steak	Filetsteak
small tenderloin/fillet steak	Tournedos
very small tenderloin/fillet steak	Filet mignon
tenderloin/fillet goulash	Filetgulasch
tennis court	Tennisplatz
tepid	lauwarm
terminal	Halle
terminal hotel	Hotel am Flughafen, Bahnhof …
terms and conditions	allgemeine Geschäftsbedingungen
terrace	Terrasse
terrapin	Süßwasserschildkröte
to thaw	auftauen
theft protection	Diebstahlversicherung
thermal spa	Thermalbad
thermos (flask)	Thermoskanne
thick	dick, sämig
thick soup	Einmachsuppe, gebundene Suppe
to thicken, to bind	binden (z. B. mit Mehl oder Stärke), eindicken, legieren
thickening agent	Bindemittel
thigh	Hühnerkeule
thin/thin-bodied	leer
thirsty	durstig
thorough	gründlich
thread	Faden
through	durch
through the lobby	durch die Halle
to throw away	wegwerfen

English	German
thrushes	Drosseln
thunderstorm	Gewitter
Thursday	Donnerstag
thyme	Thymian
thyme butter	Thymianbutter
thyme sauce	Thymiansauce
tick	Häkchen
to tick	abhaken
tidbit, titbit, tasty	Schmankerl, Leckerbissen
tie	Krawatte
tile	Fliese
tilting frying pan	Kippbratpfanne
tilting kettle	Kippkochkessel
timbale	Timbale, Pastete
time	Stoppuhr
time switch	Zeitschaltuhr
time zones clock	Zeitzonenuhr
tin (can)	Dose
tin (can) opener	Dosenöffner
tinned	konserviert
tinned beer	Dosenbier
tinplate	Weißblech
tip	Trinkgeld
tissue	Papiertaschentuch
to toast	toasten, rösten (Brot)
toast rack	Toastständer
toasted sandwich (with ...)	Toast (mit ...)
toasty	nach Karamell schmeckend
tobacco	Tabak, nach Tabak
tobacconist	Trafik
toboggan	Rodel
to toboggan	rodeln, Schlitten fahren
toddler	Kleinkind
toddler's pool	Planschbecken
toilet brush	Klobürste
toilet paper	Toilettenpapier
toilet paper holder	Toilettenpapier-Halter
toilet roll	Toilettenpapier
tomato	Tomate
tomato and mozzarella salad	Caprese, Tomaten-Mozzarella-Salat
tomato purée	Tomatenmark
(raw) tomato sauce	(rohe) Tomatensauce
tongs	Zange
tongue	Zunge
tonic water	Tonic
tonight's specials	Abendkarte
tool	Werkzeug, Gerät

toothbrush	Zahnbürste
toothbrush cup	Zahnputzbecher
toothpaste	Zahnpaste
toothpick	Zahnstocher
top floor	oberste Etage
top-fermented	obergärig (Bier)
topped with ...	bedeckt mit ...
topping	Belag
topside of veal	Kalbsnuss
torso	Rumpf
tortilla (thin flat maize cake)	Tortilla (Maisfladen)
tortoise	Schildkröte
to toss	vermischen, schütteln, schwenken (in heißem Fett)
to toss salad	Salat anmachen
total amount	Gesamtbetrag
tough	zäh
tourist	Tourist/in
tourist menu	Touristenmenü
tournedos	kleine Filetsteaks
towel	Handtuch
towel rack, towel rail	Handtuchhalter
town hall	Rathaus
traceability	Rückverfolgbarkeit
to trace	zurückführen
to be traced to	zurückzuführen auf
trademark	Markenzeichen, Handelsmarke
traffic lights	Ampel
trainee	Praktikant/in
training programme	Ausbildungsprogramm
transparent	durchsichtig
transparent film	Klarsichtfolie
travel agency	Reisebüro
travel card	Tageskarte
travel data	Reisedaten
traveller	Reisende/r
traveller's check	Reisescheck
to pay in traveller's checks	mit Reiseschecks zahlen
tray	Tablett, Fach
tray table	Klapptisch
treacle, golden syrup, molasses	Melasse, Zuckersirup
to treat	behandeln
treatment	Behandlung
triangle	Dreieck
to trim	zuputzen, parieren, wegschneiden
trip	Reise
Have a nice trip!	Gute Reise!
tripe	Kutteln, Kaldaunen
trivet	Untersetzer

trolley	Wagen, Servierwagen
trout	Forelle
rainbow trout	Regenbogenforelle
lake trout	Seeforelle
brook trout	Bachforelle
salmon trout	Lachsforelle
sea trout	Meerforelle
farmed trout, trout from the fish-tank	Zuchtforelle
truffle	Trüffel
black truffle	schwarze Trüffel
truffle sauce	Trüffelsauce (Sauce périgueux)
to truss	dressieren (Geflügel)
trussing needle	Bridiernadel
truthful	wahrheitsliebend
Tuesday	Dienstag
tumbler	Tumbler
tunny, tuna	Thunfisch
turbot	Steinbutt
tureen	Terrine
turkey	Truthahn
turkey fillets	Truthahnschnitzel
turkey hen	Pute
turmeric	Kurkuma, Gelbwurz
to turn	drehen, tournieren
to turn into decorative shapes	tournieren
to turn over	umkippen
turnover	Umsatz
turnspit	Bratenwender
turnip	weiße Rübe
turnip cabbage	Kohlrabi
turtle	Schildkröte
turtle sauce (Madeira sauce with essence of herbs)	Schildkrötensauce (Madeirasauce mit Auszug von Kräutern), Tortue
turtle soup	Schildkrötensuppe
turtle soup Lady Curzon (flavoured with curry and covered with whipped cream)	Schildkrötensuppe Lady Curzon (mit Curry gewürzt und mit Schlagobers bedeckt)
mock turtle soup	falsche Schildkrötensuppe
tweezers	Pinzette
twin(-bedded) room	Zweibettzimmer
twine	Küchengarn
two-pronged fork	zweizinkige Gabel
Tyrolean fried potatoes	Tiroler Gröstl
Tyrolean sauce	Tiroler Sauce (Sauce tyrolienne)
Tyrolean sirloin steak (with tomatoes and fried onion rings)	Entrecote nach Tiroler Art (mit Tomaten und Zwiebelringen)

U

udder	Euter
umbrella	Regenschirm
unattended	unbeaufsichtigt
unbreakable	unzerbrechlich
to uncork	entkorken
underground/tube	U-Bahn
underside/bottom side	Unterseite
understanding	verständnisvoll
undiluted	unverdünnt
unemployed	arbeitslos
unfiltered	naturtrüb
unflinching	entschlossen
unfortunately	leider
unleavened bread	ungesäuertes Brot
to unmold	stürzen (z. B. aus der Backform)
unrefined sugar	Rohzucker
unripe	unreif, grün
unripe grain (of spelt)	Grünkern
unsaturated fatty acids	ungesättigte Fettsäuren
unsavoury	fade, geschmacklos (Essen)
unsweetened	ungezuckert
unwilling	widerwillig
upside-down cake	gestürzter Apfelkuchen, Tarte Tatin
upstairs	die Treppe hinauf
use	Gebrauch
usually	normalerweise, gewöhnlich
utensil	Gerät, Werkzeug

V

V-8 juice	Multivitaminsaft
vacancy	freie Stelle
vacant	frei, verfügbar
vaccination	Impfung
vacherin (rounds of meringue alternated with whipped cream), meringue cake	Vacherin (Schichttorte aus Meringeböden und Schlagobers), Baisertorte
to vacuum	staubsaugen
vacuum cleaner/hoover	Staubsauger
valet	Diener
valet service	Reinigung, Wäscherei
valuables	Wertsachen
vanilla	Vanille
vanilla crescents	Vanillekipferl

vanilla pod/bean	Vanilleschote
vanilla sugar	Vanillezucker
to vary	variieren
varied	abwechslungsreich
various	unterschiedlich, verschieden
vase	Vase
VAT = value-added tax	Mehrwertsteuer
veal	Kalbfleisch
veal (purée) soup	Kalbspüreesuppe
veal chop	Kalbskotelette
veal medallions	Kalbsmedaillons
veal noisette	Kalbsnuss
veal steak	Kalbssteak
veal stew	Kalbsragout
veal stew in paprika sauce	Kalbsgulasch
veal stock	Kalbsfond
veal and ham pie	Kalbfleischpastete
veal roulades (slice of veal rolled up with stuffing and stewed)	Kalbsrouladen
veal sausage	Weißwurst
vegetables, veggies	Gemüse
vegetable	pflanzlich
vegetable juices	Gemüsesäfte
vegetable knife	Gemüsemesser
vegetable peeler	Gemüseschäler
vegetable stock	Gemüsefond
vegetable strips	Gemüsestreifen
vegetarian	Vegetarier/in, vegetarisch
velouté (basic white sauce)	Velouté (weiße Grundsauce), Samtsauce
velvet swim crabs	Schwimmkrabben
velvety	samtig
Venetian sauce (white wine sauce with purée of herbs)	venezianische Sauce (Weißweinsauce mit Kräuterpüree)
venison	Wild, Wildbret
leg of venison	Rehkeule
roast saddle of venison	Rehrücken
roast venison	Hirschbraten, Rehbraten
venison sauce	Wildsauce
ventilation	Lüftung
venus mussel	Venusmuschel
to verify	verifizieren, nachprüfen
vermicelli	Fadennudeln, Vermicelli
vermouth	Wermut
vervain tea	Eisenkrauttee
vichyssoise (iced potato-leek cream soup)	Vichyssoise (Kartoffel-Lauch-Suppe, kalt serviert)
vicinity	Nähe
video recorder	Videorekorder

video surveillance	Videoüberwachung
video-monitored	videoüberwacht
vigilant	aufmerksam, wachsam
vigorous	lebhaft, energisch
Villeroi sauce (white sauce with essence of mushrooms)	Villeroi-Sauce (weiße Sauce mit Champignonfond)
vinaigrette/vinaigrette sauce/ vinaigrette dressing	Vinaigrette (Essig-Kräutersauce)
vine	Weinstock
vine leaf, leaves (pl.)	Weinblatt, -blätter
vineyard	Weinberg
vinegar	Essig
vinegar essence	Essigessenz
vintage (year)	Jahrgang (Wein)
violet	Veilchenblüte
visitor's tax	Kurtaxe
viticulture	Weinbau
vocational school	Berufsschule
voice mail	Sprachmitteilung
Voisin potatoes (cake of potato, butter and cheese)	Voisin-Kartoffeln (Kartoffeltörtchen mit Butter und Käse)
vol-au-vent	Blätterteigpastete, Vol-au-Vent
chicken vol-au-vent	– mit Geflügel
seafood vol-au-vent	– mit Meeresfrüchten
mushroom vol-au-vent	– mit Pilzen
volume	Volumen, Inhalt
voucher	Gutschein, Coupon
voyage	Reise, Seereise, Törn

W

wafer potatoes	Waffel-, Gitterkartoffeln
wafers, waffles	Waffeln
waffle iron	Waffeleisen
wages	Lohn
waiter/waitress	Kellner/Kellnerin
waiting period/time	Wartezeit
wake-up call	Weckruf
Waldorf salad (apples, celeriac and walnuts, mayonnaise)	Waldorfsalat (Äpfel, Knollensellerie, Walnüsse, Mayonnaise)
walk-in fridge	Kühlhaus
wall cupboard	Wandschrank
walnut	Walnuss
walnut kernel	Walnusskern
walnut sauce, nut sauce	Walnusssauce
wardrobe	Garderobe, Kleiderschrank
warm	warm
warm beverages	warme Getränke

W | English – German

English	German
warm butter sauces	warme Buttersaucen
warm pudding	warmer Pudding
to warm	erwärmen
warning lamp	Kontrolllampe
warranty	Garantie
to wash	waschen
to wash up (crockery)	(Geschirr) spülen
washbasin	Waschbecken
washcloth	Waschlappen
washing-up room	Geschirrspülraum
waste basket/wastepaper bin	Papierkorb
waste disposal	Müllbeseitigung
water glass	Wasserglas
water melon	Wassermelone
water tap	Wasserhahn
watercress	Brunnenkresse
watercress sauce	Kressesauce
watery	wässrig
wax bean	Wachsbohne
to weave	flechten
wedding	Hochzeit
wedding anniversary	Hochzeitstag
Wednesday	Mittwoch
weekly market	Wochenmarkt
(greater) weever	Petermännchen, Drachenfisch
to weigh	wiegen
weighing	Wiegen
weighing machine, scales	Waage
weight	Gewicht
by weight	nach Gewicht
well-balanced	ausgeglichen, ausgewogen
well-being	Wohlergehen
well-bred	gut erzogen, wohlerzogen
well-done	durchgegart, durchgebraten
well-flavoured	aromatisch
well-organised	gut organisiert, ordentlich
well-presented	gut aussehend, vorzeigbar
welsh rabbit (dish of melted cheese on toast)	Welsh Rabbit (geröstetes Brot, mit heißem Käse belegt)
to wet	befeuchten
wet tissue/wipe	Feuchttuch
wether	Hammel
wheat	Weizen
wheel	Rad
wheelchair	Rollstuhl
whetstone	Wetzstein
whey	Molke
to whip	schlagen (schaumig)
whipped cream	Schlagobers (geschlagen)

English	German
whisk	Schneebesen
to whisk	verquirlen
whisk(e)y	Whisk(e)y
Irish whiskey	irischer Whiskey
Scotch whisky	schottischer Whisky
Canadian whisky	kanadischer Whisky
American whiskey	amerikanischer Whiskey
bourbon	– mit mind. 51 % Mais
rye	– mit mind. 51 % Roggen
grain whisky	Whisky aus verschiedenen Getreidearten
malt whisky	Whisky nur aus Gerste
blended whisky	gemischter Whisky (malt und grain)
whisk(e)y glass, old-fashioned	Whisk(e)yglas
white beans	weiße Bohnen
white bread	Weißbrot
white bread dumplings	Semmelknödel
white cabbage	Kraut, Weißkraut
white lamb stew	Lammeingemachtes
white radish	Rettich
white sauce	weiße Sauce
white stock	weißer Fond
white wine	Weißwein
white wine sauce (white fish stock)	Weißweinsauce (Fischeinmachsauce)
white/dark meat	helles/dunkles Fleisch
whiteboard pen	Stift für weiße Kunststofftafel
whitefish, whiting	Weißfisch, Wittling, Merlan
Whitsun	Pfingsten
whole	ganz
on the whole	im Ganzen
wholemeal	Schrot, Vollkorn
wholemeal bread	Vollkornbrot
wholemeal flour	Vollkornmehl
wholesale	Großhandel
wholesale market	Großmarkt
wholesome	gesund (Nahrung), wohltuend
wide range of	breites Angebot
widowed	verwitwet
wild boar	Wildschwein
wild duck	Wildente
wild fowl	Wildgeflügel, Federwild
wild garlic, ramson	Bärlauch
wild garlic butter	Bärlauchbutter
wild garlic sauce	Bärlauchsauce
wild goose	Wildgans
wild mushrooms	Waldpilze
wild rice	Wildreis

wild salmon	Wildlachs
wild strawberries	Walderdbeeren
wild thyme	Feldthymian
Williams/Bartlett pear	Williamsbirne
willing	wollend, bereit
window	Fenster
wine	Wein
wine jelly	Weingelee
wine cellar	Weinkeller
wine cooler	Weinkühler
wine cradle	Weinflaschen-Korb
wine from the barrel/wood	Wein vom Fass
wine list	Weinkarte
wine of foreign growth	Wein aus dem Ausland/ausländischer Wein
wine steward	Weinkellner
wine storage cabinet	Klimaschrank
wine tasting	Weinprobe
wine tavern	Weinkeller (Lokal)
wine waiter	Sommelier
wine yeast	Weinhefe
wine-grower	Winzer/in
wing, winglet	Flügel
winkles, periwinkles	Strandschnecken
winter squash	Kürbis
winter vegetables	Wintergemüse
to wipe (clean)	abwischen
wire rack	Drahtgestell
wireless internet connection	drahtlose Internetverbindung
wish	Wunsch
to wish	wünschen
withdraw	Geld abheben, entziehen, abheben
withered	verdorrt, vertrocknet
within	innerhalb
wok	Wok
wood-burning oven	Holzofen
woodgrouse	Auerhahn
woodcock	Schnepfe
woodruff	Waldmeister
wood-stove baked bread	Holzofen-Brot
wood-stove baked pizza	Holzofen-Pizza
wooly hat	Haube
Worcestershire sauce	Worcestershire-Sauce
word processing	Textverarbeitung
to work (on sth)	(be)arbeiten
workforce	Arbeiterschaft
working hours	Arbeitszeiten
workshop	Workshop
workstation	Computerarbeitsplatz

to wrap	einhüllen
to wrap (a)round	umwickeln
to wrap in bacon	bardieren
to wrap up	verpacken
wrapping	Verpackung
wrapping film	Frischhaltefolie
wrasse	Lippfisch
wreath	Kranz
to write down	aufschreiben
wrongdoing	Vergehen

X

X-ray machine	Röntgengerät

Y

year of production	Jahrgangsangabe
indicating the year of production	mit Jahrgangsangabe
yeast	Germ, Hefe
yeast buns	Buchteln
yeast cake	Hefekuchen
yeast dough	Germteig, Hefeteig
yeast dumpling	Germknödel
yeast pastry	Hefegebäck
yeasty/yeast-like	unruhig, hefig
yellow boletus	Steinpilz
yielding	nachgiebig
yolk	Eigelb
young	jung
young wild boar	Frischling
young/green wine	neuer Wein, Primeur
young/new wine	Heuriger
youth hostel	Jugendherberge

Z

zappy	animierend, anregend
zest (of citrus fruit)	Schale
zester	Zestenreißer
zestful	lebenslustig
zingara sauce (tomatoed sauce with strips of ham, ox-tongue, mushrooms)	Zigeunersauce (Tomatensauce mit Paprika, Champignons, Zunge und Schinken)
zip code	Postleitzahl

zuppa pavese (beef broth with slices of fried bread and a poached egg)	Zuppa pavese (Bouillon mit gerösteten Brotscheiben, darauf ein pochiertes Ei)
zwieback, rusks, biscuit rusks	Zwieback

We speak English

Phrases

Redewendungen

Elements of a letter of application

1. Refer to the advertisement / telephone conversation

in reference to our yesterday's telephone conversation	bezugnehmend auf unser gestriges Telefonat
with reference to your advertisement in the "Rolling Pin"	bezugnehmend auf Ihr Inserat in der „Rolling Pin“
I read your advertisement in the "Rolling Pin" of November with interest.	Ich habe Ihr Inserat in der „Rolling Pin“ von November mit Interesse gelesen.

2. Mention the position and apply for it

I wish to apply for the position of ...	Ich möchte mich für die Position als ... bewerben.

3. Why are you applying?

Personally I am convinced that I could contribute a great deal to your service team.	Persönlich bin ich davon überzeugt, dass ich einen wertvollen Beitrag zu Ihrem Serviceteam leisten kann.
My personal commitment would be a benefit to the kitchen team.	Mein persönliches Engagement würde ein Nutzen für das gesamte Küchenteam sein.
I am sure that your company will benefit from my education and practical experience.	Ich bin sicher, dass Ihre Firma von meiner Ausbildung und meinen persönlichen Erfahrungen profitieren wird.
I would welcome the challenge of working in a creative team.	Ich würde die Herausforderung, in einem kreativen Team zu arbeiten, begrüßen.

4. Highlights of education / job experience / personal qualities (related to the position offered)

I would particularly draw your attention to ...	Ich würde gerne Ihre Aufmerksamkeit speziell auf ... lenken.
the fact that I passed my final exam with honours	die Tatsache, dass ich meine Lehrabschlussprüfung mit Auszeichnung bestanden habe
I speak three European languages fluently.	Ich spreche drei europäische Sprachen fließend.
frequent periods of residence abroad	häufige Saisonen im Ausland
I have acquired skills in ...	Ich habe mir Fähigkeiten im Bereich von ... angeeignet.
my experience in my former job and various holiday jobs	meine Erfahrungen in meinem ehemaligen Job und diversen Ferialjobs
I gained valuable experience during my employment at ... as ...	Ich habe während meiner Beschäftigung bei ... als ... wertvolle Erfahrung gewonnen.

5. Reason for leaving your current position (be positive)

I am seeking a more challenging position in the field.	Ich suche eine herausfordernde Position im Bereich.
At the firm where I am currently employed my duties are ...	In der Firma, in der ich derzeit arbeite, sind meine Aufgaben ...

6. Ask for a personal interview

I am available for an interview at any time.	Ich stehe jederzeit für ein Bewerbungsgespräch zur Verfügung.

I look forward to being invited to a job interview.

Ich freue mich, zu einem Bewerbungsgespräch eingeladen zu werden.

I would be glad to meet with you personally to discuss the matter.

Ich würde mich freuen, Sie persönlich zu treffen, um die Angelegenheit zu besprechen.

Elements of a CV / resume

1. **Contact details (name, address, telephone number, e-mail contact)**
2. **Education** – starting with the most recent item (reverse chronological)
3. **Employment** – starting with the most recent item (reverse chronological)
4. **Additional activities or skills**
5. **Personal data**
6. **References**

Phrases

Taking a complaint

I am sorry to hear about ...	Es tut mir leid ... zu hören
Let me take the full particulars of what happened.	Lassen Sie mich die Einzelheiten über das Geschehene zusammenfassen.
I fully understand.	Ich verstehe vollkommen.
I'll do my best to sort it out.	Ich werde mein Bestes tun, um es zu regeln.
Let me start by apologising for ...	Lassen Sie mich beginnen, indem ich mich entschuldige für ...

I assure you we will have the problem solved in no time.	Ich versichere Ihnen, wir werden das Problem in kürzester Zeit gelöst haben.
I'm sorry. This is not usual for our company.	Es tut mir leid. Das ist nicht typisch für unser Unternehmen.
I'll be more than happy to get things straightened out.	Ich werde mehr als erfreut sein, die Angelegenheit in Ordnung zu bringen.
I'm sorry you've been put in this predicament.	Es tut mir leid, dass Sie in diese prekäre Lage gebracht wurden.
I'm sorry sir; I will take full responsibility for the situation.	Mein Herr, es tut mir sehr leid; ich werde die volle Verantwortung für diese Angelegenheit übernehmen.
We will do our best to make your remaining stay as comfortable as possible.	Wir werden unser Bestes geben, um Ihren restlichen Aufenthalt so angenehm wie möglich zu gestalten.
Please accept our apologies for the inconveniences caused.	Bitte akzeptieren Sie unsere Entschuldigung für die Ihnen entstandenen Unannehmlichkeiten.
Should there be any further troubles please contact me immediately.	Bei weiteren Schwierigkeiten kontaktieren Sie mich bitte unverzüglich.
I'll get right on top of that.	Ich werde es sofort in den Griff bekommen.
I'm afraid there's been a terrible mix-up.	Ich fürchte, hier gab es eine verheerende Verwechslung.
Due to the circumstances beyond our control ...	Aus besonderem Anlass außer unserer Kontrolle ...
I have thoroughly investigated the situation and ...	Ich habe die Angelegenheit sorgfältig überprüft und ...
Please accept my sincere apologies for ...	Ich bitte vielmals um Entschuldigung für ...

I will personally make sure.	Ich werde mich persönlich davon vergewissern.
I can assure you this will never happen again.	Ich kann Ihnen versichern, dass dies nie wieder vorkommen wird.

Handling a complaint

Many people working at front office are terrified of dealing with complaints. But why? The truth is because they are hardly ever trained how to deal with complaints positively.

There are two points we should remember when dealing with complaining guests:

1. The customers are doing us a favour by giving us an opportunity to put things right! They could just walk out the door and never come back – not even to mention the negative word of mouth and all the gossip. But instead, they have chosen to let us try to solve the problem, and if we do, they will probably become loyal and regular customers.
2. Keep in mind: Customer is king – he is always right!

Correct way of dealing with customers' complaints

1. **Listen:** The customer wants to complain, wants to get it all off his chest and the angrier he is, the more he wants to tell his story. Thus you listen first and you don't interrupt except to show him that you are listening and understanding what he is saying.

2. **Take notes:** Let the customer realise that this is not just a speech on his part, but the supplying of evidence which you are going to take down in order not to forget a single detail.

3. **Apologize:** When the customer has finally finished getting it all off his chest, you have to apologise. Whether it was entirely his own fault or not, whether the hotel is 100 % in the right or not, you still have to apologise. Otherwise the customer loses face and has to admit to you that he was wrong and most customers will try to build their complaints out of all proportion, rather than admit that. **Remember: the customer is always right – even if he's wrong.**

4. **Take action:** Last but not least, be sure to do something about it! See that the customer is satisfied with the explanation, has accepted the apology and is content. If it is a serious complaint, bring it to the attention of the manager, so that he can speak to the customer or write to him.

If you promised to change something before their return to the hotel/company, make sure you do. If they come back and nothing has been done, they probably won't give you the opportunity to put it right a second time. They will simply quit.

Thus remember: the objective with complaining customers is not just to get them to go away. Your guests should leave satisfied and happy. The way you can be sure that they will not only return again and again, but that they will also tell their friends and colleagues how professional and caring your hotel/company is.

Phrases

Elements of an apology letter

1. Acknowledge receipt of the letter

We received your letter dated ...	Wir haben Ihren Brief vom ... erhalten.
In response to your letter from the ...	Als Antwort auf Ihren Brief vom ...
I have read your letter to us.	Ich habe Ihren Brief an uns gelesen.

2. Express thanks for the letter

We highly appreciate you taking the time to write us.	Wir begrüßen es sehr, dass Sie sich die Zeit genommen haben, uns zu schreiben.
... and would like to express our thanks for taking the time to write us about your experience.	... und möchten uns herzlich bedanken, dass Sie sich die Zeit genommen haben, Ihre Erfahrungen mit uns zu teilen.
I would like to thank you for giving me the opportunity to apologise.	Ich möchte mich bedanken, dass Sie mir die Möglichkeit geben, mich zu entschuldigen.

3. Apologise for the mistake

I am sorry that your stay at our hotel was not to your complete satisfaction.	Es tut mir leid, dass Ihr Aufenthalt in unserem Hotel nicht zu Ihrer vollen Zufriedenheit war.
I deeply regret you having had this experience with us	Ich bedauere zutiefst, dass Sie eine derartige Erfahrung mit unserem Betrieb gemacht haben
I would like to express my sincere apologies for your negative experience in our establishment.	Ich möchte meine aufrichtige Entschuldigung für Ihre negative Erfahrung in unserem Unternehmen ausdrücken.
I am sorry that we were unable to offer you our full line of quality service.	Es tut mir leid, dass wir Ihnen nicht unser Service in höchster Qualität bieten konnten.

Phrases

4. Give a brief explanation, but don't go into details

Normally we would never ... but on this particular day ...	Normalerweise würden wir niemals ... aber an dem besagten Tag ...
Unfortunately on this day ...	Bedauernswerterweise/leider war an diesem Tag ...
Though this is unusual for our company, we were forced to ...	Obwohl dies für unser Unternehmen ungewöhnlich ist, waren wir gezwungen ...

5. Briefly explain customer service (mission statement)

We are known for our customer service.	Wir sind für unser Kundenservice bekannt.
Our customers are very important for us.	Unsere Kunden sind uns sehr wichtig.
We place full emphasis on making our customers feel at home in our establishment.	Wir legen großen Wert darauf, dass sich unsere Kunden bei uns wie zu Hause fühlen.

We usually pride ourselves on our quality service.	Gewöhnlich sind wir sehr stolz auf unser Kundenservice.
We place full emphasis on our customers.	Der Kunde steht bei uns im Mittelpunkt.
In our hotel, the customer is king.	In unserem Hotel ist der Kunde König.
We have made it to our mission statement to ...	Wir haben es zu unserem Leitbild gemacht, dass ...

6. Suggest a remedy/compensation

We would like to invite you.	Wir würden Sie gerne einladen.
If you accept our apology, we would be delighted to offer you ...	Wenn Sie unsere Entschuldigung annehmen, würden wir Ihnen gerne ... anbieten.
May I offer you as a small compensation ...?	Darf ich Ihnen als kleine Wiedergutmachung ... anbieten?
We would like to apologise by offering you ...	Wir würden uns gerne bei Ihnen entschuldigen, indem wir Ihnen ... anbieten.

7. Restore goodwill (close politely)

Please come by to see us again in order to convince yourself of our usual high standards.	Kommen Sie doch bitte vorbei, um sich von unserem gewöhnlich hohen Standard zu überzeugen.
I would, once again, like to apologise for the mishap and hope that you can forgive us.	Ich möchte mich erneut für den Zwischenfall entschuldigen und hoffe, Sie können uns verzeihen.

Elements of a first inquiry

ATTENTION

You are always selling and representing yourself and your company!

1. Mention how you obtained your potential supplier's name

Your name has been given to us by Mr Hinterbuchner / our associates ...	Ihr Name wurde uns von Herrn Hinterbuchner/unserem Partner ... gegeben.
We have seen / We refer to your advertisement in ...	Wir haben Ihre Annonce gesehen/ Wir beziehen uns auf Ihre Annonce in ...
We are writing in connection with ...	Wir schreiben Ihnen in Zusammenhang mit ...
further to	bezugnehmend auf
with reference to	in Bezug auf
I am writing to enquire about ...	Ich schreibe Ihnen, um mich nach ... zu erkundigen.

2. Introduce your company

Could you please send us your catalogue and current price list for ...	Könnten Sie uns bitte Ihren Katalog und Ihre aktuelle Preisliste für ... senden.
We would appreciate more details / full particulars / detailed information on ...	Wir würden weitere Details/ genaue Einzelheiten /detaillierte Information über ... begrüßen.
Please quote your best offer.	Bitte geben Sie uns Ihr bestes Angebot bekannt.
We need / require / are looking for ...	Wir brauchen/benötigen/ suchen ...
Please let us know your earliest date of delivery.	Bitte teilen Sie uns Ihren ehestmöglichen Liefertermin mit.

Will you please let us have a sample of the product?	Würden Sie uns bitte ein Muster Ihres Produkts zukommen lassen?
A visit of your representative would be appreciated.	Ein Besuch Ihres Vertreters wäre uns sehr willkommen.
We would like to reserve one of your conference rooms with seating capacity for 80 people.	Wir würden gerne einen Ihrer Konferenzräume mit 80 Sitzplätzen reservieren.

3. Say what you require

I would like to reserve ... in the name of ...	Ich würde gerne ... auf den Namen von ... reservieren.
We also need the following equipment and services: ...	Weiters bräuchten wir folgende Ausstattung und Leistungen: ...
Would you mind if ...	Würde es Ihnen etwas ausmachen, wenn ...
Would you be so kind as to ...	Wären Sie so freundlich ...
We would appreciate it if you could send us more detailed information / an offer	Wir würden uns sehr freuen, wenn Sie uns ausführlichere Informationen/ein Angebot zusenden könnten.
I would be grateful if you could ...	Ich wäre Ihnen sehr dankbar, wenn Sie ... könnten.
Would you please send me ...	Würden Sie mir freundlicherweise ... zusenden.
We are interested in receiving ...	Wir sind daran interessiert ... zu erhalten.
Could you recommend ...?	Können Sie ... empfehlen?
You are urgently requested to ...	Sie werden dringlichst gebeten ...
What is your current price list for ...?	Wie lautet Ihre aktuelle Preisliste für ...?

We understand from your advertisement that you offer ...

Wir haben Ihrer Werbung entnommen, dass Sie ... anbieten.

It is our intention to ...

Wir beabsichtigen ...

4. Indicate sales opportunities in your area

If your prices are reasonable ...

Wenn Ihre Preise entsprechen/angebracht sind ...

If the quality meets our expectations ...

Wenn die Qualität unseren Erwartungen entspricht ...

5. Closing remarks (ask for action)

We look forward to hearing from you soon.

Wir freuen uns, bald von Ihnen zu hören.

We would appreciate a prompt reply.

Wir würden eine rasche Antwort begrüßen.

Elements of an offer

ATTENTION

It's your first important step for entering serious relationship!

1. Thank for the preceding inquiry

We refer to your letter of ... and are glad to quote as follows: ...

Wir beziehen uns auf Ihr Schreiben vom ... und freuen uns, Ihnen Folgendes anbieten zu können: ...

We thank you for your inquiry and are pleased to inform you ...

Wir danken für Ihre Anfrage und informieren Sie gerne ...

In reply to your inquiry of ... we wish to make you the following offer: ...

Stellung nehmend zu Ihrer Anfrage vom ... unterbreiten wir Ihnen gerne folgendes Angebot: ...

Many thanks for sending ...	Vielen Dank für die Zusendung ...
Your request will be processed as quickly as possible.	Ihre Anfrage wird so rasch wie möglich bearbeitet.

2. Confirm that you sell the goods indicated

a) This offer is subject to confirmation by ...	Dieses Angebot ist vorbehaltlich Bestätigung bis ...
This offer is firm subject to immediate acceptance, otherwise without engagement.	Dieses Angebot ist vorbehaltlich umgehender Akzeptanz, anderer-seits freibleibend.
Please find enclosed our current catalogue and price list.	Anbei finden Sie bitte unseren gül-tigen Katalog und die Preisliste.
b) Unfortunately we are fully booked over the requested period.	Leider sind wir zum gefragten Zeitpunkt bereits ausgebucht.
We regret there are no rooms / is no table available that day.	Wir bedauern, aber es ist an die-sem Tag kein Zimmer/Tisch frei.

3. Indicate terms and conditions (price, discounts, terms of payment, terms of delivery)

The prices are net, service and taxes are not included.	Die Preise verstehen sich netto, Service und Steuern sind nicht inbegriffen.
The prices are quoted net.	Preise sind netto angegeben.
Our prices are subject to a 2 % discount for cash.	2 % Skonto bei Barzahlung.
Payment within 30 days from the date of invoice.	Zahlung innerhalb 30 Tage ab Rechnungsdatum.
We can offer this room at a special price / on very favourable terms.	Wir können dieses Zimmer zu einem Sonderpreis/zu besonders günstigen Bedingungen anbieten.

Offer is valid until ...	Das Angebot ist gültig bis ...
It is our company policy to invoice only in euros.	Gemäß unserer geschäftlichen Richtlinie rechnen wir ausschließlich in Euro ab.

4. Mention one or two selling points convincing the prospect to do business with you – be ready-oriented!

We are sure that our offer meets your requirements and look forward to your confirmation.	Wir sind sicher, dass unser Angebot Ihren Erwartungen entspricht, und freuen uns auf Ihre Bestätigung.

5. Stimulate action – ask for an order

We are looking forward to welcoming you in our hotel / restaurant soon.	Wir freuen uns, Sie bald in unserem Hotel/Restaurant begrüßen zu dürfen.
If you require more information, please don't hesitate to contact us.	Sollten Sie weitere Information benötigen, zögern Sie nicht, uns zu kontaktieren.
We appreciate your business.	Wir schätzen Sie als Kunden.
Please contact me – my direct number is ...	Bitte kontaktieren Sie mich, meine direkte Nummer ist ...
If you need any additional assistance, please contact me. / Should you require any further information, please do not hesitate to contact me.	Für weitere Auskünfte stehe ich Ihnen gerne zur Verfügung.
If we can be of any further assistance, please let us know.	Sollten wir Ihnen weiter behilflich sein können, lassen Sie es uns bitte wissen.
Please answer reply as soon as possible because ...	Bitte antworten Sie umgehend, da ...
I look forward to the possibility of working together.	Ich freue mich auf die Zusammenarbeit.

Orders

Confirm an order

We would like to place an order ...	Wir möchten eine Bestellung aufgeben ...
Enclosed is our firm order for ...	Beiliegend finden Sie unsere verbindliche Bestellung für ...
Enclosed you will find our order.	Beiliegend erhalten Sie unsere Bestellung.
Would you be able to accept an order for ... at a price of ...?	Wäre es Ihnen möglich, eine Bestellung zu einem Preis von ... entgegenzunehmen?
Please confirm in writing.	Bitte bestätigen Sie schriftlich.
Could you please confirm price and date by fax?	Könnten Sie bitte Preis und Datum per Fax bestätigen?
We hereby confirm your reservation / order.	Hiermit bestätigen wir Ihre Reservierung/Bestellung.
This is to confirm our verbal reservation of today.	Hiermit bestätigen wir unsere mündliche Bestätigung von heute.
We accept your terms of payment and cancellation.	Wir erklären uns mit den Zahlungs- und Stornobedingungen einverstanden.
We have just received your fax and confirm your reservation as stated.	Wir haben soeben Ihr Fax erhalten und bestätigen Ihre Reservierung wie angegeben.

Change an order

Would it be possible to reduce / increase / change our order / reservation from ... to ...?	Wäre es möglich, unsere Bestellung/Reservierung von ... auf ... zu reduzieren/erhöhen/ändern?
Would it be possible to change the date of the booking to ...?	Wäre es möglich, das Reservierungsdatum auf ... zu ändern?

Unfortunately I already have a booking / I am double-booked that day. Would any other date be possible?	Leider haben wir bereits eine Buchung/haben wir zwei Termine gleichzeitig vergeben. Wäre ein anderes Datum möglich?
I am afraid I must ask you to change / alter my booking from ... to ...	Leider muss ich Sie bitten, meine Reservierung vom ... auf den ... umzubuchen.
I would like to reserve an additional room where lunch will be served after the meeting.	Ich würde gerne ein zusätzliches Zimmer reservieren, in dem das Mittagessen nach der Besprechung serviert wird.

Cancel an order

Unfortunately we cannot accept your offer because ...	Leider können wir Ihr Angebot nicht annehmen, da ...
We would like to cancel our order. The order number is ...	Wir würden unsere Bestellung gerne stornieren. Die Bestellnummer ist ...
We are forced to cancel our order due to ...	Wir müssen unsere Bestellung leider stornieren, da ...
We see no other alternative but to cancel our reservation / order for ...	Wir sehen leider keine andere Alternative, als unsere Reservierung/Bestellung von ... zu stornieren.
I am afraid I have to cancel our reservation for ... because ...	Leider muss ich unsere Reservierung für ... stornieren, weil ...
Owing to ... I am afraid that I have to cancel my booking.	Aufgrund von ... muss ich meine Reservierung leider stornieren.
Unfortunately I have to cancel our reservation for a conference room and a three-course dinner.	Leider muss ich unsere Reservierung für einen Konferenzraum und ein dreigängiges Abendessen stornieren.

Sending an invoice

For our services we kindly request the following payment ...	Für unsere geleisteten Dienste erlauben wir uns, folgenden Betrag in Rechnung zu stellen ...
Please find enclosed invoice No. ... for ...	Beigefügt finden Sie bitte Rechnung Nr. ... für ...
The pro forma invoice will be sent to you by e-mail.	Wir werden Ihnen die Pro-forma-Rechnung per E-Mail zusenden.
The total amount payable comes up to / is ...	Der Gesamtbetrag beläuft sich auf ...

Phrases

Reminder

May we remind you that your payment for ... is overdue.	Wir möchten Sie daran erinnern, dass Sie mit der Zahlung für ... in Verzug sind.
This is to remind you that the above invoice is still unpaid.	Hiermit möchten wir Sie daran erinnern, dass die oben genannte Rechnung noch offen ist.
According to our records, we have not yet received a remittance for the above invoice.	Gemäß unseren Unterlagen konnten wir für oben genannte Rechnung noch keinen Zahlungseingang verzeichnen.
We would appreciate if you cleared your account within the next few days.	Wir würden uns freuen, wenn Sie Ihre Rechnung innerhalb der nächsten Tage begleichen würden.
Our records show that the invoice still has not been paid.	Laut unseren Unterlagen ist die Rechnung noch nicht bezahlt worden.
Please send your payment promptly.	Bitte tätigen Sie Ihre Zahlung umgehend.

We have not yet received payment for ...	Wir haben Ihre Zahlung für ... noch nicht erhalten.
Our accounting department will only release this order for delivery upon receipt of a copy of your transfer / cheque.	Unsere Buchhaltung wird die Bestellung erst nach Erhalt einer Überweisungsbestätigung freigeben.
If you have already sent your payment, please disregard this letter.	Sollten Sie den Betrag bereits beglichen haben, beachten Sie dieses Schreiben bitte als gegenstandslos.

Closing formulas

Yours faithfully / sincerely	Mit freundlichen Grüßen
Respectfully yours	Hochachtungsvoll
Kind/best regards	Herzliche Grüße
Regards	Grüße
Fond regards	Alles Liebe (Grußformel für gute Freunde)
Thanking you in advance	Vielen Dank im Vorhinein
I look forward to discussing this with you.	Ich freue mich darauf, dies mit Ihnen zu besprechen.
With best wishes	Mit besten Grüßen
Kindest regards	Beste Grüße
All the best	Alles Gute
Say hello to ... from me.	Bitte grüße ... von mir.

Appointments

Making an appointment

I would like an appointment with ..., please.	Ich möchte Sie um einen Termin mit ... bitten.
When would it suit you?	Wann würde es Ihnen passen?
Can we arrange a meeting?	Können wir ein Treffen vereinbaren?
I think we should meet.	Ich denke, wir sollten uns treffen.
Asap (As soon as possible).	So bald wie möglich.

Postpone a meeting

I wonder whether we can postpone our meeting.	Wäre es möglich, unsere Besprechung zu verschieben?
I cannot make it tomorrow at 10:00 am. Can we make it a bit later, say 11:00?	Ich schaffe es morgen um 10:00 Uhr leider nicht. Würde es ein wenig später passen, sagen wir 11:00 Uhr?
Would it be possible to set another date?	Wäre es möglich, ein anderes Datum zu vereinbaren?
I have to postpone our meeting until ...	Ich muss unsere Besprechung bis zum ... verschieben.
Unfortunately I am double-booked on the day we arranged to meet. Would it be possible to make another date?	Leider habe ich zwei Termine zur gleichen Zeit an dem Tag, den wir ausgemacht hätten. Wäre ein anderes Datum möglich?
I am forced to change the date of our meeting.	Ich muss leider unsere Besprechung verschieben.
Could we make it a bit earlier / later?	Könnten wir uns etwas früher/später treffen?

Cancel a meeting

I could not reach you on the phone so I am writing you this e-mail to inform you that I have to cancel our appointment for tomorrow. I'm very sorry for any inconvenience caused.	Ich konnte Sie telefonisch leider nicht erreichen, daher schreibe ich Ihnen dieses E-Mail, um Ihnen mitzuteilen, dass ich unsere morgige Besprechung absagen muss. Eventuelle Unannehmlichkeiten ersuche ich Sie zu entschuldigen.
Regretfully I have to inform you that I will not be able to attend our proposed meeting and shall thus have to cancel.	Leider muss ich Ihnen mitteilen, dass ich unseren Termin nicht wahrnehmen kann und diesen somit absagen muss.
I am afraid I have to cancel our appointment for ...	Leider muss ich unseren Termin für ... absagen.
Owing to ... I am afraid I have to cancel our appointment.	Aufgrund von ... muss ich leider unseren Termin absagen.

At the restaurant

Booking a table

A table for ..., please.	Ein Tisch für ..., bitte.
Do you have any free tables?	Haben Sie freie Tische?
I'd like to make a reservation.	Ich möchte reservieren.
I'd like to book a table, please.	Ich möchte einen Tisch reservieren, bitte.
When for?	Für wann?
For what time?	Für welche Zeit?
Do you have a reservation?	Haben Sie eine Reservierung?
I've got a reservation.	Ich habe eine Reservierung.

Can you recommend a good restaurant?	Können Sie mir ein Restaurant empfehlen?
Are there any good / cheap restaurants around here?	Gibt es gute/preiswerte Restaurants in der Nähe?
We'll come at ... o'clock.	Wir kommen um ... Uhr.
Could we have a table for ...	Können wir einen Tisch für ... haben.
in the corner	in der Ecke
by the window	am Fenster
outside	draußen
on the terrace	auf der Terrasse

Taking an order

Are you ready to order?	Sind Sie bereit zu bestellen?
Can I get you any drinks?	Darf ich Ihnen etwas zu trinken bringen?
Would you like ...?	Möchten Sie ...?
May I take your order?	Darf ich Ihre Bestellung aufnehmen?
Do you prefer ...?	Bevorzugen Sie ...?
May I serve you ...?	Darf ich Ihnen ... servieren?
May I recommend ...	Darf ich empfehlen ...?
May I suggest ...?	Darf ich vorschlagen ...?
Would you like anything else?	Darf es sonst noch etwas sein?
Can I get you anything else?	Darf ich Ihnen noch etwas bringen?
How about ...?	Wie wäre es mit ...?

Should I put the rest in a doggy bag for you?	Soll ich Ihnen den Rest der Mahlzeit einpacken?
Enjoy your meal!	Mahlzeit!/Guten Appetit!
Here you are.	Bitte sehr!
You are welcome.	Keine Ursache./Bitte. (Antwort auf „Danke“)
Could I see the menu / the wine list, please?	Kann ich die Speisekarte/Weinkarte sehen, bitte?
I'll take ...	Ich nehme ...
I'll have the ...	Ich nehme ...
The same for me.	Dasselbe für mich.
I'd prefer ...	Ich bevorzuge ...
Do you have any specials?	Haben Sie Spezialitäten?
What do you recommend?	Was empfehlen Sie?
What's the soup of the day?	Was ist die Suppe des Tages?
I'm allergic to ...	Ich reagiere allergisch auf ...
I'm a vegetarian.	Ich bin Vegetarier/in.
How long will it take?	Wie lange wird es dauern?
For my starter I'll have ...	Als Vorspeise nehme ich ...
For my main course I'll have ...	Als Hauptspeise nehme ich ...
May I please have the menu?	Darf ich bitte die Speisekarte haben?
a set menu	Tagesgedeck
local dishes / specialities	(lokale) Spezialitäten
a children's menu	ein Kindermenü

Giving information about wine

Which wine goes well with ...?	Welcher Wein passt zu ...?
I'd prefer a light, dry red wine. Which one do you recommend?	Ich bevorzuge einen leichten, roten Wein. Welchen können Sie mir empfehlen?
I'd recommend / suggest the Traminer with the poultry.	Ich würde den Traminer zum Geflügel empfehlen.
With its fruit flavours the Cabernet goes very well with the spices in this dish.	Mit seinen fruchtigen Aromen passt der Cabernet sehr gut zu den Gewürzen in diesem Gericht.
The dish calls for a light / heavy / fruity wine.	Das Gericht verlangt nach einem leichten/schweren/fruchtigen Wein.
The Cabernet Sauvignon has strong tannins that counterbalance spiced dishes.	Der Cabernet Sauvignon hat starke Tannine die ein Gegengewicht zu gewürzten Speisen bieten.

Problems with orders

I'm sorry, we're out of that.	Entschuldigung, es ist leider ausgegangen.
This isn't what I ordered.	Das ist nicht, was ich bestellt habe.
This food is cold / salty.	Das Essen ist kalt/salzig.
This doesn't taste right.	Es schmeckt nicht richtig.
We have been waiting a long time.	Wir haben lange gewartet.
Is our meal on the way?	Ist das Essen bereits auf dem Weg?
May I change this?	Können Sie mir dafür etwas anderes bringen?
overdone / underdone / too tough	zu stark gebraten/zu wenig gebraten/zäh

bitter / salty / sweet	bitter/salzig/süß
What is taking so long?	Was dauert so lange?
Where are our drinks?	Wo sind unsere Getränke?
This isn't clean / fresh.	Das ist nicht sauber/frisch.
Would you ask the head waiter / restaurant manager to come over?	Würden Sie den Oberkellner/ Restaurantleiter zu uns bitten?

Giving information / asking for information

Breakfast / lunch / dinner is served from ... to ...	Frühstück/Mittagessen/Abendessen wird von ... bis ... serviert.
We have a variety of ...	Wir haben eine Vielzahl von ...
The soup of the day is ...	Die Tagessuppe ist ...
Each order includes ...	Jedes Gericht beinhaltet ...
I can offer you ...	Ich kann Ihnen anbieten ...
Would you like to taste the wine?	Möchten Sie den Wein probieren?
How would you like your steak? Rare, medium-rare, medium or well-done?	Wie möchten Sie Ihr Steak?
Would you like any coffee or dessert?	Möchten Sie Kaffee oder ein Dessert?
Was everything alright?	War alles in Ordnung?

Paying

Could we have the bill, please?	Können wir bitte die Rechnung haben?
The bill, please!	Die Rechnung, bitte!
Can I pay by ...?	Kann ich mit ... bezahlen?

Do you take credit cards?	Nehmen Sie Kreditkarten?
How are you paying?	Wie bezahlen Sie?
I'd like to pay in cash / a foreign currency / by credit card / by debit card / by ec-card.	Ich bezahle bar/in fremder Währung/mit Kreditkarte/mit Bankomatkarte/mit EC-Karte.
Can we pay separately?	Können wir getrennt bezahlen?
Is service included?	Ist der Service/die Bedienung inkludiert?
How much is ...?	Wie viel kostet ...?
The total amount / exchange rate is ...	Der gesamte Betrag ist ...
Service and value-added tax are included.	Service und Steuern sind inklu-diert.
Would you like to put it on your hotel bill?	Möchten Sie es auf die Hotel-rechnung setzen?
Keep the change.	Der Rest ist für Sie.
That was a very good meal.	Das Essen war sehr gut.
We enjoyed it, thank you.	Es hat gut geschmeckt danke.

At the hotel

Checking availability / questions before booking

Do you have any vacancies / free rooms?	Haben Sie freie Unterkünfte/ Zimmer?
We're are looking for ...	Wir suchen ...
For how many nights?	Für wie viele Nächte?
When for?	Für wann?

How long will you be staying for?	Wie lange möchten Sie bleiben?
What's the price per night?	Was ist der Preis pro Nacht?
Can you offer me any discount?	Können Sie mir Rabatt gewähren?
Is breakfast included?	Ist das Frühstück dabei?
Have you got anything cheaper / bigger / more quiet room?	Haben Sie ein günstigeres/ größeres/ruhigeres Zimmer?
Half board or full board?	Halb- oder Vollpension?

Booking a room

Phrases

I'd like to make a reservation.	Ich möchte eine Reservierung vornehmen.
I'd like to book ...	Ich möchte ... buchen.
What type of room would you like? A single room? A double room? A twin-bedded room with shower/ bath?	Welches Zimmer wünschen Sie? Ein Einzelzimmer? Ein Doppelzimmer? Ein Zimmer mit zwei Betten mit Dusche/Badezimmer?
I'd like a ... room.	Ich möchte ein ...zimmer.
I'd like a room with a shower / a bath / a sea view / a balcony.	Ich möchte ein Zimmer mit Du-sche/Bad/Meeresblick/Balkon.
Could we have an extra bed?	Könnten wir ein zusätzliches Bett bekommen?
I can confirm your booking.	Ich kann Ihre Buchung bestätigen.

At the front office

Can I / may I help you?	Kann ich behilflich sein?
Do you have a reservation?	Haben Sie eine Reservierung?
What's your name?	Wie ist ihr Name?

Can you give me your name, please?	Können Sie mir Ihren Namen geben, bitte?
How long will you be staying?	Wie lange bleiben Sie?
Would you fill this registration form?	Würden Sie dieses Formular ausfüllen?
Here's your key / key card.	Hier ist Ihr Schlüssel/Ihre Schlüsselkarte.
Please sign here.	Bitte unterschreiben Sie hier.
May I see your passport, please?	Kann ich Ihren Pass sehen, bitte?
Have you got any identification?	Haben Sie Papiere zur Identifikation?
You have room number ...	Sie haben Zimmernummer ...
Your room number is ...	Ihre Zimmernummer ist ...
The porter will show you to your room.	Der Portier wird Ihnen das Zimmer zeigen.
The porter will carry your luggage.	Der Portier wird Ihr Gepäck tragen.
Have a nice trip!	Gute (Weiter-)Reise!

About facilities

Does the room have television / air condition / internet access?	Hat das Zimmer Fernsehen/eine Klimaanlage/Internetzugang?
Do you allow pets?	Erlauben Sie Haustiere?
Is there a gym / swimming pool / sauna?	Gibt es ein Fitnessstudio/einen Swimmingpool/eine Sauna?
Is there enough parking space?	Gibt es ausreichend Parkplätze?

Tourism

Finding accommodation

We're looking for accommodation / a hotel.	Wir suchen eine Unterkunft/ein Hotel.
We need somewhere to stay.	Wir benötigen eine Unterkunft.
Do you have a list of hotels / youth hostels / B&Bs / campsites?	Haben Sie eine Liste von Hotels/Jugendherbergen/Campingplätzen?
What sort of accommodation are you looking for?	Welche Art von Unterkünften suchen Sie?

Asking for information about sightseeing, activities, events

Do you have a map of ...?	Habe Sie eine Karte von ...?
Where is the ...?	Wo ist ...?
What's the best way of getting around?	Wie ist die beste Art herumzukommen?
Where can I hire a car?	Wo kann ich ein Auto buchen?
What are you interested in?	Wofür interessieren Sie sich?
Are there any guided tours / excursions / trips?	Gibt es Besichtigungstouren/Exkursionen/Ausflüge?
Can I book tickets here?	Kann ich hier Tickets buchen?
Do you have any brochures of ...?	Haben Sie Broschüren über ...?
Could you recommend a good restaurant?	Können Sie uns ein Restaurant empfehlen?

Wine vocabulary

Wein-Fachausdrücke

Quality classes of wine

Tafelwein	can come from more than one region; 10.7°KMW
Landwein	a Tafelwein that comes from just one region; 14°KMW; < 11.5% alcohol
Qualitätswein	comes from a single wine district; > 15°KMW; > 9% alcohol
Kabinettwein	no sugar added; > 17°KMW
Prädikatswein	covers the range from Spätlese to Eiswein; range from dry to high natural sweetness; no sugar addition permitted
Spätlese	wine not released until 1st March after harvested; > 19°KMW; usually dry – can be sweet
Auslese	"Selection" – bad grapes removed; no sugar added; can be dry – usually sweet; minimum sugar content 21°KMW
Beerenauslese	"Grape selection" – bad grapes removed; no sugar added; naturally sweet; minimum sugar content 25°KMW
Ausbruch	botrytised grapes, grape juice or late harvest wine may be added to assist the pressing operation; minimum sugar content 27°KMW; naturally sweet
Trockenbeeren-auslese	"Dry Berry Selection" – completely botrytised grapes; sweetest wine of all; minimum sugar content 30°KMW
Eiswein	"Ice wine" – made from naturally frozen grapes; minimum sugar content 25°KMW
Strohwein/ Schilfwein	made from grapes dried on straw mats; > 25°KMW

Wachau Classification

The "Vinea Wachau Nobilis Districtus" has three categories, all for dry wines:

Steinfeder	"Stone feather" – named after a grass that grows in the vineyards; < 11,5% alcohol
Federspiel	11.5–12.5% alcohol; minimum sugar content 17°KMW; roughly equivalent to Kabinett
Smaragd	> 12.5% alcohol; < 9g/litre residual sugar; some of the best dry white wines in Austria; named after a lizard that lives in the vineyards

Famous grape varieties in Austria

Blauer Portugieser	A red grape which has its origins in Fortugal und grows in the Thermenregion and the north-western Weinviertel. Characteristics: simple, neutral, light-coloured.
Blaufränkisch	Red grape which grows mainly in Mittelburgenland. Characteristics: rich, prominent tannins, with berry or cherry notes.
Cabernet Sauvignon	A red grape which has its origin in France and needs warm sides. Characteristics: strong, powerful bouquet with strong tannins; when matured notes of black currant and roasted notes.
Grüner Veltliner	Most important white grape variety in Austria with its origin in Austria. Characteristics: lean, fruity, sometimes spicy and peppery, acidity-toned.
Müller-Thurgau (Rivaner)	A white grape with its origin in Germany; characteristics: mild with a slight Muscat taste.

Muskat Ottonell	White grape which grows mainly at Neusiedlersee, Burgenland. Characteristics: nutmeg flavour, delicious with sweet dishes.
Muskateller	One of the oldest grape varieties; characteristics: nutmeg flavour; delicious as aperitif and with appetizers.
Neuburger	Austrian white grape with a neutral taste. Characteristics: mild, sometimes flowery.
Riesling	One of the top white grapes with its origin in Germany. Characteristics: fruity, notes of stone fruit;
Rotgipfler	Crossing of Traminer and Roter Veltliner which needs a warm climate for growing. Characteristics: fine bouquet, light acidity.
Sauvignon Blanc	A white grape which grows worldwide and has a characteristic bouquet.
Traminer (Gewürztraminer, Roter und Gelber Traminer)	A sweet and spicy white grape which was already known by the Romans. Characteristics: low in acidity, but rich in aromas.
Welschriesling	A white grape of origin in Northern Italy; good for the production of sparkling wine. Welschriesling can be fresh and acidity-toned, but also sweet and fruity.
Zweigelt	A red grape which is the most widespread in Austria. The characteristics can range from light with soft tannins to mature and full-bodied. Sometimes wine is matured in barriques.
Gemischter Satz	It is one of Austria's most traditional wines which popularity has increased during the last years because of strict quality policy and new cultivation regulations. It is pushed by a group of Viennese winemakers known as "WienWein".

How to describe wine

acetic	essigsauer
acidic	säurereich
ample	üppig, großzügig
aromatic	aromatisch
austere	herb
balanced	ausgeglichen, ausgewogen
big, full-bodied	Wein mit einem intensiven, vollen Aroma
bitter	bitter
body	beschreibt den Eindruck der „Schwere“ eines Weins; light – medium – full-bodied
concentrated	intensiv im Geschmack
corked	nach Kork schmeckend
crisp	frischer, säurebetonter Wein
deep	komplex, reichhaltig
dull	stumpf
easy-drinking	leichter, fruchtiger Wein mit geringem Tanningehalt
elegant	elegant, raffiniert
flabby	schlaff, säurearm
fleshy	dicht
fresh	frisch
fruity	fruchtig
grassy	Aroma von frisch geschnittenem Gras
full	volles Aroma
green	negativ: jung, unreif; positiv: frisch – fruchtig
harsh	rau, herb aufgrund von Säure/Tanningehalt
heavy	schwer, voll
herbal	Wein mit Kräuteraromen
honeyed	Aroma von Honig

lean / thin	dünner, säurebetonter, wenig aromatischer Wein
light	leicht
long	Wein mit langsamen Abgang
mature	reif
nutty	nussig
oxidized	oxidiert, von Sauerstoff beeinträchtig
powerful	kräftig
racy	rassig
rich	reichhaltig
ripe	reif
rounded	rund, ausgeglichen
simple	einfach, wenig komplex
smooth / soft	lieblich
sparkling	Schaumwein, Sekt
spicy	würzig
subtle	subtil, raffiniert
sweet	süß
tannic	stark tanninhaltig
woody	holzig
stemmy	grüner, herber Wein
supple	weich, ausgeglichen, lieblich
hollow	flach, leer

European countries

Europäische Länder

Albania
(AL)

Capital: Tirana
People: Albanian
Languages: Albanian

Andorra
(AND)

Capital: Andorra la Vella
People: Andorran
Languages: Catalan

Austria
(A)

Capital: Vienna
People: Austrian
Languages: German

Belarus
(BY)

Capital: Minsk
People: Belarusian
Languages: Belarusian

Belgium
(B)

Capital: Brussels
People: Belgian
Languages: French / Dutch

Bosnia and Herzegovina
(BIH)

Capital: Sarajevo
People: Bosnian
Languages: Bosnian / Croatian / Serbian

Bulgaria
(BG)

Capital: Sofia
People: Bulgarian
Languages: Bulgarian

Croatia
(HR)

Capital: Zagreb
People: Croat
Languages: Croatian*

Cyprus
CY

Capital: Lefkosia (Nicosia)
People: Cyprian / Cypriote
Languages: Greek / Turkish

Czech Republic
CZ

Capital: Prague
People: Czech
Languages: Czech

Denmark
DK

Capital: Copenhagen
People: Dane
Languages: Danish

Estonia
EST

Capital: Tallinn
People: Estonian
Languages: Estonian

Finland
FIN

Capital: Helsinki
People: Finn
Languages: Finnish

France
F

Capital: Paris
People: Frenchman (-woman)
Languages: French

Germany
D

Capital: Berlin
People: German
Languages: German

Greece
GR

Capital: Athens
People: Greek
Languages: Greek

Hungary
H

Capital: Budapest
People: Hungarian
Languages: Hungarian

Iceland
IS

Capital: Reykjavík
People: Icelander
Languages: Icelandic

Ireland
IRL

Capital: Dublin
People: Irish
Languages: Gaelic / English

Italy
I

Capital: Rome
People: Italian
Languages: Italian

Latvia
LV

Capital: Riga
People: Latvian
Languages: Latvian

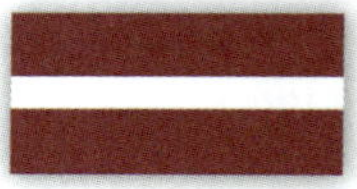

Liechtenstein
FL

Capital: Vaduz
People: Liechtensteiner
Languages: German

Lithuania
LT

Capital: Vilnius
People: Lithuanian
Languages: Lithuanian

Luxembourg
L

Capital: Luxembourg
People: Luxembourger
Languages: French / German / Luxembourgish*

Macedonia
MK

Capital: Skopje
People: Macedonian
Languages: Macedonian

Malta
M

Capital: Valletta
People: Maltese
Languages: Maltese / English

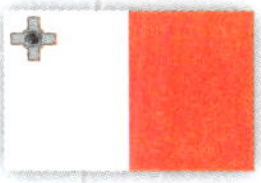

Moldova
MD

Capital: Chişinău
People: Moldavian
Languages: Moldavian

Monaco
MC

Capital: Monaco
People: Monacan / Monégasque
Languages: French

Montenegro
MNE

Capital: Podgorica
People: Montenegrin
Languages: Montenegrin / Serbian

(the) Netherlands / Holland
NL

Capital: Amsterdam (official), The Hague (administrative capital)
People: Netherlander / Dutchman (-woman)
Languages: Netherlands-Dutch

Norway
N

Capital: Oslo
People: Norwegian
Languages: Norwegian

Poland
PL

Capital: Warsaw
People: Pole
Languages: Polish

Portugal
P

Capital: Lisbon
People: Portuguese
Languages: Portuguese

Romania
RO

Capital: Bucharest
People: Romanian
Languages: Romanian

Russia
RUS

Capital: Moscow
People: Russian
Languages: Russian*

San Marino
RSM

Capital: San Marino
People: San Marinese
Languages: Italian

Serbia
SRB

Capital: Belgrade
People: Serb
Languages: Serbian*

Slovakia
SK

Capital: Bratislava
People: Slovak
Languages: Slovakian

Slovenia
SLO

Capital: Ljubljana
People: Slovenian
Languages: Slovenian

Spain

E

Capital:	Madrid
People:	Spaniard / Catalan / Basque / Galician
Languages:	Spanish / Catalan / Basque / Galician

Sweden

S

Capital:	Stockholm
People:	Swede
Languages:	Swedish

Switzerland

CH

Capital:	Bern
People:	Swiss
Languages:	German / French / Italian / Romansh

Turkey

TR

Capital:	Ankara
People:	Turk
Languages:	Turkish

Ukraine

UA

Capital:	Kiev
People:	Ukrainian
Languages:	Ukrainian

United Kingdom of Great Britain and Northern Ireland

GB

Capital:	London
People:	Englishman / Welshman / Scotsman / Irishman (-woman)
Languages:	English / Welsh / Scots Gaelic

Vatican City

V

Capital:	Vatican City
People:	Inhabitant of Vatican City
Languages:	Italian* / Latin

* official language

Numerical Expressions

Zahlen

Cardinal numbers

1	one
2	two
3	three
4	four
5	five
6	six
7	seven
8	eight
9	nine
10	ten
11	eleven
12	twelve
13	thirteen
14	fourteen
15	fifteen
16	sixteen
17	seventeen
18	eighteen
19	nineteen
20	twenty
21	twenty-one
30	thirty
31	thirty-one
40	forty
41	forty-one
50	fifty
51	fifty-one
60	sixty
61	sixty-one
70	seventy
71	seventy-one
80	eighty
81	eighty-one
90	ninety
91	ninety-one
100	one hundred
101	one hundred and one
200	two hundred
1,000	one thousand
1,000,000	one million
1,000,000,000	one billion

Ordinal numbers

1st	first
2nd	second
3rd	third
4th	fourth
5th	fifth
6th	sixth
7th	seventh
8th	eighth
9th	ninth
10th	tenth
11th	eleventh
12th	twelfth
13th	thirtheenth
14th	fourteenth
15th	fifteenth
16th	sixteenth
17th	seventeenth
18th	eighteenth
19th	nineteenth
20th	twentieth
21st	twenty-first
30th	thirtieth
31st	thirty-first
40th	fortieth
41st	forty-first
50th	fiftieth
51st	fifty-first
60th	sixtieth
61st	sixty-first
70th	seventieth
71st	seventy-first
80th	eightieth
81st	eighty-first
90th	ninetieth
100th	one hundredth
101st	one hundred and first
1,000th	one thousandth

NOTES